THE NEW TESTAMENT

CONTENTS

First published as Découvrir la Bible 1983
First edition © Librairie Larousse 1983
English translation © Daan Retief Publishers 1990
24-volume series adaptation by Mike Jacklin © Knowledge Unlimited 1994
Current edition printed as a 24-volume series © 1995 OM Publishing
New Testament series reprinted as a combined volume1999

05 04 03 02 01 00 99 7 6 5 4 3 2 1

OM Publishing is an imprint of Paternoster Publishing,
PO Box 300, Carlisle, Cumbria, CA3 0QS, UK
Website: www.paternoster-publishing.com

Series editor: D.Roy Briggs
English translation: Bethan Uden

British Library Cataloguing in Publication Data
A catalogue record for this book is available from the British Library
ISBN 1-85078-325-X

Cover Design by Mainstream, Lancaster
Printed in Singapore by Star Standard Industries Pte. Ltd.

JOHN THE BAPTIST AND JESUS
IN THE TIME OF KING HEROD THERE WAS IN JERUSALEM A TEMPLE PRIEST CALLED ZACHARIAH. HE WAS ALWAYS BEGGING GOD TO BLESS HIM AND HIS WIFE WITH A CHILD, EVEN THOUGH THEY WERE BOTH OLD.
SCENARIO: Etienne DAHLER
DRAWING: Paolo ELEUTERI-SERPIERI
ZACHARIAH, THE LOT'S FALLEN TO YOU TO BURN THE INCENSE IN THE HOUSE OF THE LORD.
BLESSED BE THE HOLY ONE OF ISRAEL!
ZACHARIAH WENT INTO THE TEMPLE TO CARRY OUT HIS PRIESTLY DUTIES.
HE'S A LONG TIME ... WHAT'S GOING ON?
AS LONG AS HE'S NOT BEEN OVER-WHELMED BY THE LORD'S PRESENCE! IT'S HAPPENED TO OTHER PEOPLE...
HERE HE COMES!
HE'S DUMB! HE CAN'T SAY ANYTHING!
HE MUST HAVE HAD A VISION!

WHEN ZACHARIAH HAD COMPLETED HIS DUTY AT THE TEMPLE, HE WENT BACK TO HIS VILLAGE CLOSE TO JERUSALEM.

A FEW MONTHS LATER...

ZACHARIAH, THE LORD'S ANSWERED OUR PRAYER. I'M EXPECTING A CHILD.

MEANWHILE IN NAZARETH, A GALILEAN VILLAGE SOME 160 KILOMETRES NORTH OF JERUSALEM...

LET'S GO BACK NOW, MARY. THE SUN'S SETTING...

MY BASKET'S FULL TOO.

WAIT FOR ME! I'M COMING!

OH, MARY, YOUR FIANCÉ JOSEPH WAS HERE. HE'LL COME BACK LATER.
MARY WENT HOME AND FOUND HER MOTHER ANNE IN THE DOORWAY WAITING FOR HER...

THAT EVENING...

TODAY WE DREW UP OUR MARRIAGE CONTRACT WITH THE RABBI.
THAT'S GOOD! I'M HAPPY TO HAVE A DESCENDANT OF DAVID AS A SON-IN-LAW!

IT WAS ALREADY LATE BEFORE JOSEPH WENT HOME.
ANNE AND MARY, MAY THE LORD BLESS THIS HOME AND PROTECT YOU THROUGH THE NIGHT.
PEACE BE WITH YOU, JOSEPH!
YOUR FIANCÉ IS A GOOD MAN, MARY. I'M SURE YOU'LL BE WORTHY OF HIM.
MARY COULD NOT SLEEP BECAUSE SHE WAS SO HAPPY. SUDDENLY SHE HEARD A GENTLE RUSTLING...
AND ALL AT ONCE...
BE FULL OF JOY! GOD'S VERY PLEASED WITH YOU! THE LORD'S WITH YOU!
DON'T BE AFRAID, MARY... YOU'LL BECOME PREGNANT AND GIVE BIRTH TO A SON, AND YOU'LL CALL HIM JESUS*... THE LORD WILL GIVE HIM THE THRONE OF HIS ANCESTOR DAVID, FOR EVER. HE'LL BE CALLED SON OF THE MOST HIGH.
* In Hebrew, YESHOUA, 'The Lord saves'

WHO'S SHE TALKING TO? I CAN'T SEE ANYBODY...

I'M THE SERVANT OF THE LORD: LET IT HAPPEN TO ME AS YOU HAVE SAID.

AND THE MESSENGER LEFT HER...

A FEW DAYS LATER...

JOSEPH, DID YOU KNOW THAT MARY'S GONE?

SHE'S GONE TO JUDAEA... HER COUSIN ELIZABETH'S GOING TO HAVE A BABY.

ELIZABETH! AT HER AGE? EXPECTING A CHILD!

AFTER A JOURNEY OF SEVERAL DAYS...
ZACHARIAH! ELIZABETH! YOUR COUSIN MARY IS HERE!
PEACE BE WITH YOU, ELIZABETH!
...AND WITH YOU, MARY.
YOU ARE THE MOST BLESSED OF ALL WOMEN AND BLESSED IS THE CHILD YOU WILL BEAR.
BUT HOW DO YOU KNOW, ELIZABETH?
AND YOU, MARY? NOBODY ELSE KNOWS THAT I'M EXPECTING A CHILD!
THE LORD'S GREAT! I DANCE WITH JOY FOR MY GOD WHO HAS SAVED ME!

ABOUT THREE MONTHS LATER...
IT'S A BOY!
WHAT A BLESSING, ELIZABETH!
QUICKLY! BRING ZACHARIAH!
EVEN IF YOU CAN'T SPEAK, I KNOW HOW HAPPY YOU ARE, ZACHARIAH!
EIGHT DAYS LATER FRIENDS AND NEIGHBOURS GATHERED FOR THE BOY'S CIRCUMCISION.
I SUPPOSE HE'LL BE CALLED ZACHARIAH, LIKE HIS FATHER.
NO, HIS NAME'S JOHN!
BUT NO ONE IN THE FAMILY HAS THAT NAME...
I THINK ZACHARIAH WANTS TO WRITE SOMETHING...
YES, IT'S FOR HIM TO DECIDE.
JOHN

BLESSED BE THE LORD, THE GOD OF ISRAEL! HE COMES TO SET HIS PEOPLE FREE!
LISTEN TO THAT! ZACHARIAH CAN SPEAK AGAIN!
JOHN
AND YOU, LITTLE CHILD, WILL BE CALLED PROPHET OF THE MOST HIGH; BECAUSE YOU WILL GO AHEAD OF THE LORD TO PREPARE HIS ROAD FOR HIM.
AFTER THESE EVENTS, MARY WENT BACK TO NAZARETH.
HERE WE ARE, AT LAST! AND NOW I MUST TELL JOSEPH.
BUT, MARY! WHAT ARE YOU SAYING! WHAT CAN I...
IT'S THE TRUTH, JOSEPH...
BE BRAVE, MARY. JOSEPH'S HEART WILL OPEN.

MARY... IT'S IMPOSSIBLE... MARY...
JOSEPH WENT TO GET ADVICE FROM THE RABBI.
IT'S VERY SIMPLE, JOSEPH. IF THE CHILD'S YOURS, THE TORAH DOESN'T CONDEMN YOU. YOU ARE, IN FACT, MARRIED. BUT IF THE CHILD ISN'T YOURS, YOU MUST CANCEL THE CONTRACT WITH MARY, AND...
AND?
...SHE'LL BE STONED... THAT'S THE LAW.
THAT SAME NIGHT JOSEPH WAS DEEPLY DISTURBED, WHEN...
JOSEPH, DON'T BE AFRAID TO TAKE MARY AS YOUR WIFE. THE CHILD SHE CARRIES IS THE FRUIT OF THE HOLY SPIRIT.
IT WILL BE A BOY. YOU'LL CALL HIM JESUS.*

* God saves.

SOMETIME LATER JOSEPH AND MARY WERE MARRIED, AND HE TOOK HER TO HIS HOME.
MAY THE LORD BLESS YOU!
MAY HE PROTECT YOUR HOME!
THE MONTHS PASSED...
HAVE YOU HEARD THE LATEST ABOUT THOSE ROMANS? THEY WANT TO COUNT US LIKE SHEEP!
SO THAT THEY CAN SHEAR US BETTER!
A CENSUS, I SUPPOSE?
YES, JOSEPH, EVERYONE MUST BE REGISTERED IN HIS HOME TOWN.
THEN I'LL HAVE TO GO TO BETHLEHEM WITH MARY.
AFTER A WEEK OF DIFFICULT TRAVELLING...
THERE'S BETHLEHEM! WE'RE SURE TO FIND A PLACE IN THE FAMILY HOME...
I HOPE SO...

I'M SORRY, JOSEPH! OUR PLACE HAS BEEN FULL FOR SEVERAL DAYS!
...BUT MARY COULD GIVE BIRTH AT ANY TIME!
YOU'LL BE BETTER OFF IN THE CAVES... ONE OF THE CHILDREN WILL GO WITH YOU.
THERE! IT SERVES AS THE SHELTER FOR SHEPHERDS AND THEIR FLOCKS.
EPHRAIM, GO AND LOOK FOR TWIGS. WE'LL LIGHT A FIRE IN THE OTHER CORNER.
JOSEPH! THE BABY...
LITTLE ONE, RUN TO THE HOUSE TO GET HELP!

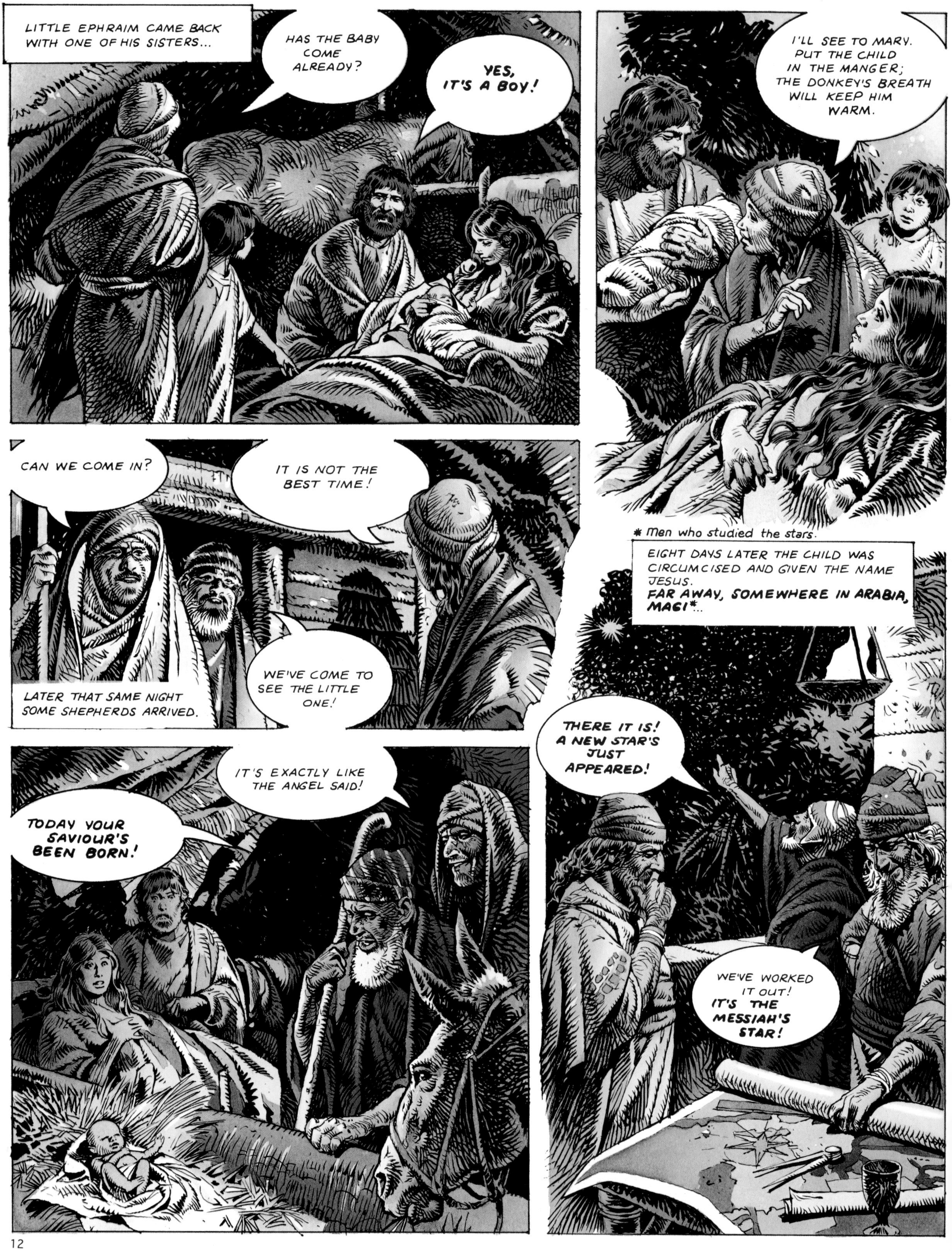

I'LL SEE TO MARY. PUT THE CHILD IN THE MANGER; THE DONKEY'S BREATH WILL KEEP HIM WARM.

EIGHT DAYS LATER THE CHILD WAS CIRCUMCISED AND GIVEN THE NAME JESUS.
FAR AWAY, SOMEWHERE IN ARABIA, MAGI*...

THERE IT IS! A NEW STAR'S JUST APPEARED!

WE'VE WORKED IT OUT! IT'S THE MESSIAH'S STAR!

* Men who studied the stars.

FORTY DAYS LATER THE CHILD WAS PRESENTED BY HIS PARENTS IN THE TEMPLE OF JERUSALEM.
THIS IS A BIG DAY FOR YOU, MY SON: YOU'RE GOING TO THE TEMPLE FOR THE FIRST TIME.
JESUS? RIGHT! PUT YOUR OFFERING HERE.
GIVE ME THE CHILD.
THERE WAS A HOLY MAN IN JERUSALEM CALLED SIMEON WHO WAS WAITING FOR ISRAEL TO BE SAVED. LED BY THE SPIRIT, HE WENT TO THE TEMPLE.
NOW, MASTER, LET YOUR SERVANT GO IN PEACE: I'VE SEEN YOUR SALVATION WITH MY OWN EYES!
TURNING TO MARY, SIMEON SAID TO HER...
THIS CHILD WILL BE A SIGN PEOPLE WILL REJECT. AND AS FOR YOU, MARY, A SHARP SWORD WILL PIERCE YOUR HEART.

NOT LONG AFTERWARDS, THE MAGI ARRIVED IN JERUSALEM. THIS NEWS REACHED KING HEROD.
THEY'VE COME TO WORSHIP THE KING OF THE JEWS...
HE'S JUST BEEN BORN. THEY READ IT IN THE SKY!
CALL TOGETHER THE PRIESTS AND THE SCRIBES!
WHERE WILL THE MESSIAH COME FROM?
FROM THE TRIBE OF JUDAH.
FROM BETHLEHEM IN FACT. THE PROPHET MICAH SAID THAT IT'S FROM THERE A LEADER WILL COME TO GUIDE ISRAEL.
MY FRIENDS, YOU MUST GO TO BETHLEHEM! COME BACK THIS WAY... I'M VERY INTERESTED IN THAT CHILD!
THEN HEROD RECEIVED THE MAGI IN SECRET.
THE STAR SEEMS TO POINT THAT WAY.

THE STAR STOPPED ABOVE THE CAVE AND THE MAGI WENT IN.
AND NOW?
NOTHING'S TOO FINE FOR THE MASTER OF THE UNIVERSE!
THEN THE MAGI LEFT, TRAVELLING EASTWARDS.
WE MUSTN'T GO BACK TO SEE HEROD... THAT MAN IS DANGEROUS.
I AGREE.
LET'S TAKE THE TRADE-ROUTE AND AVOID JERUSALEM.
JOSEPH!
JOSEPH! TAKE THE CHILD AND HIS MOTHER, AND ESCAPE INTO EGYPT.
THAT DAY EGYPT, LAND OF EXILE AND REFUGE FOR THE CHILDREN OF ISRAEL, RECEIVED ONE OF ABRAHAM'S SONS WHO WAS ALREADY PURSUED BY HATRED.

YOUR MAJESTY, THE MAGI LEFT THE COUNTRY.
TRAITORS! THEY'VE ESCAPED ME!
KILL ALL THE CHILDREN LESS THAN TWO YEARS OLD IN AND AROUND BETHLEHEM!
A MESSIAH? WE'LL SEE ABOUT THAT!
IN JERUSALEM...
CARRY OUT THE KING'S ORDERS!
A SOUND IS HEARD IN RAMAH, THE SOUND OF BITTER WEEPING. RACHEL IS CRYING FOR HER CHILDREN: SHE REFUSES TO BE COMFORTED, FOR THEY ARE DEAD.
JEREMIAH 31:15

TWO YEARS LATER, AFTER VISITING THE SPRINGS OF CALLIRHOE, KING HEROD DIED IN HIS PALACE IN JERICHO ON THE DAY OF PASSOVER. HIS BODY WAS TAKEN TO THE HERODION, THE FORTIFIED PALACE, NEAR TO JERUSALEM.
GALILEE
PHILIP
SAMARIA
JUDAEA
HEROD ANTIPAS
ARCHELAUS
FAR AWAY...
WE CAN GO BACK TO **NAZARETH, MARY.** THOSE WHO WANTED TO KILL JESUS ARE DEAD.
HEROD'S KINGDOM WAS DIVIDED AMONG THREE OF HIS SONS. THE REIGN OF ARCHELAUS BEGAN WITH SERIOUS RIOTING IN JERUSALEM. ROMAN LEGIONS, STATIONED IN SYRIA, HAD TO RESTORE ORDER.
DO YOU SEE? THERE'S NAZARETH. WE'LL BE ABLE TO LIVE THERE IN PEACE.

A FEW YEARS LATER, IN NAZARETH.
AND NOW, MY BOY, GO AND REST. YOU'LL NEED YOUR STRENGTH TOMORROW MORNING!
WHEN YOU COME OUT OF THE SYNAGOGUE, YOU'LL BE A MAN!
THE NEXT DAY...
I WILL SUBDUE THE SEA, THE RIVERS BENEATH MY RIGHT HAND WILL CALL ME 'MY FATHER', 'MY GOD', 'THE ROCK WHICH SAVES ME'.*
NOW, JESUS, YOU'RE A SON OF THE LAW.
GOD BE PRAISED!
AMEN!
* Psalm 89:25-26
THE PASSOVER PILGRIMS SOON SET OFF.
GLORY TO GOD!
ALLELUIA!
FROM NOW ON YOU'LL COME WITH US TO JERUSALEM FOR THE FESTIVALS.
MAY GOD GUARD US! MAY THE SINGING OF THE PSALMS GIVE US COURAGE!

AFTER A JOURNEY OF ONE WEEK...
JERUSALEM!
THE TEMPLE! THAT'S MY HOME TOO NOW!
YES, IT'S HOME TO ALL JEWS, AND ONE DAY IT WILL BE HOME TO ALL PEOPLE.
MY FRIENDS, MOSHE'S GONE TO BUY THE LAMBS. JESUS, LEVI, SAMUEL AND MICHAEL, THE YOUNGEST IN OUR COMPANY, WILL CARRY THEM TO THE TEMPLE.
MAY THE BLOOD OF THE LAMB DELIVER US FROM ALL EVIL AND SLAVERY.
AMEN!
THE CROWD GATHERED ROUND THE TEMPLE ENTRANCE.
WHEN I SEE SO MANY PEOPLE, I'M ALWAYS AFRAID OF FRESH RIOTS.
NOT THIS YEAR! ROME'S GOT EVERYTHING UNDER CONTROL!
IN FACT THE EMPEROR AUGUSTUS HAD RECEIVED SO MANY COMPLAINTS THAT HE HAD BANISHED ARCHELAUS TO GAUL AND PLACED HIS TERRITORY UNDER ROMAN RULE.

THE SAME NIGHT THEY GATHERED FOR THE PASSOVER MEAL.
BLESSED BE THE LORD OUR GOD, KING OF THE UNIVERSE, WHO DELIVERED OUR ANCESTORS FROM EGYPT, AND HAS ENABLED US TO REACH THIS NIGHT AND TO EAT THE PASSOVER BREAD.

SOON IT WAS TIME TO SET OUT BACK TO NAZARETH.
JESUS? HE MUST BE WITH THE YOUNGSTERS AT THE BACK.
NO, I'VE BEEN THERE. NO ONE'S SEEN HIM...
THEY ASKED EVERYWHERE, BUT NO ONE COULD HELP THEM.
YOU MUST GO BACK TO JERUSALEM.

IN THE END, AFTER SEARCHING FOR THREE DAYS...
WHERE DO YOU COME FROM, MY BOY, AND WHERE DID YOU LEARN ALL THESE THINGS?
HE KNOWS THE SCRIPTURES PERFECTLY, AND HAS AN ANSWER TO EVERY QUESTION!
THERE HE IS!

MY CHILD, YOU HAD US SO WORRIED!
WHY DID YOU HUNT FOR ME? DIDN'T YOU KNOW I WOULD BE IN MY FATHER'S HOUSE?
YOUR SON'S AMAZED US WITH HIS WISDOM! WATCH OVER HIM CARE-FULLY!

IN ROME, IN THE YEAR 14, THE EMPEROR TIBERIUS SUCCEEDED AUGUSTUS. THE TWO SONS OF HEROD, ANTIPAS AND PHILIP, STILL RULED THE AREA AROUND GALILEE AND ITURAEA. AS FOR JUDAEA, IT ALREADY HAD A NEW GOVERNOR, ONE PONTIUS PILATE.
JOSEPH DIED PEACEFULLY IN NAZARETH. JESUS STAYED WITH HIS MOTHER. IN THE FIFTEENTH YEAR OF THE REIGN OF TIBERIUS, JESUS' COUSIN JOHN BEGAN TO PREACH.
REPENT! BECAUSE THE KINGDOM OF HEAVEN IS NEAR!
WHO ARE YOU, TO TALK LIKE THAT?
I'M THE VOICE OF HIM WHO SHOUTS IN THE DESERT, 'MAKE THE WAY STRAIGHT FOR THE LORD!'
MANY PEOPLE CAME FROM JERUSALEM AND ALL JUDAEA TO BE BAPTIZED IN THE JORDAN.
ALL YOUR SINS ARE WASHED AWAY.

BUT JOHN THE BAPTIST ATTACKED THOSE WHO WERE HOSTILE TO HIM...
BROOD OF VIPERS! YOU HOPE TO ESCAPE FROM THE ANGER WHICH IS COMING! ALL THE TREES THAT DON'T PRODUCE FRUIT WILL BE CUT DOWN AND THROWN IN THE FIRE.
AND WE, WHAT MUST WE DO?
HE WHO HAS TWO TUNICS MUST SHARE WITH HIM WHO HAS NONE.
YOU YOURSELF SAY THAT YOU'RE NOT THE MESSIAH, OR ELIJAH, OR MOSES...
...WELL, THEN, WHY DO YOU BAPTIZE?
FOR MYSELF I BAPTIZE WITH WATER, BUT SOMEONE IS COMING WHO IS MUCH GREATER THAN I. HE WILL BAPTIZE YOU WITH THE HOLY SPIRIT.
HE'S THE ONE CHOSEN BY GOD! I'M NOT WORTHY TO UNTIE THE STRAPS OF HIS SANDALS!

SO JOHN DID WHAT JESUS ASKED: HE BAPTIZED HIM IN THE JORDAN.

YOU ARE MY BELOVED SON.

MY FAVOUR RESTS ON YOU.

Eleuteri Serpieri 83

JESUS in Galilee
SCENARIO: Etienne DAHLER
DRAWING: Paolo ELEUTERI-SERPIERI
THEN THE SPIRIT SENT JESUS INTO THE DESERT. HE WAS TEMPTED BY SATAN FOR 40 DAYS.
BE GONE, SATAN! FOR IT IS WRITTEN: YOU SHALL NOT TEMPT THE LORD YOUR GOD!

THEN JESUS WENT BACK TO THE JORDAN VALLEY.

IT IS HE, ANDREW; I'M SURE. THE BAPTIST POINTED HIM OUT TO US!

WELL, COME ON THEN!

WE'RE BOTH DISCIPLES OF JOHN THE BAPTIST, AND...

RABBI, WHERE ARE YOU STAYING?

COME AND SEE.

TOMORROW I MUST GO AND TELL MY BROTHER **SIMON** ABOUT YOU.

WHILE ANDREW SET OFF FOR LAKE TIBERIAS, TWO MEN CAME TO JOHN THE BAPTIST ON THE BANKS OF THE JORDAN.
JOHN! HEROD'S GUARDS ARE COMING TO ARREST YOU!
QUICKLY! YOU STILL HAVE TIME TO ESCAPE!
NO, THE TIME HAS COME.

HE MUST BECOME GREATER, WHILE I BECOME LESS.
ARREST HIM!

THOSE WERE JOHN THE BAPTIST'S LAST WORDS BEFORE THEY TOOK HIM AWAY.
I'M SURE HE WAS TALKING ABOUT YOU.
IT WILL BE BETTER IF WE LEAVE, AND RETURN TO GALILEE.
A LITTLE WHILE LATER, ANDREW...
SIMON! IT'S JESUS OF NAZARETH- THE ONE I TOLD YOU ABOUT!
COME WITH ME; I'LL MAKE YOU FISH FOR PEOPLE.
AND STRAIGHT AWAY THEY LEFT THEIR NETS AND FOLLOWED JESUS.
THAT SAME NIGHT JESUS AND HIS FRIENDS GATHERED AT SIMON'S HOUSE IN CAPERNAUM.
TOMORROW WE ARE GOING TO CANA; WE'VE ALL BEEN INVITED TO A WEDDING.

THE NEXT DAY, SIMON...
MOVE BACK! LET HIM THROUGH!

YOU, FOLLOW ME!
IT'S PHILIP, MASTER! HE LIVES NEARBY.

MASTER, LET ME GO ON AHEAD...
NATHANAEL! NATHANAEL!
NATHANAEL, WE'VE FOUND THE ONE THE LAW AND THE PROPHETS SPEAK OF: IT'S **JESUS OF NAZARETH!**
CAN ANYTHING GOOD COME OUT OF NAZARETH, PHILIP?
COME AND SEE FOR YOURSELF, NATHANAEL!

LOOK, NATHANAEL, HE'S COMING!
HERE'S A REAL ISRAELITE! THERE'S NOTHING FALSE ABOUT HIM.
HOW DO YOU KNOW ME?
I SAW YOU BEFORE PHILIP CALLED YOU, WHEN YOU WERE SITTING UNDER THE FIG TREE!
RABBI, YOU'RE THE SON OF GOD, THE KING OF ISRAEL!
YOU BELIEVE, BECAUSE I SAID THAT I SAW YOU UNDER THE FIG TREE! NATHANAEL, YOU'LL SEE MUCH GREATER THINGS THAN THAT...
ON THE THIRD DAY, JESUS AND HIS DISCIPLES REACHED CANA. THERE THEY MET MARY, JESUS' MOTHER.
LET'S MAKE FOR THE WEDDING.
WE'VE BEEN WAITING FOR YOU.
I KNEW YOU'D BE AT THE WEDDING TOO.

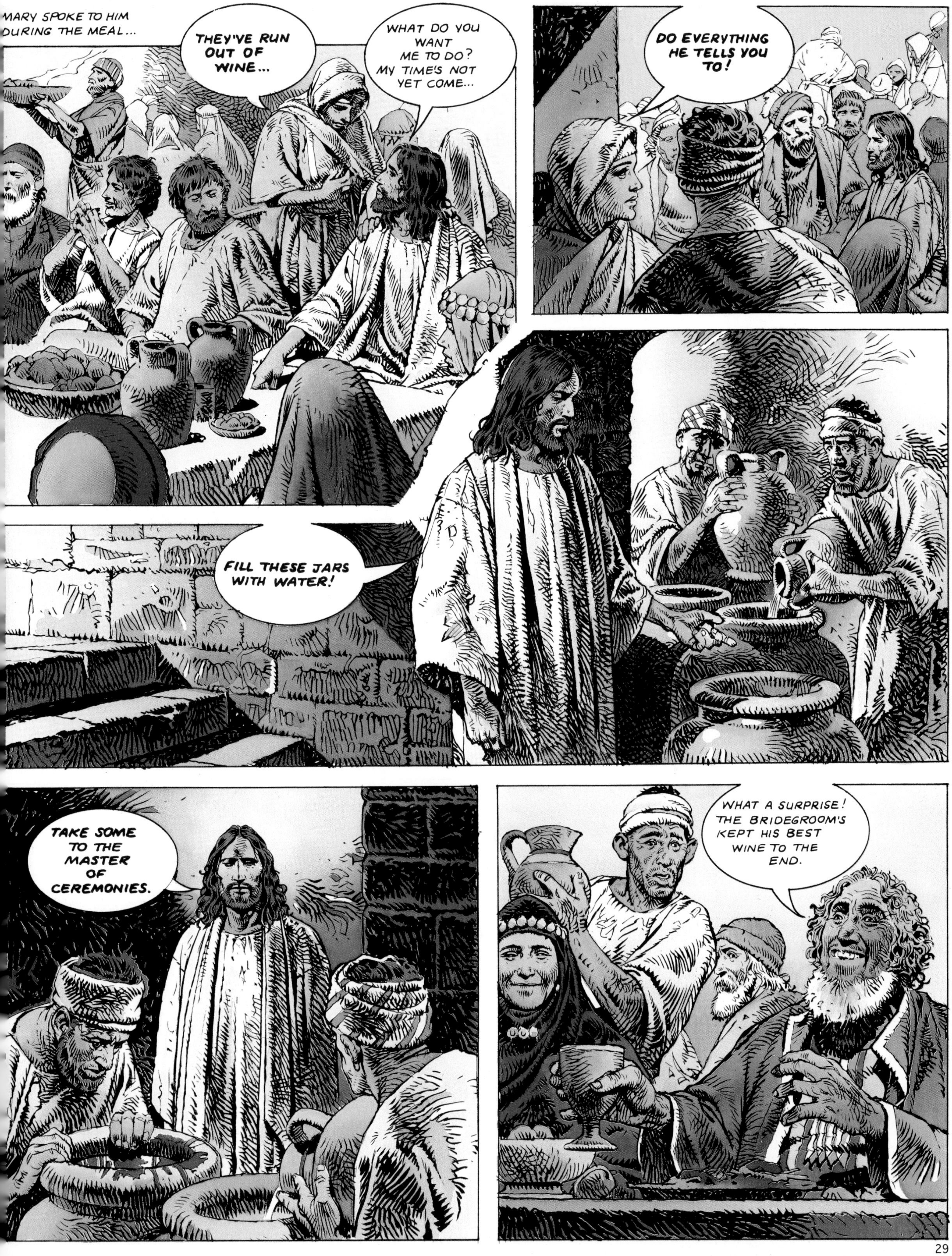

MARY SPOKE TO HIM DURING THE MEAL...

THEY'VE RUN OUT OF WINE...

WHAT DO YOU WANT ME TO DO? MY TIME'S NOT YET COME...

DO EVERYTHING HE TELLS YOU TO!

FILL THESE JARS WITH WATER!

LEAVING CANA, JESUS SET OUT FOR NAZARETH.
THE KINGDOM OF HEAVEN IS LIKE A MUSTARD-SEED. IT'S THE SMALLEST SEED, BUT ONCE IT IS IN THE GROUND...
...IT QUICKLY BECOMES SUCH A BIG TREE THAT ALL THE BIRDS COME TO SHELTER IN ITS BRANCHES.
JESUS WENT TO THE SYNAGOGUE ON THE SABBATH.
AND NOW I AM GOING TO READ THE SCROLL OF THE PROPHET ISAIAH...
RABBI, MAY I READ IT?
THE LORD HAS FILLED ME WITH HIS SPIRIT. HE HAS CHOSEN ME TO BRING THE GOOD NEWS TO THE POOR. HE HAS SENT ME TO ANNOUNCE RELEASE TO PRISONERS,
TO GIVE BACK THEIR SIGHT TO THE BLIND, TO SET FREE THE OPPRESSED AND TELL PEOPLE THAT THE TIME HAS COME FOR THE LORD TO SAVE THEM.

THEY CHASED HIM OUT OF THE TOWN, AND DRAGGED HIM TO THE EDGE OF A CLIFF TO THROW HIM OVER.

THEN THEY LET HIM GO.

ON THE WAY BACK TO CAPERNAUM...
THE KINGDOM OF GOD IS ALSO LIKE A NET THROWN IN THE SEA ... IT GATHERS ALL SORTS OF FISH...
...THEN THE FISHER-MEN PULL IT ONTO THE BANK AND SORT THE FISH - THAT'S WHAT IT'LL BE LIKE AT THE END OF THE WORLD.
IT'S JESUS! HE'S COME BACK!
A FEW DAYS LATER...
SIMON! ROW OUT INTO THE DEEP WATER AND CAST YOUR NET.
BUT... RABBI... WE'VE FISHED ALL NIGHT AND CAUGHT NOTHING!
SIMON! DO WHAT HE SAYS!
AND THEN SIMON...
HEY! COME AND HELP US. OUR NETS ARE FULL TO BREAKING-POINT!

LEAVE ME, LORD, I'M A SINFUL MAN.
DON'T BE AFRAID, SIMON! I'LL MAKE YOU ALL FISH FOR PEOPLE... FOLLOW ME!
SIMON, FROM NOW ON YOU'LL BE CALLED PETER.
WHAT A CATCH!
I'VE NEVER SEEN SO MANY FISH!
BUT... WHERE ARE THEY GOING?
LEAVING THEIR NETS, THEY FOLLOWED HIM STRAIGHT AWAY.
IN CAPERNAUM, THE FOLLOWING SABBATH.
I'VE NOT COME TO DO AWAY WITH THE LAW AND THE PROPHETS, BUT TO FULFIL THEM.
WHAT DO YOU WANT OF US, JESUS OF NAZARETH? HAVE YOU COME TO DESTROY US?
I KNOW WHO YOU ARE... THE HOLY ONE OF GOD.
SILENCE, UNCLEAN SPIRIT! COME OUT OF THIS MAN!
EVEN THE EVIL SPIRITS OBEY HIM!

LEAVING THE SYNAGOGUE, HE SET OFF FOR PETER'S HOUSE.
LET'S SPEND THE SABBATH AT MY HOME.
PETER'S MOTHER-IN-LAW'S IN BED WITH A BAD FEVER.
DON'T WORRY!
MAY THIS FEVER LEAVE YOU, AS I WANT IT TO!
BUT YOU'RE UP AGAIN!
YES, I'M HEALED... I'LL GO AND PREPARE A MEAL FOR YOU.
DON'T WORRY ABOUT FOOD AND DRINK AND CLOTHES... FIRST LOOK FOR THE KINGDOM OF GOD AND HE'LL GIVE YOU EVERYTHING YOU NEED.

THAT EVENING...
THE SUN'S SET. THE SABBATH IS OVER!
LET'S SET OFF RIGHT AWAY.
FROM ALL AROUND THEY BROUGHT THE SICK TO JESUS.
I CAN SEE YOU! I'M HEALED!
JESUS! MAKE ME BETTER TOO!
JOHN, THE KINGDOM'S RIGHT HERE - AMONGST US!
YES, PETER, AND THIS IS ONLY THE BEGINNING!
GO! AND REMEMBER: DO TO OTHER PEOPLE WHAT YOU WOULD LIKE THEM TO DO TO YOU, BECAUSE THAT'S WHAT THE LAW AND THE PROPHETS TEACH US.
JESUS SPOKE TO THOSE HE'D CURED.

THE NEXT MORNING, AFTER HE'D PRAYED FOR A LONG TIME ...
WE MUST MOVE ON! OTHER TOWNS MUST ALSO HEAR ABOUT THE KINGDOM OF GOD.
JESUS PREACHED IN THE SYNAGOGUES ALL OVER GALILEE, HEALING THE SICK AND DRIVING OUT EVIL SPIRITS.
ALL THOSE PEOPLE AROUND HIM! IT WORRIES ME...
I WONDER WHAT JERUSALEM'S GOING TO THINK.
ALONG THE ROAD...
JESUS! IT'S A LEPER! KEEP BACK!
COME BACK! HE'S UNCLEAN!
YOU CAN MAKE ME CLEAN, IF YOU WANT TO.
I WILL! BE HEALED!
GO, SHOW YOURSELF TO THE PRIEST, AND MAKE THE OFFERING FOR YOUR HEALING, AS MOSES LAID DOWN.

A FEW DAYS LATER JESUS RETURNED TO CAPERNAUM.
IT'S NOT WHAT'S ON THE OUTSIDE OF A PERSON THAT MAKES HIM DIRTY, BUT RATHER WHAT'S IN HIS HEART.
WHEN THEY HEARD THAT JESUS WAS THERE, THE CROWD SURGED INTO THE HOUSE.
WE'LL NEVER GET THROUGH!
I HAVE AN IDEA! LET'S GO TO THE BACK.
PUSH THE PLANKS APART. WE'LL GET HIM DOWN THAT WAY.
MY ROOF!
OH! LOOK!
LET THEM CARRY ON.
FRIEND, YOUR SINS ARE FORGIVEN.
HOW CAN HE SAY SUCH A THING! ONLY GOD CAN FORGIVE SINS!

WHY DO YOU CRITICIZE ME? IS IT EASIER TO SAY: 'YOUR SINS ARE FORGIVEN', OR 'GET UP AND WALK'?
KNOW THIS! THE SON OF MAN HAS THE POWER TO FORGIVE. THAT'S WHY I CAN ALSO SAY, 'GET UP, PICK UP YOUR BED, AND GO HOME.'
GOD BE PRAISED! WE'VE NEVER SEEN ANYTHING LIKE IT!
HOW CAN HE TALK LIKE THAT?
SO YOU MUST BE MERCIFUL, AS YOUR FATHER IS MERCIFUL.

MATTHEW WAS SITTING AT THE CUSTOMS OFFICE AT THE ENTRANCE TO CAPERNAUM.
IS THAT ALL YOU HAVE IN YOUR CART?
JUST WHAT I'VE TOLD YOU!
LISTEN: TWO MEN WENT UP TO THE TEMPLE TO PRAY...
...ONE WAS A PHARISEE, THE OTHER A TAX-COLLECTOR. THE FIRST THANKED GOD THAT HE WASN'T A CHEAT AND A BAD MAN LIKE THE OTHER...
AND MY CHANGE?
...BUT THE TAX-COLLECTOR SAID: 'HAVE MERCY, LORD! I'M A SINNER.'
HERE, KEEP THE LOT!
WHAT'S COME OVER HIM?
WELL, THEN! IT WAS THAT MAN WHOM GOD HEARD, NOT THE OTHER. WHOEVER MAKES HIMSELF GREAT, WILL BE CUT DOWN TO SIZE, WHILE THE PERSON WHO'S HUMBLE WILL BE LIFTED UP.
MATTHEW! FOLLOW ME!

SO MATTHEW GAVE A FEAST IN HIS HOUSE IN HONOUR OF JESUS.
MY FRIENDS! I LISTENED TO THE RABBI THIS AFTER-NOON AND MY HEART WAS TURNED INSIDE OUT. NOW YOU TOO MUST LISTEN TO HIM.
WHY DOES YOUR MASTER EAT WITH SINNERS?
IT'S SICK PEOPLE WHO NEED A DOCTOR, NOT THOSE WHO ARE HEALTHY.
WHICH OF YOU, IF HE HAD 100 SHEEP, AND LOST ONE, WOULDN'T LEAVE THE 99 OTHERS, TO LOOK FOR IT?
...AND WHEN HE'S FOUND IT, HE INVITES ALL HIS FRIENDS TO CELEBRATE WITH HIM.
I TELL YOU, THERE'S MORE JOY IN HEAVEN OVER ONE SINNER WHO REPENTS THAN OVER 99 GOOD PEOPLE WHO DON'T NEED TO REPENT.

THE NEXT SABBATH JESUS WAS TEACHING IN THE SYNAGOGUE. THERE WAS A MAN WHOSE RIGHT HAND WAS PARALYSED.
STAND UP, AND COME HERE!
IF HE DARES TO HEAL HIM, WE'LL BE ABLE TO ACCUSE HIM.

I ASK YOU: WHICH IS RIGHT - TO DO EVIL ON THE SABBATH, OR TO DO GOOD?

THE PHARISEES KEPT QUIET...
GOOD! THEN STRETCH OUT YOUR HAND!

HE'S HEALED!
ALLELUIA!
GOD IS ALL-POWERFUL!
NOW WE KNOW ENOUGH.

HE CLAIMS TO BE LORD OF THE SABBATH, AND BEHAVES LIKE IT TOO!

THAT'S BLASPHEMY! GOD ALONE IS LORD OF THE SABBATH!

WORST OF ALL, HE ATTRACTS CROWDS. EVERY DAY MORE PEOPLE FOLLOW HIM.

WE MUST ACT QUICKLY, BEFORE THEY BECOME TOO POWERFUL.

JESUS SPENT THE NEXT NIGHT ON THE MOUNTAIN, PRAYING.

WHEN DAYLIGHT CAME, HE BROUGHT HIS DISCIPLES TOGETHER AND CHOSE 12 OF THEM. HE CALLED THEM APOSTLES.

PETER AND ANDREW, JAMES AND JOHN, PHILIP AND BARTHOLOMEW, MATTHEW, THOMAS, JAMES...

... SIMON, JUDE, AND JUDAS...
THE ISCARIOT? BUT HE'S NOT EVEN A GALILEAN!
THAT'S WHAT I SAID: JUDAS ISCARIOT!

WHEN HE WENT BACK DOWN TOWARDS THE TOWN...
MASTER! THEY'VE COME FROM EVERYWHERE TO SEE YOU, FROM JUDAEA AND JERUSALEM, TYRE AND SIDON.
JESUS! HEAL ME! ...IF ONLY I COULD TOUCH HIM...
WHAT SHALL WE DO?
MAKE THEM SIT DOWN, PETER.
AFTER HEALING MANY SICK PEOPLE, JESUS TAUGHT THE CROWD.
HAPPY ARE THE POOR, THE KINGDOM OF GOD IS THEIRS. HAPPY ARE THE MEEK, THEY WILL INHERIT THE EARTH. HAPPY ARE THOSE WHO MOURN, THEY WILL BE COMFORTED...
HAPPY ARE THOSE WHO HUNGER AND THIRST FOR JUSTICE, THEY WILL BE SATISFIED. HAPPY ARE THE MERCIFUL, GOD WILL BE MERCIFUL TO THEM. HAPPY ARE THE PURE IN HEART, THEY WILL SEE GOD.
HAPPY ARE THOSE WHO WORK FOR PEACE, GOD WILL CALL THEM HIS CHILDREN. HAPPY ARE THOSE WHO ARE PERSECUTED FOR THE SAKE OF JUSTICE, THE KINGDOM OF HEAVEN IS THEIRS. HAPPY ARE YOU, WHEN PEOPLE HATE YOU BECAUSE OF ME.

AS JESUS CAME INTO CAPERNAUM, A ROMAN CENTURION MET HIM...
LORD! MY SERVANT'S SERIOUSLY ILL. HE'S IN GREAT PAIN.
I'LL COME AND CURE HIM.
NO! I'M NOT GOOD ENOUGH FOR YOU TO COME TO MY HOUSE. JUST SAY THE WORD, AND HE'LL BE HEALED.
I TELL YOU, I HAVEN'T FOUND FAITH LIKE THIS, EVEN IN ISRAEL.
LOOK AT THAT! NOW HE'S FRIENDLY WITH THE ROMANS.
I TOLD YOU, WE CAN'T COUNT ON HIM TO FREE US FROM THE ROMANS.
GO HOME. BECAUSE OF YOUR FAITH HE'LL BE HEALED.
AND AT THAT VERY MOMENT, THE SERVANT WAS HEALED.

SOME TIME LATER, A PHARISEE CAME TO SEE JESUS.
MY NAME'S SIMON. I LIVE NEARBY. WILL YOU COME AND EAT AT MY TABLE?
OF COURSE, SIMON! I NEVER REFUSE TO GO WHERE I'M INVITED.
THAT EVENING, DURING THE MEAL...
WOMAN, WHAT ARE YOU DOING HERE? IN THE HOUSE OF A GOOD MAN?
I DON'T UNDERSTAND. YOU SAY THAT YOU FULFIL THE LAW, BUT YOU SEEM TO SCORN IT...
IF HE WERE A PROPHET, HE'D KNOW WHAT SORT OF WOMAN WAS TOUCHING HIM!

SIMON, I'VE SOMETHING TO SAY TO YOU... A CREDITOR HAD 2 DEBTORS; THE ONE OWED HIM A LARGE AMOUNT, THE OTHER TEN TIMES AS MUCH. HE FORGAVE BOTH THE DEBTS. WHICH ONE LOVED HIM MORE?
THE ONE WHO OWED MORE.
THAT'S RIGHT! THIS WOMAN CAN NOW GO IN PEACE. HER MANY SINS ARE FORGIVEN.
WHO IS THIS MAN...
...WHO EVEN FORGIVES SINS...?
I'VE NEVER MET ANYONE WHO LOVES LIKE THIS...
AND JESUS CONTINUED TO PREACH THE GOOD NEWS OF THE KINGDOM OF GOD IN TOWN AFTER TOWN.
Eleuteri Serpieri 84

JESUS
AND THE TWELVE
TRAVELLING THROUGHOUT GALILEE, JESUS OF NAZARETH, ACCOMPANIED BY THE TWELVE APOSTLES CONTINUES TO WORK WONDERS AND MIRACLES... EVEN THOUGH THE SCRIBES AND THE PHARISEES ARE AGAINST HIM.
HE'S JUST DELIVERED MY SON OF AN EVIL SPIRIT!
HARDLY SURPRISING! HE HIMSELF SERVES THE PRINCE OF DEVILS!
A COUNTRY AT WAR WITH ITSELF WILL BE DESTROYED. IF SATAN'S FIGHTING AGAINST HIMSELF, HOW CAN HE CONTINUE TO LIVE?
HE'S RIGHT! YOUR ACCUSATIONS DON'T MAKE SENSE!
SCENARIO: Etienne DAHLER
DRAWING: José BIELSA
EITHER THAT MAN COMES FROM GOD, OR HE'S SENT BY SATAN...
YOU STILL DARE TO ASK THAT QUESTION AFTER WHAT YOU'VE JUST SEEN?

JESUS! WAIT!
DON'T GO LIKE THIS... COME AND EAT IN MY HOUSE.
VERY WELL... TAKE US TO YOUR HOME.
DID YOU SEE? HE DIDN'T WASH HIS HANDS BEFORE THE MEAL.
YES. HE'S EATING WITH UNCLEAN HANDS...
THIS IS WHAT YOU'RE LIKE, YOU PHARISEES. YOU CLEAN THE OUTSIDE OF THE CUP! BUT THE INSIDE REMAINS DIRTY WITH LIES AND SLANDER!
FOOLS! DIDN'T HE WHO MADE THE OUTSIDE ALSO MAKE THE INSIDE?
José Zielba

WOE TO YOU, PHARISEES! YOU RESPECT TRADITION, BUT NEGLECT JUSTICE AND THE LOVE OF GOD!
YOU WERE SAYING THAT THIS MAN HAD TO BE SENT EITHER BY GOD OR BY SATAN...
YOU WERE RIGHT... HE'S SENT BY SATAN!
THEN JESUS WENT BACK TO THE SHORES OF LAKE TIBERIAS...
WOE ALSO TO THE DOCTORS OF THE LAW WHO PUT LOADS ON OTHER PEOPLE THEY THEMSELVES WON'T CARRY!
CROWDS CAME FROM ALL AROUND TO LISTEN TO HIM.
GET INTO THIS BOAT, MASTER, AND SPEAK TO THESE PEOPLE.
SIT DOWN, ALL OF YOU!
LISTEN: A SOWER WENT OUT TO SOW...

...AND AS HE SOWED, SOME OF THE SEED FELL ON THE PATH AND THE BIRDS ATE IT.
SOME OF IT FELL ON ROCKY GROUND. IT SPROUTED QUICKLY, BUT HAVING NO SOIL, IT WAS BURNT UP BY THE SUN... THE THIRD PORTION FELL AMONG THISTLES WHICH CHOKED THE PLANTS SO THEY COULDN'T GROW.
FINALLY, SOME FELL ON GOOD GROUND. IT PRODUCED CORN, WITH 30, 60 OR EVEN 100 GRAINS IN EACH EAR.
THOSE WHO HAVE EARS TO HEAR, LET THEM HEAR!

A LITTLE LATER...
RABBI, NOT ALL OF US UNDERSTOOD YOUR PARABLE...
YET IT'S QUITE SIMPLE: THE SOWER SOWS GOD'S WORD...
josé Zielsa

... SOME HEAR IT, BUT THEN SATAN COMES AND SNATCHES IT AWAY...
LIKE THE SCRIBES AND THE PHARISEES THE OTHER DAY!

... OTHERS DON'T LET IT TAKE ROOT, SO THEY DON'T LAST LONG. WHEN THE FIRST TEST COMES, THEY GIVE UP.

... IN OTHERS THEIR WORRIES AND DESIRES CHOKE THE WORD.

BUT EVERYONE HAS SOME GOOD SOIL.
YOU'RE RIGHT, JOHN, BUT THIS GROUND NEEDS TO BE WORKED...

JESUS AGAIN TAUGHT THE CROWDS FOR A LONG TIME, THEN...
NOW LET'S GO TO THE OTHER SIDE OF THE LAKE.

AND WHILE THE DISCIPLES SENT THE CROWD AWAY...
HERE, MASTER!
I'M COMING WITH YOU!
GO HOME, ALL OF YOU.

SUDDENLY, DURING THE CROSSING...
HEY, PETER, THE WIND'S GETTING STRONGER...
THERE'S A STORM COMING. WE'RE IN DANGER...!

SOON THE STORM BROKE...
PETER! WE'RE ALL GOING TO DIE!
MASTER! WAKE UP! DO SOMETHING!
LOOK OUT!

THEN JESUS CALLED OUT...
SILENCE!
THE WATER AND THE WIND DIED DOWN, AND THERE WAS A GREAT CALM.

WHY WERE YOU FRIGHTENED? DO YOU STILL HAVE NO FAITH?
WHO IS THIS MAN? EVEN THE WIND AND THE SEA OBEY HIM!
AFTER A FEW DAYS IN THE LAND OF THE GADARENES,* JESUS CROSSED BACK TO CAPERNAUM.
* People of Gadara, south-east of Lake Tiberias.
A LARGE CROWD WAS ALREADY WAITING FOR HIM.
RABBI, MY DAUGHTER'S DYING! COME AND LAY YOUR HANDS ON HER, AND SAVE HER LIFE!
JAIRUS, TAKE ME TO HER.
JAIRUS IS AN OFFICIAL IN THE SYNAGOGUE IN CAPERNAUM.
JESUS! HEAL ME!
HAVE PITY, MASTER!
THERE WAS ALSO A WOMAN WHO HAD BEEN BLEEDING BADLY FOR 12 YEARS...
IF I COULD JUST TOUCH HIS CLOAK, I'M SURE I'D BE CURED.

SHE MANAGED TO REACH HIM...
...AND IMMEDIATELY SHE WAS HEALED.
PETER, WHO TOUCHED ME?
YOU SEE THE CROWD PRESSING ALL ROUND YOU, AND YOU ASK WHO TOUCHED YOU!
I DID, MASTER.
MY DAUGHTER, YOUR FAITH HAS SAVED YOU. GO IN PEACE!
JAIRUS, YOUR DAUGHTER IS DEAD!
DON'T BE AFRAID... ONLY BELIEVE.
PETER, JAMES AND JOHN, COME WITH ME. EVERYONE ELSE STAY HERE.
THEY SOON REACHED JAIRUS'S HOUSE...
ALAS! ALAS!

BUT THE NEWS SOON SPREAD THROUGH THE WHOLE REGION.

A LITTLE LATER...

YOU SEE, PETER? THE SMALLEST VILLAGE WELCOMES ME... AND MY OWN PEOPLE REJECT ME... BUT I CAN'T ABANDON THEM... LET'S GO BACK TO NAZARETH!

ON THE SABBATH JESUS WENT TO THE SYNAGOGUE IN NAZARETH. HE'D ATTENDED IT FOR NEARLY 30 YEARS, SO HE KNEW IT WELL.

THE LAW OF MOSES TEACHES THAT ANYONE COMMITTING A CRIME MUST BE PUNISHED BY THE JUDGES...

...BUT I SAY TO YOU: WHOEVER IS ANGRY WITH HIS BROTHER, DESERVES PUNISHMENT JUST AS MUCH.
YOU'VE COME TO GIVE US A LESSON, YOU WORKER OF MIRACLES?
YOU CAN SEE HE'S GONE MAD!

ANYONE WHO CALLS HIS BROTHER A FOOL, DESERVES TO BE THROWN INTO THE FIRE OF GEHENNA!
SILENCE!

JESUS, YOU'RE ONE OF US... BUT YOU MUST UNDERSTAND THAT WE CAN'T ACCEPT WHAT YOU'RE SUGGESTING.
I TELL YOU THE TRUTH. A PROPHET'S REJECTED ONLY IN HIS OWN LAND.

THEN JESUS AND THE TWELVE LEFT NAZARETH.
HOW CAN PEOPLE BE SO STUBBORN?

MASTER, IF THESE PEOPLE DON'T WANT THE KINGDOM OF GOD, TELL OTHERS ABOUT IT...
YES, JOHN, THERE'S A HUGE HARVEST, BUT THERE ARE FEW WORKERS!

SO PRAY THAT THE LORD OF THE HARVEST WILL SEND LABOURERS TO REAP HIS HARVEST.
A WEEK OR TWO LATER...
FROM TOMORROW YOU'LL LEAVE TWO BY TWO. DON'T CARRY ANYTHING FOR THE JOURNEY...
BUT WHAT WILL WE DO WITHOUT YOU?
DON'T BE AFRAID. I'LL GIVE YOU POWER OVER EVIL SPIRITS.
AND IF ANY PLACE DOESN'T WELCOME YOU, LEAVE IT, AND SHAKE ITS DUST FROM YOUR SANDALS.
THE NEXT DAY PETER...
ANDREW, YOU KNOW WHEREVER WE GO, THE MASTER WILL BE WITH US!
THEY WENT FROM VILLAGE TO VILLAGE, PREACHING THAT PEOPLE SHOULD TURN AWAY FROM THEIR SINS. THEY DROVE OUT DEMONS, AND CURED THE SICK.
José Zielsa

ONE DAY THE DISCIPLES OF JOHN THE BAPTIST CAME TO FIND JESUS.

MASTER, WE'VE TERRIBLE NEWS FOR YOU. **JOHN'S DEAD!**
HEROD ANTIPAS HAD HIM EXECUTED.
EXECUTED? HOW CAN THAT BE?

IT'S INCREDIBLE! HEROD WAS GIVING A PARTY FOR HIS BIRTHDAY...
HERODIAS, THE WIFE HE'D TAKEN FROM HIS BROTHER PHILIP, WAS THERE.

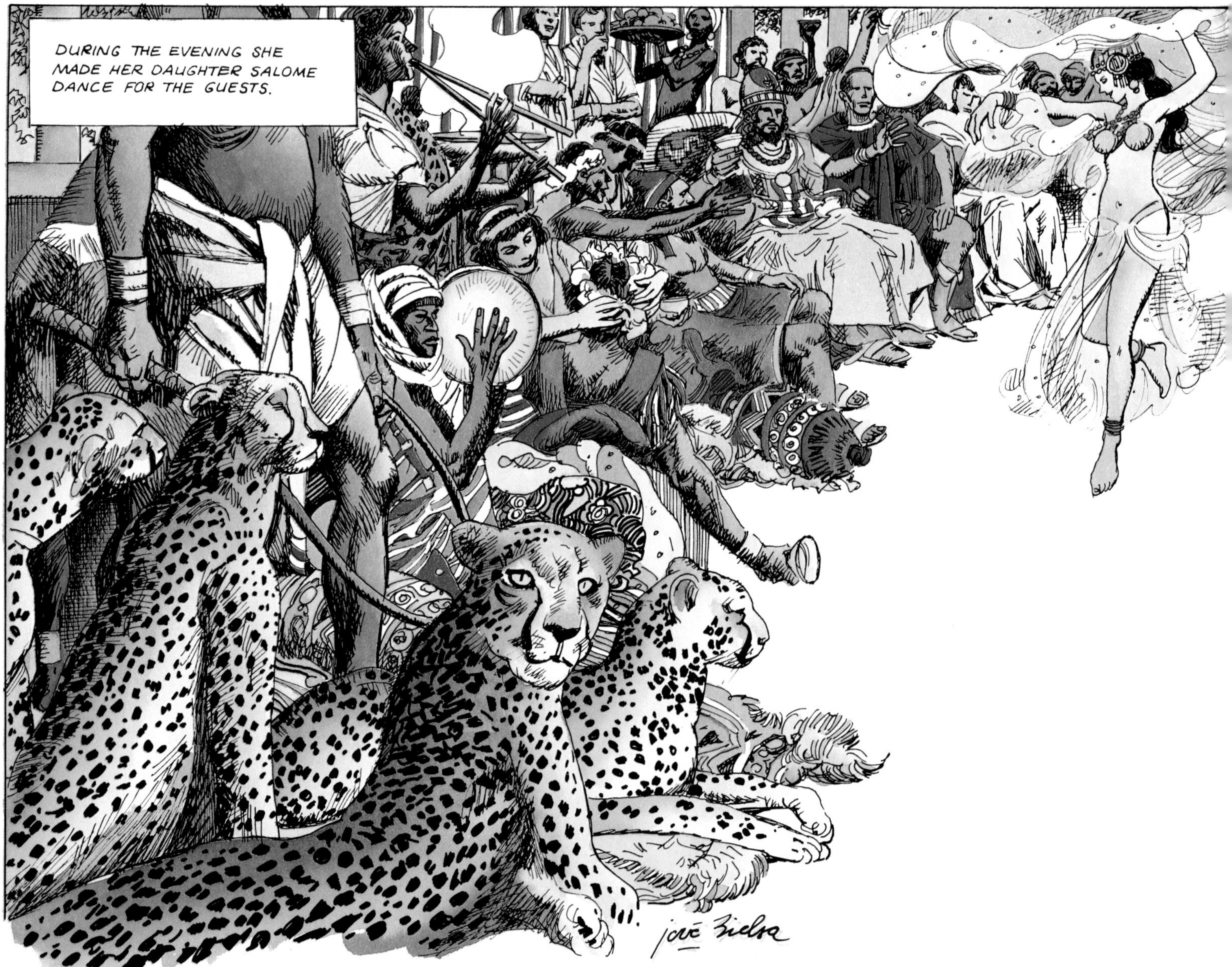

DURING THE EVENING SHE MADE HER DAUGHTER SALOME DANCE FOR THE GUESTS.

THEN...
YOU'VE DANCED SUPERBLY. I'LL GIVE YOU ANYTHING YOU WANT!
SALOME WENT OUT FOR A FEW MOMENTS TO ASK HER MOTHER ...

WHEN SHE CAME BACK...
I WANT THE HEAD OF JOHN THE BAPTIST ON A DISH!
WHAT?

WHAT ARE YOU SAYING?
HERODIAS HAD NEVER FORGIVEN JOHN THE BAPTIST FOR PUBLICLY CONDEMNING HER ADULTERY.
HEROD WAS CAUGHT IN A TRAP.

VERY WELL, THEN...

JOHN WAS MORE THAN A PROPHET. IT WAS HE OF WHOM IT WAS WRITTEN: I WILL SEND MY MESSENGER TO PREPARE THE WAY FOR ME.*

I TELL YOU, AMONG ALL HUMAN BEINGS THERE'S NO ONE GREATER THAN JOHN.

* Malachi 3:1

WEEKS WENT BY. SPRING WAS ALREADY COVERING THE HILLS OF GALILEE WHEN THE DISCIPLES RETURNED FROM THEIR MISSION.
MASTER, IT'S WONDERFUL TO SEE YOU AGAIN!
WELL?
WHEREVER WE WENT, MANY TURNED BACK TO GOD, AND THE SICK WERE HEALED!
SOON ALL THE TWELVE WERE BACK, AND TOLD THEIR STORIES...
BUT SOMETIMES THEY CHASED US AWAY...
AND NOW WHAT ARE WE GOING TO DO? CAN WE ALWAYS LIVE BY BEGGING OUR BREAD, WITHOUT EVEN KNOWING IN THE MORNING WHERE WE'LL SLEEP THAT NIGHT?
HE'S RIGHT. WE HAVE FAMILIES, CHILDREN... WE MUST SEE TO THEIR NEEDS.
THE BIRDS OF THE SKY DON'T SOW OR REAP, BUT GOD FEEDS THEM...

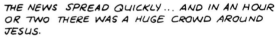

THE LILIES DON'T SPIN OR WEAVE, BUT NOT EVEN SOLOMON IN ALL HIS SPLENDID ROBES WAS EVER DRESSED LIKE ONE OF THESE.
YOUR FATHER KNOWS WHAT YOU NEED. FIRST LOOK FOR THE KINGDOM OF GOD, AND HE'LL GIVE YOU EVERYTHING YOU NEED.
JESUS AND THE TWELVE WENT AWAY TO BETHSAIDA.

BUT VERY SOON...
JESUS AND HIS DISCIPLES ARE BACK! I'VE JUST SEEN THEM!
LET'S GO!
LET'S FOLLOW THEM!

THE NEWS SPREAD QUICKLY... AND IN AN HOUR OR TWO THERE WAS A HUGE CROWD AROUND JESUS.

THERE HE IS!
HURRY! HURRY!

JESUS TAUGHT THEM, AND HEALED MANY SICK PEOPLE. BUT IT WAS GETTING LATE...
LORD, SEND THEM AWAY, SO THEY CAN GO AND BUY SOMETHING TO EAT.
NO, YOU GIVE THEM SOMETHING TO EAT.

200 SILVER COINS WOULDN'T BUY ENOUGH BREAD TO FEED ALL THESE PEOPLE!
THERE'S A LAD HERE WHO HAS 5 BARLEY LOAVES AND 2 FISH...
MAKE THE CROWD SIT DOWN.

BUT ... WHAT CAN YOU DO WITH SO LITTLE?
ANDREW, DON'T ARGUE!

THANK YOU, FATHER, FOR TAKING CARE OF YOUR CHILDREN!

NOW SHARE THIS AMONG THE PEOPLE.

HELP YOURSELVES-
AS MUCH AS
YOU LIKE!
MATTHEW,
MY BASKET'S
EMPTY...
GET SOME
MORE FROM THE
MASTER.
PETER!
MATTHEW!
COME AND SEE!
EVERYONE
HAD
ENOUGH!
IT'S UNBELIEVABLE!
AND THERE MUST BE
5000 MEN, NOT
COUNTING WOMEN
AND CHILDREN.

MASTER, THEY'VE ALL EATEN THEIR FILL, AND THERE'S STILL SOME BREAD AND FISH LEFT OVER.
GATHER UP THE PIECES SO THAT NOTHING'S WASTED.
THEY FILLED 12 BASKETS WITH WHAT WAS LEFT!
NOW, PETER, LET THESE PEOPLE GO HOME, AND YOU CROSS THE LAKE. I'LL MEET YOU THERE.
WHEN THE CROWD HAD GONE, JESUS WENT UP ONTO THE MOUNTAIN TO PRAY.

MEANWHILE, PETER ON HIS SHIP, IN THE MIDDLE OF THE NIGHT...
THE WIND'S AGAINST US!
WELL, ROW HARDER THEN!

SUDDENLY...
AAAAH!! A GHOST!

CHEER UP! IT'S I. DON'T BE AFRAID.
MASTER, IF IT REALLY IS YOU, ORDER ME TO COME TO YOU.

COME!
BUT PETER, YOU AREN'T GOING TO...

... WALK ON THE WATER!
I'M FRIGHTENED!

THE NEXT DAY THE CROWD SET OFF TO LOOK FOR JESUS.

WHEN THE CROWD MET HIM AT CAPERNAUM...
YOU'RE LOOKING FOR ME BECAUSE YOU HAD ENOUGH TO EAT.
BUT MY FATHER WANTS YOU TO HAVE THE BREAD OF HEAVEN, WHICH GIVES LIFE TO THE WORLD.
LORD, GIVE US THIS BREAD FOR EVER.
I AM THE BREAD OF LIFE. THOSE WHO COME TO ME WILL NEVER BE HUNGRY AGAIN; THOSE WHO BELIEVE IN ME WILL NEVER BE THIRSTY AGAIN.
BUT THAT'S JOSEPH OF NAZARETH'S SON! HOW CAN HE SAY THAT HE COMES FROM HEAVEN?

A LITTLE LATER, IN THE SYNAGOGUE IN CAPERNAUM, WHERE MANY WERE TURNING AGAINST JESUS...
YOUR FATHERS ATE MANNA IN THE DESERT AND THEY DIED. BUT THOSE WHO EAT THE BREAD OF HEAVEN WILL LIVE FOR EVER.

AND THIS BREAD IS MY FLESH WHICH I GIVE FOR THE LIFE OF THE WORLD.
HOW CAN HE GIVE US HIS FLESH TO EAT?

THOSE WHO EAT MY FLESH AND DRINK MY BLOOD HAVE ETERNAL LIFE. I WILL RAISE THEM UP TO LIFE ON THE LAST DAY.
THAT'S TOO MUCH!

OUTSIDE THE SYNAGOGUE THE DISCIPLES TRIED TO WORK THIS OUT...
IT'S VERY DIFFICULT! HOW CAN WE UNDERSTAND IT?
AND HOW CAN HE SAY THAT?

THE WORDS I'VE SPOKEN TO YOU ARE SPIRIT AND LIFE. BUT THERE ARE MANY AMONG YOU WHO DON'T BELIEVE IT!

FROM THAT TIME MANY OF THOSE WHO HAD FOLLOWED HIM, LEFT HIM.
AND YOU, DO YOU WANT TO LEAVE ME TOO?
PETER REPLIED...
LORD, TO WHOM SHOULD WE GO? YOU HAVE THE WORDS OF ETERNAL LIFE!
WE BELIEVE, AND WE KNOW YOU ARE THE HOLY ONE OF GOD.
YET ONE OF YOU WILL BETRAY ME!

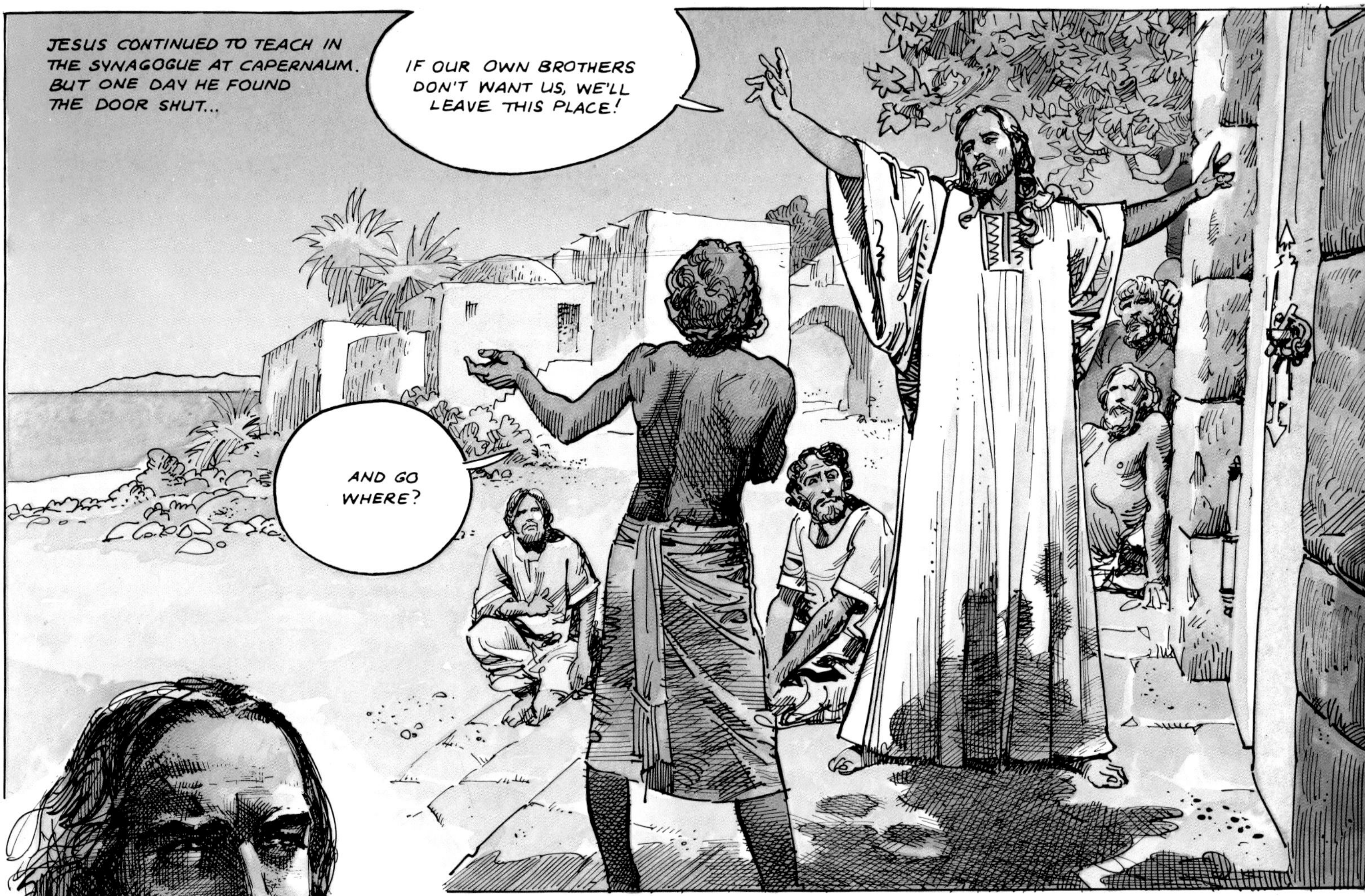

JESUS CONTINUED TO TEACH IN THE SYNAGOGUE AT CAPERNAUM. BUT ONE DAY HE FOUND THE DOOR SHUT...

IF OUR OWN BROTHERS DON'T WANT US, WE'LL LEAVE THIS PLACE!

AND GO WHERE?

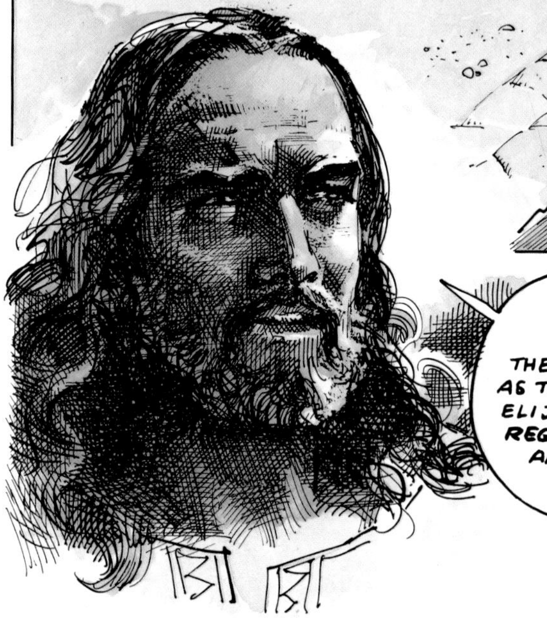

THE SAME WAY AS THE PROPHET ELIJAH, TO THE REGION OF TYRE AND SIDON.

JESUS
AMONG THE PAGANS

SCENARIO : Etienne DAHLER
DRAWING: Pierre FRISANO

NEAR A VILLAGE...
MASTER! SON OF DAVID! HAVE PITY ON ME!
HOW DOES SHE KNOW THE MASTER?
TAKE PITY ON ME! A DEMON'S TORMENTING MY DAUGHTER.
DON'T BOTHER THE MASTER!
A LITTLE FURTHER ON...
SEND HER BACK!
SHE KEEPS ON SHOUTING... THE WHOLE VILLAGE IS COMING.
LORD, WHY NOT ANSWER THIS WOMAN'S PRAYER?
NO, JOHN. I'VE BEEN SENT ONLY TO THE LOST SHEEP OF THE HOUSE OF ISRAEL.
HELP ME, LORD!
DON'T YOU KNOW THAT BREAD MEANT FOR CHILDREN ISN'T TO BE THROWN DOWN FOR LITTLE DOGS!
YES, LORD... BUT SURELY LITTLE DOGS CAN HAVE THE CRUMBS THAT FALL FROM THEIR MASTER'S TABLE!
WOMAN, YOU HAVE GREAT FAITH! WHAT YOU ASK FOR WILL BE GRANTED.
AND AT THAT MOMENT HER CHILD WAS CURED.

THE WHOLE COUNTRY SOON HEARD ABOUT JESUS.

LITTLE ONE, I WANT YOU TO BE HEALED!

THAT NIGHT...

JESUS, MANY OF THESE PEOPLE WANT TO FOLLOW US...
WELL AND GOOD! LET THEM COME WITH US!

BUT... THEY'RE NOT JEWS!
JAMES, THE KINGDOM IS FOR THEM ALSO!

DIDN'T THE PROPHET ISAIAH SAY: YOU WILL CALL THE NATIONS WHOM YOU DO NOT KNOW AND THEY WILL RUN TO YOU, BECAUSE OF THE LORD YOUR GOD?
IT'S TIME TO GET A LITTLE REST. TOMORROW WE'LL MOVE EASTWARDS.

DON'T BE AFRAID, LITTLE FLOCK... YOUR FATHER'S SEEN FIT TO GIVE YOU THE KINGDOM.

THE NEXT DAY JESUS AND HIS DISCIPLES SET OFF INTO THE INTERIOR OF THE COUNTRY.
WE'LL CROSS THAT MOUNTAIN.

LOOK! A CARAVAN OF CAMELS!

THE KINGDOM'S LIKE THIS. THE ROAD TO DESTRUCTION IS WIDE, WITH PLENTY OF ROOM, AND THAT'S WHY MANY TAKE IT...

...BUT THE ROAD TO LIFE IS STEEP AND DIFFICULT... FEW PEOPLE FIND THAT ROAD!

THE LITTLE GROUP CONTINUED ON THEIR WAY, BUT SUDDENLY...
JESUS, WE CAN'T GET THROUGH!

THE DOOR'S NARROW. MANY WANT TO ENTER, BUT WON'T SUCCEED; THEN THERE'LL BE TEARS AND GRINDING OF TEETH.
BUT WHY, MASTER?
BECAUSE SOME WILL SEE THE PATRIARCHS AND THE PROPHETS IN THE KINGDOM OF GOD, AND THEN THEY'LL BE THROWN OUT.
ARE YOU SAYING THAT VERY FEW WILL BE SAVED?
NO! MANY PEOPLE WILL COME FROM EAST AND WEST, FROM NORTH AND SOUTH, AND TAKE THEIR PLACE AT THE DINNER PARTY IN THE KINGDOM OF GOD!
BUT THERE, THOSE WHO ARE LAST WILL BE FIRST AND THOSE WHO ARE FIRST WILL BE LAST.
WELL, BARTHOLOMEW, YOU'RE LUCKY!

AT THE TOP OF THE MOUNTAIN...
AND THIS SIDE IS SYRIA?
YES, PETER, IT'S OVER THERE.
WHAT A BEAUTIFUL COUNTRY!
LET'S REST HERE, BEFORE GOING ON.
RIGHT! WE COULDN'T GO ON UNDER THIS SUN WITHOUT SALT.
HERE, TAKE YOUR SALT RATION. DON'T FORGET TO TAKE IT, OR ELSE YOU'LL DRY OUT LIKE AN OLD FIG!
...AND YOU'RE THE SALT OF THE EARTH!
BUT IF SALT LOSES ITS FLAVOUR, IT'S WORTHLESS, AND IS THROWN OUT AND TRAMPLED UNDER FOOT.
YOU'RE ALSO THE LIGHT OF THE WORLD! A TOWN BUILT ON A MOUNTAIN CAN'T BE HIDDEN!
SO LET YOUR LIGHT SHINE BEFORE PEOPLE; THEN THEY CAN SEE YOUR GOOD WORKS AND GLORIFY YOUR HEAVENLY FATHER.

GOING DOWN THE SYRIAN SIDE, JESUS AND HIS DISCIPLES PASSED THROUGH A VERY FERTILE AREA.

IT'S TIME TO GO BACK TO GALILEE.

IN ONE VILLAGE...
MASTER, THEY TOLD US YOU COULD DO SOMETHING FOR THIS MAN.
HE'S DEAF, AND CAN HARDLY SPEAK.

JESUS TOOK HIM ON ONE SIDE...
THEN TOUCHED HIS TONGUE
EPHPHATHA!*

HE'S HEALED ME!
I CAN HEA
THE GOD OF ISRAEL LIVES!
AND THERE'S NO LIMIT TO HIS POWER!

* Open up!

Sidon
PHOENICIA
SYRIA
Caesarea Philippi
Tyre
GALILEE
Bethsaida
Capernaum
Tiberias
Shechem
Jericho
Jerusalem
JUDAEA
A FEW WEEKS LATER...
DADDY, JESUS IS BACK!
JESUS OF NAZARETH?
YES! AND WHEN HE GOT TO BETHSAIDA, HE EVEN CURED JACOB! I SAW IT ALL...
QUICK! TELL ME!
CAN YOU SEE ANYTHING?
YES, LIKE SHADOWS... YOU COULD SAY TREES... BUT WALKING!
LORD, I SEE YOU...! SEE YOUR EYES... YOUR FACE...
NOW GO HOME, JACOB, AND PRAISE GOD IN YOUR HEART.
HE EVEN SAID HE MUSTN'T GO BACK TO BETHSAIDA!
REALLY?
HE PROBABLY DIDN'T TRUST THE PHARISEES...

AFTER A BRIEF STAY BESIDE LAKE TIBERIAS, THE LITTLE GROUP WENT BACK UP THE JORDAN VALLEY TOWARDS **CAESAREA PHILIPPI.**

LOOK THERE! ANOTHER PAGAN TEMPLE!

YOU'LL SEE PLENTY MORE WHEN WE REACH PANEAS*

*Temple of Pan, later called Banias.

AT ONE OF THE SOURCES OF THE JORDAN...

THIS IS WHERE PAGANS CELEBRATE THE WAY LIFE SPRINGS UP...

... AND END UP WORSHIPPING THIS RIVER!

AS IF WATER COULD BE GOD!

AND ME: WHO DO PEOPLE SAY THAT I AM?
SOME SAY YOU'RE JOHN THE BAPTIST.
OTHERS THAT YOU'RE ELIJAH.
I'VE HEARD THEM SAYING THAT YOU'RE THE PROPHET JEREMIAH!

BUT YOU, WHO DO YOU SAY I AM?
YOU'RE THE CHRIST*, THE SON OF THE LIVING GOD.
YOU'RE BLESSED, SIMON! MY FATHER REVEALED THIS TO YOU, NOT YOUR OWN THOUGHTS.

*The Messiah, that is, God's Anointed.

YOU'RE PETER, AND ON THIS ROCK I'LL BUILD MY CHURCH, AND NOT EVEN DEATH WILL EVER BE ABLE TO OVERCOME IT.
I WILL GIVE YOU THE KEYS OF THE KINGDOM OF HEAVEN: WHAT YOU FORBID ON EARTH, WILL BE FORBIDDEN IN HEAVEN...
...AND WHAT YOU PERMIT ON EARTH, WILL BE PERMITTED IN HEAVEN...
MEANWHILE, DON'T TELL ANYONE THAT I'M **THE CHRIST**.
A FEW DAYS LATER, NOT FAR FROM CAESAREA PHILIPPI...
LET'S SPEND THE NIGHT HERE.
SOON I MUST GO TO JERUSALEM. THERE I'LL BE REJECTED BY THE PRIESTS AND THE SCRIBES, AND PUT TO DEATH...

...BUT I'LL RISE AGAIN ON THE THIRD DAY.
GOD FORBID! THAT MUSTN'T HAPPEN TO YOU!

GET BEHIND ME, SATAN! YOUR THOUGHTS DON'T COME FROM GOD!

A LITTLE LATER...
LORD, A CROWD'S FOLLOWING US...
THEY'RE WAITING FOR A WORD OR A SIGN FROM YOU...
GOOD. LET THEM SIT DOWN HERE!

IF ANYONE WANTS TO COME WITH ME, HE MUST FORGET HIMSELF, CARRY HIS CROSS EACH DAY, AND FOLLOW ME!
AND YOU, DO YOU FOLLOW HIM?
YES... WE'VE FOLLOWED HIM FOR A LONG TIME.

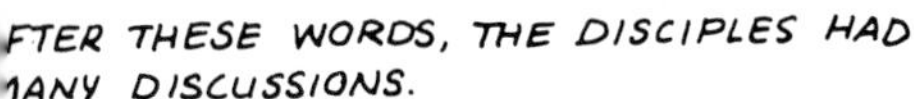

SUDDENLY...

MOSES! ELIJAH!

MASTER, IT'S GOOD TO BE HERE! SO THAT GOD'S GLORY STAYS WITH US, LET'S BUILD THREE BOOTHS,* FOR YOU, FOR MOSES, AND FOR ELIJAH.
THIS IS MY OWN DEAR SON WITH WHOM I AM PLEASED. LISTEN TO HIM.
GET UP; DON'T BE AFRAID!
* Huts made of branches for the festival of Succoth.

WHEN THEY WENT BACK INTO THE VALLEY...
THEY SOUND VERY EXCITED!
WELL, NOW! WHAT'S GOING ON?
MASTER, I'VE BROUGHT MY SON. HE'S TORTURED BY AN EVIL SPIRIT; IT THROWS HIM TO THE GROUND AND HURLS HIM ABOUT.
I ASKED YOUR DISCIPLES TO DRIVE IT OUT, BUT THEY COULDN'T.
PEOPLE WITHOUT FAITH! HOW LONG WILL I HAVE TO STAY HERE AND PUT UP WITH YOU? BRING THE BOY TO ME!
AS SOON AS HE SAW JESUS, THE LAD THREW A FIT.
HOW LONG HAS THIS BEEN GOING ON?
SINCE HIS CHILDHOOD... IF YOU CAN DO SOMETHING, HELP US!
... IF YOU CAN! EVERYTHING'S POSSIBLE FOR SOMEONE WHO BELIEVES!
LORD, I BELIEVE.

SPIRIT OF DARKNESS, I ORDER YOU TO COME OUT OF THIS BOY, AND NEVER ENTER HIM AGAIN!

HE'S DEAD!
MY SON! MY ONLY CHILD!

NOW GET UP.
JESUS, YOU'VE CURED HIM!

WHEN THE CROWD HAD GONE...
WHY COULDN'T WE DRIVE OUT THAT SPIRIT?
BECAUSE OF YOUR LACK OF FAITH... IF YOU HAD FAITH ONLY AS BIG AS A MUSTARD SEED...

...YOU COULD SAY TO THIS MOUNTAIN, 'MOVE FROM HERE TO THERE...' AND IT WOULD MOVE.

THEY LEFT THAT PLACE AND CROSSED GALILEE ON THE WAY BACK TO CAPERNAUM.
I SAY PETER'S THE GREATEST AMONG US.
YOU'RE FORGETTING JOHN. JESUS LOVES HIM DEARLY.
NO, I THINK ANDREW'S THE GREATEST. HE WAS THE FIRST TO FOLLOW THE MASTER, AND BEFORE THAT HE WAS JOHN THE BAPTIST'S DISCIPLE.
AT THE END OF THEIR JOURNEY, IN PETER'S HOUSE...
WHAT WERE YOU TALKING ABOUT ON THE ROAD?
IF ONE OF YOU WANTS TO BE FIRST, LET HIM BE THE LAST, THE SERVANT OF ALL.
THE DISCIPLES WERE QUIET.
SAMUEL, COME HERE.
TRULY, I TELL YOU, UNLESS YOU BECOME LIKE LITTLE CHILDREN, YOU WILL NEVER ENTER THE KINGDOM OF HEAVEN.

A LITTLE LATER, BY THE LAKE...
IF ANYONE SHOULD MAKE ONE OF THESE LITTLE ONES GO WRONG, IT WOULD BE BETTER FOR HIM TO BE THROWN INTO THE SEA WITH A MILLSTONE ROUND HIS NECK!
BE CAREFUL NOT TO LEAD OTHERS INTO WRONG.
WHAT SHOULD WE DO, MASTER? WE CAN'T BE PERFECT!
IF YOUR EYE LEADS YOU INTO TROUBLE, TEAR IT OUT! IT WOULD BE BETTER TO LIVE WITH ONLY ONE EYE THAN TO HAVE TWO AND BE THROWN INTO THE FIRES OF GEHENNA!
JESUS IS SAYING DIFFICULT THINGS TO US TODAY!
MASTER, IF SOMEONE DOES SOMETHING WRONG TO ME, HOW OFTEN MUST I FORGIVE HIM? AS MANY AS SEVEN TIMES?
NO, PETER, UP TO SEVENTY TIMES SEVEN!

THEN THE PHARISEES CAME TO HIM.
YOU MUST GET AWAY FROM HERE! HEROD WANTS TO KILL YOU.
HE'S FRIGHTENED OF YOU. HE THINKS YOU'RE JOHN THE BAPTIST COME BACK FROM THE DEAD!
GO AND TELL THAT FOX I'M LEAVING HIS TERRITORY...
..NOT TO ESCAPE HIM, BUT TO FULFIL GOD'S WILL...
...BECAUSE IT IS NOT FITTING THAT A PROPHET SHOULD DIE OUTSIDE JERUSALEM.
PETER, TELL THE OTHERS. WE'RE LEAVING CAPERNAUM TODAY.
SOME HOURS LATER...
WOE TO YOU, CHORAZIN! WOE TO YOU, BETHSAIDA!
IF TYRE AND SIDON HAD SEEN THE MIRACLES WORKED IN YOU, THOSE TOWNS WOULD HAVE LONG AGO BEEN SORRY FOR THEIR SINS.
AS FOR YOU, CAPERNAUM!
YOU'LL GO DOWN TO THE PLACE OF THE DEAD. I TELL YOU, ON THE JUDGEMENT DAY, SODOM WILL BE TREATED WITH MORE MERCY THAN YOU.
COME BACK SOON, JESUS!

THEY LANDED AT THE SOUTHERN END OF THE LAKE.
MASTER, YOU MUST REST A LITTLE.
NO, WE'LL GO ON. WHEN IT'S THIS HOT, IT'S BETTER TO WALK AT NIGHT.

THE NEXT DAY, AT THE GATES OF THE TOWN OF NAIN...
THAT POOR WIDOW'S LOST HER ONLY SON.

DON'T CRY!
UNCOVER HIM!

YOUNG MAN, I SAY, 'GET UP!'

LADY, HERE'S YOUR SON, ALIVE AGAIN.
THE NEWS ABOUT JESUS SPREAD THROUGH THE WHOLE REGION.

ON THE ROAD TO SAMARIA JESUS CROSSED THE PLAIN OF JEZREEL.
WHAT MARVELLOUS CROPS!
NO WONDER THEY CALL IT THE GRANARY OF THE KINGDOM!
SOON, IN A MARKET PLACE...
SELL WHAT YOU HAVE, AND GIVE IT TO THE POOR. THEN YOU'LL STORE UP TREASURE IN HEAVEN.
... BECAUSE YOUR HEART WILL BE WHEREVER YOUR TREASURE IS.
OH, COME ON! WEALTH'S ALWAYS BEEN A SIGN OF GOD'S BLESSING.
THAT WON'T CHANGE OVERNIGHT! HA! HA! HA!
NO ONE CAN SERVE TWO MASTERS! YOU CAN'T SERVE GOD AND MONEY.

IN SAMARIA...
LORD, LOTS OF PEOPLE WANT TO FOLLOW YOU.
FOXES HAVE HOLES AND BIRDS HAVE NESTS, BUT THE SON OF MAN HAS NOWHERE TO LAY HIS HEAD.
YES, I'LL FOLLOW YOU WHEREVER YOU GO.
I ALSO WANT TO FOLLOW YOU. BUT LET ME FIRST GO AND SAY GOODBYE TO MY FAMILY.
ANYONE WHO PUTS HIS HAND TO THE PLOUGH AND THEN LOOKS BACK, ISN'T FIT FOR THE KINGDO OF GOD.
MORE AND MORE BECAME DISCIPLES... JESUS CHOSE 70 OF THEM...
GO, TWO BY TWO, AND MAKE ALL THE TOWNS AND VILLAGES YOU COME TO READY TO WELCOME ME.
EVERYWHERE THEY WENT THEY PREACHED THE GOOD NEWS, AND CAME BACK FULL OF JOY...
LORD, EVEN THE DEMONS OBEYED US IN YOUR NAME!
I KNOW. I SAW SATAN FALL FROM THE SKY LIKE A FLASH OF LIGHTNIN
I PRAISE YOU, FATHER, THAT YOU HAVE HIDDEN THESE THINGS FROM THE WISE AND WELL-EDUCATED, AND REVEALED THEM TO ORDINARY PEOPLE.

ONE DAY, AT SYCHAR, NOT FAR FROM THE ANCIENT SHECHEM, JESUS WAS RESTING BESIDE JACOB'S WELL. THE DISCIPLES HAD GONE TO BUY FOOD.

GIVE ME A DRINK OF WATER.
WHAT? YOU, A JEW, ASKING A SAMARITAN FOR A DRINK?

IF ONLY YOU KNEW WHAT GOD GIVES! IT WOULD BE YOU WHO BEGGED ME TO GIVE YOU THE WATER OF LIFE.
BUT YOU'VE NO BUCKET. WHERE WOULD YOU GET THAT WATER?

WHOEVER DRINKS THIS WATER, WILL BE THIRSTY AGAIN, BUT ANYONE DRINKING THE WATER I GIVE, WILL NEVER BE THIRSTY AGAIN.
SIR, GIVE ME THAT WATER SO I WON'T GET THIRSTY AGAIN. THEN I WON'T HAVE TO COME HERE ANYMORE!

GO AND CALL YOUR HUSBAND; THEN COME BACK!
I HAVE NO HUSBAND!

YOU'RE RIGHT! YOU'VE HAD FIVE HUSBANDS, AND THE MAN YOU'RE LIVING WITH NOW ISN'T YOUR HUSBAND!
LORD, YOU MUST BE A PROPHET!
I'M NOT CLEVER. I ONLY KNOW THAT THE MESSIAH MUST COME, AND WHEN HE DOES, HE'LL TELL US EVERYTHING.
I AM HE, I WHO AM TALKING TO YOU!
THE WOMAN RAN TO THE PEOPLE IN THE TOWN WITH HER NEWS, AND THAT DAY MANY SAMARITANS BELIEVED IN JESUS BECAUSE OF WHAT SHE HAD TO TELL.

THE ROAD TO JERUSALEM

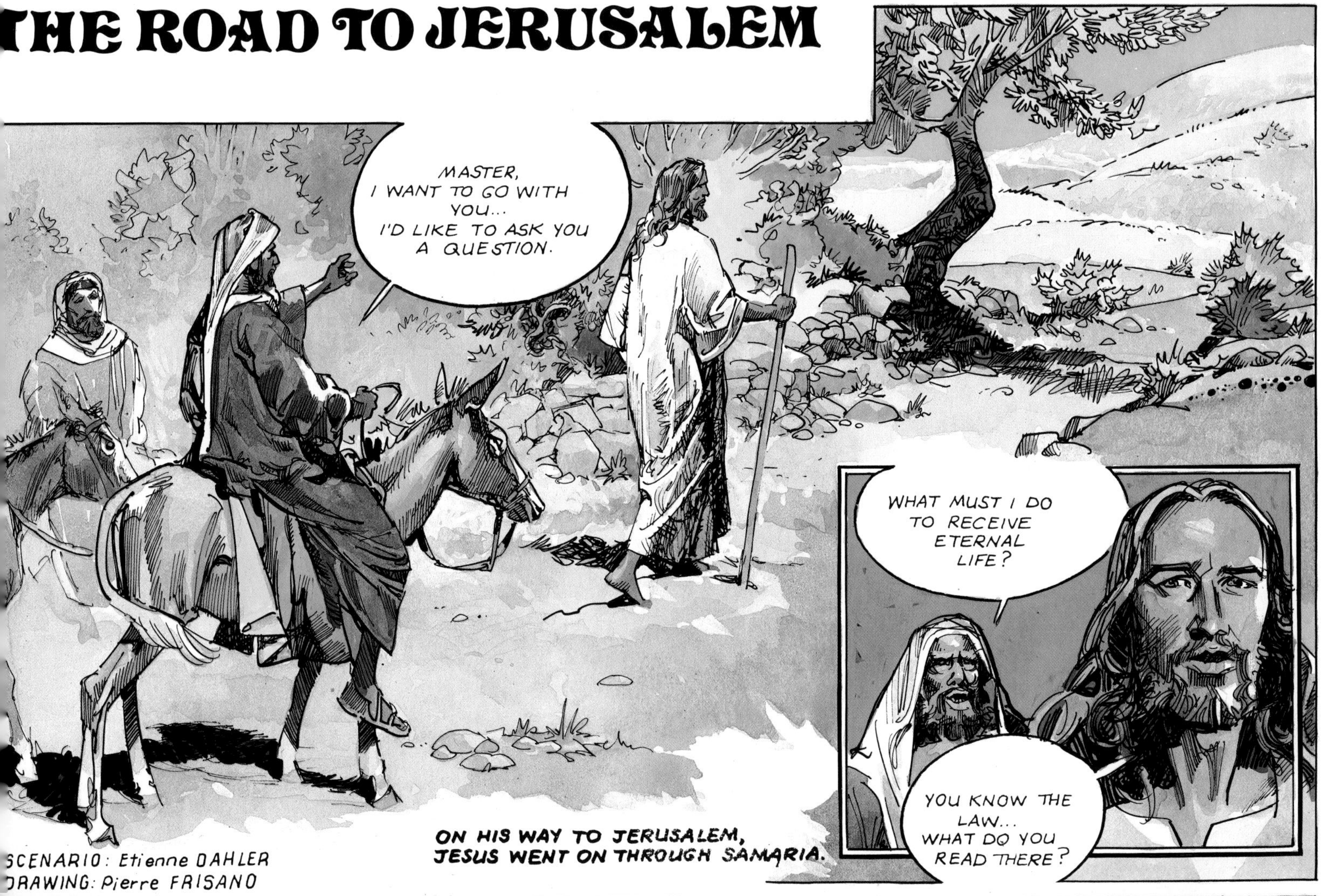

SCENARIO: Etienne DAHLER
DRAWING: Pierre FRISANO

ON HIS WAY TO JERUSALEM, JESUS WENT ON THROUGH SAMARIA.

MASTER, I WANT TO GO WITH YOU... I'D LIKE TO ASK YOU A QUESTION.

WHAT MUST I DO TO RECEIVE ETERNAL LIFE?

YOU KNOW THE LAW... WHAT DO YOU READ THERE?

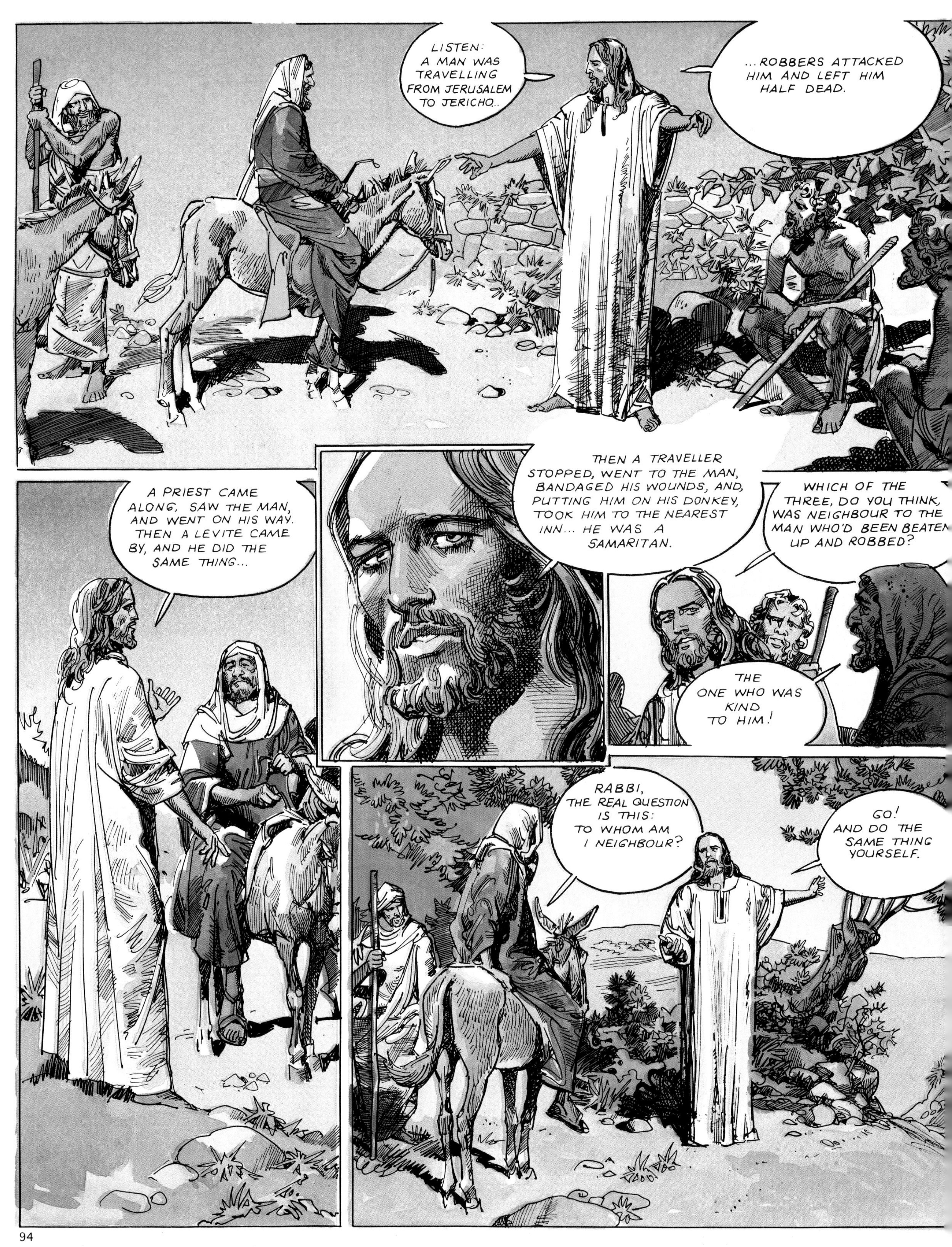
LISTEN: A MAN WAS TRAVELLING FROM JERUSALEM TO JERICHO..
...ROBBERS ATTACKED HIM AND LEFT HIM HALF DEAD.
A PRIEST CAME ALONG, SAW THE MAN, AND WENT ON HIS WAY. THEN A LEVITE CAME BY, AND HE DID THE SAME THING...
THEN A TRAVELLER STOPPED, WENT TO THE MAN, BANDAGED HIS WOUNDS, AND, PUTTING HIM ON HIS DONKEY, TOOK HIM TO THE NEAREST INN... HE WAS A SAMARITAN.
WHICH OF THE THREE, DO YOU THINK, WAS NEIGHBOUR TO THE MAN WHO'D BEEN BEATEN UP AND ROBBED?
THE ONE WHO WAS KIND TO HIM!
RABBI, THE REAL QUESTION IS THIS: TO WHOM AM I NEIGHBOUR?
GO! AND DO THE SAME THING YOURSELF.

A FEW DAYS LATER JESUS WENT TO PRAY BY HIMSELF. WHEN HIS DISCIPLES JOINED HIM...
THERE HE IS!

LORD, TEACH US HOW TO PRAY...
IT'S SIMPLE. SAY THIS:

FATHER! LET YOUR HOLY NAME BE HONOURED! LET YOUR KINGDOM COME!
GIVE US EACH DAY THE BREAD WE NEED. FORGIVE US OUR SINS, AS WE ALSO FORGIVE THOSE WHO SIN AGAINST US...

AND DO NOT BRING US TO HARD TESTING.
THE DISCIPLES WERE QUIET FOR A LONG TIME...

...THEN JESUS CONTINUED...
ASK, AND IT WILL BE GIVEN TO YOU! SEEK, AND YOU WILL FIND! KNOCK, AND IT WILL BE OPENED TO YOU!

ON THE WAY, AS THEY PASSED THROUGH A VILLAGE...

STOP, THIEF!

HE WENT THAT WAY!

IF THE MASTER OF THE HOUSE HAD KNOWN WHEN THE THIEF WAS COMING, HE WOULDN'T HAVE LET HIM BREAK THROUGH HIS WALL!

YOU MUST ALL BE READY! BECAUSE YOU DON'T KNOW WHEN THE SON OF MAN WILL COME.

AND THE KINGDOM OF GOD, WHEN WILL IT COME?
THE KINGDOM OF GOD? IT'S ALREADY AMONG YOU!

THAT DOESN'T MAKE SENSE!
ON THE OTHER HAND...
... IT SAYS A LOT ABOUT WHO HE CLAIMS TO BE...

JERUSALEM WAS NOW IN SIGHT...
A MAN HAD A FIG TREE IN HIS VINEYARD. HE WENT TO LOOK FOR FRUIT ON IT, BUT FOUND NONE...
... SO HE SAID TO HIS GARDENER,
FOR THREE YEARS RUNNING THIS TREE'S HAD NO FRUIT!
CUT IT DOWN!
WAIT ONE MORE YEAR... I'LL MANURE IT. IF IT STILL DOESN'T BEAR FRUIT, THEN YOU CAN HAVE IT CHOPPED OUT.
D THEN?
WHAT HAPPENED TO IT?
WE STILL DON'T KNOW... THE TIME'S COMING, AND THE GARDENER'S STILL HOPEFUL...
HERE WE ARE IN JERUSALEM! WHAT A CROWD!
IT'S THE FESTIVAL OF SHELTERS. MANY PILGRIMS HAVE ALREADY ARRIVED.

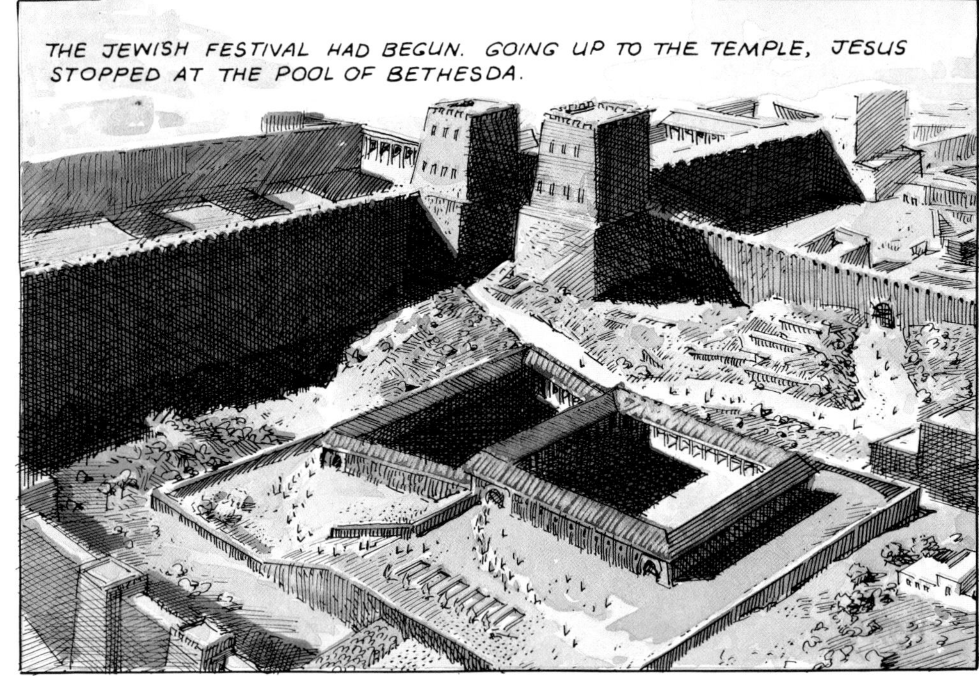

THE JEWISH FESTIVAL HAD BEGUN. GOING UP TO THE TEMPLE, JESUS STOPPED AT THE POOL OF BETHESDA.

WHY ARE ALL THESE SICK PEOPLE HERE?
BECAUSE OF THE SIGNS... NOW AND AGAIN THE WATER BUBBLES. THE FIRST TO JUMP INTO THE POOL IS CURED!

DO YOU WANT TO BE HEALED?
YES! BUT I'VE NOBODY TO THROW ME INTO THE POOL WHEN THE WATER'S STIRRED UP!

GET UP, PICK UP YOUR MAT, AND WALK!
JESUS DISAPPEARED INTO THE CROWD.

I'M WALKING! I'VE BEEN LYING DOWN FOR SUCH A LONG TIME, AND LOOK: NOW I'M WALKING!
IT'S THE SABBATH!
YOU'RE NOT ALLOWED TO CARRY YOUR MAT!*
WHO HEALED YOU? WHAT'S HIS NAME?
I DON'T KNOW. ALL I KNOW IS THAT HE CURED ME!

*The law did not allow anything to be carried on the Sabbath.

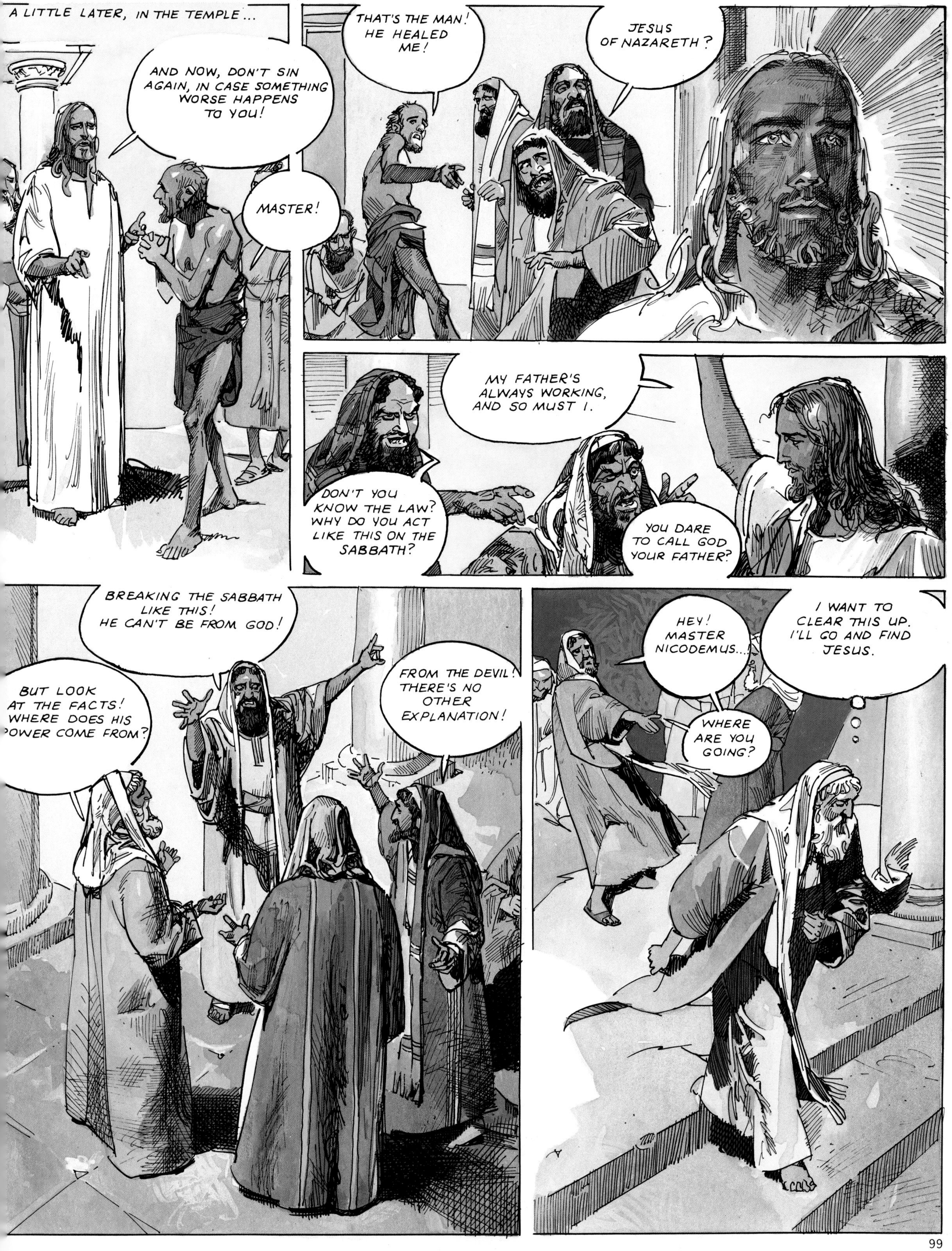

A LITTLE LATER, IN THE TEMPLE...

AND NOW, DON'T SIN AGAIN, IN CASE SOMETHING WORSE HAPPENS TO YOU!

MASTER!

THAT'S THE MAN! HE HEALED ME!

JESUS OF NAZARETH?

DON'T YOU KNOW THE LAW? WHY DO YOU ACT LIKE THIS ON THE SABBATH?

MY FATHER'S ALWAYS WORKING, AND SO MUST I.

YOU DARE TO CALL GOD YOUR FATHER?

THE SAME NIGHT, NICODEMUS...
RABBI!
RABBI! I KNOW THAT YOU'RE SENT BY GOD. NO ONE COULD DO THE THINGS YOU DO UNLESS GOD WAS WITH HIM.

TRULY, I TELL YOU! IF A MAN ISN'T BORN AGAIN, HE CAN'T SEE THE KINGDOM OF GOD!
HOW CAN A MAN BE BORN WHEN HE'S OLD?...
...CAN HE GO BACK INTO HIS MOTHER'S WOMB AND BE BOR A SECOND TIME?

I TELL YOU AGAIN; UNLESS SOMEONE IS BORN OF WATER AND OF SPIRIT, HE CAN'T ENTER THE KINGDOM...
... WHAT'S BORN OF A HUMAN BODY IS HUMAN; WHAT'S BORN OF SPIRIT IS SPIRIT.
HOW CAN THAT BE?

NICODEMUS, YOU'RE A TEACHER IN ISRAEL, AND YOU DON'T KNOW THIS?

PRAY FOR ME, JESUS!

A FEW DAYS LATER, DURING THE CEREMONY OF THE WATER...
IF ANYONE'S THIRSTY, LET THEM COME TO ME AND DRINK!
WHAT STOPS YOU FROM ARRESTING HIM?
NO ONE'S EVER SPOKEN LIKE THIS MAN!
HE'S DISAPPEARED!
NOTHING'S LOST BY WAITING!
BUT HOW CAN A MAN BE CONDEMNED BEFORE HE'S BEEN HEARD?
HAS HE FOOLED YOU TOO?
READ THE SCRIPTURES! COULD A PROPHET COME OUT OF GALILEE?
THEN JESUS LEFT JERUSALEM.

RABBI, DO US THE HONOUR OF STAYING IN OUR HOME...

WHILE JESUS WAS PASSING THROUGH THE VILLAGE OF BETHANY, A WOMAN CALLED MARTHA WENT UP TO HIM. SHE HAD A SISTER CALLED MARY.

THE KINGDOM OF HEAVEN IS LIKE A MERCHANT LOOKING FOR BEAUTIFUL PEARLS...

... WHEN HE FINDS ONE OF GREAT VALUE, HE SELLS EVERYTHING HE HAS TO BUY IT.

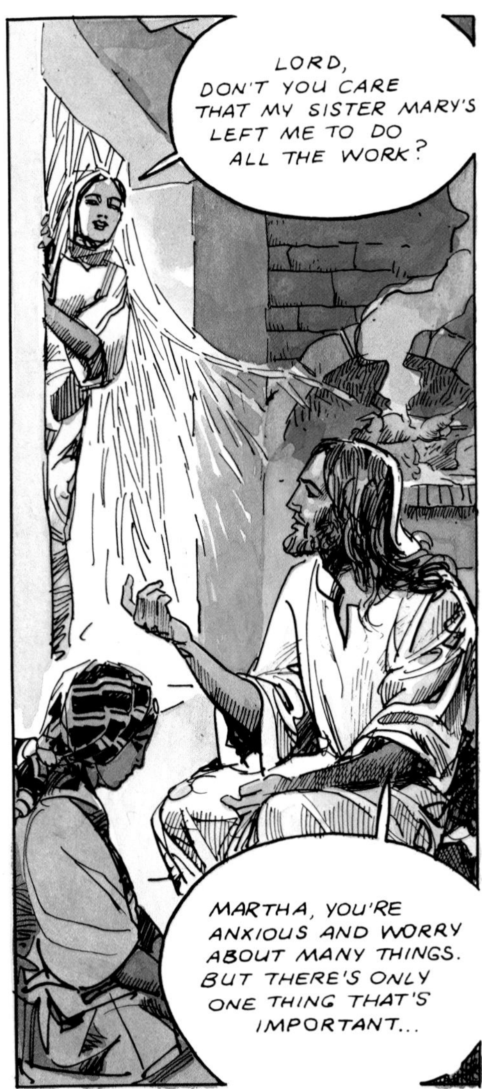

LORD, DON'T YOU CARE THAT MY SISTER MARY'S LEFT ME TO DO ALL THE WORK?
MARTHA, YOU'RE ANXIOUS AND WORRY ABOUT MANY THINGS. BUT THERE'S ONLY ONE THING THAT'S IMPORTANT...

... MARY'S CHOSEN THE RIGHT THING, AND IT WON'T BE TAKEN AWAY FROM HER.

WHO CAN LIVE A BIT LONGER BY WORRYING ABOUT IT?
LIVE FIRST FOR GOD'S KINGDOM, AND PLENTY OF EVERYTHING ELSE WILL BE GIVEN TO YOU.

IN THE EARLY MORNING JESUS WENT BACK TO THE TEMPLE. A CROWD GATHERED TO HEAR HIS TEACHING.

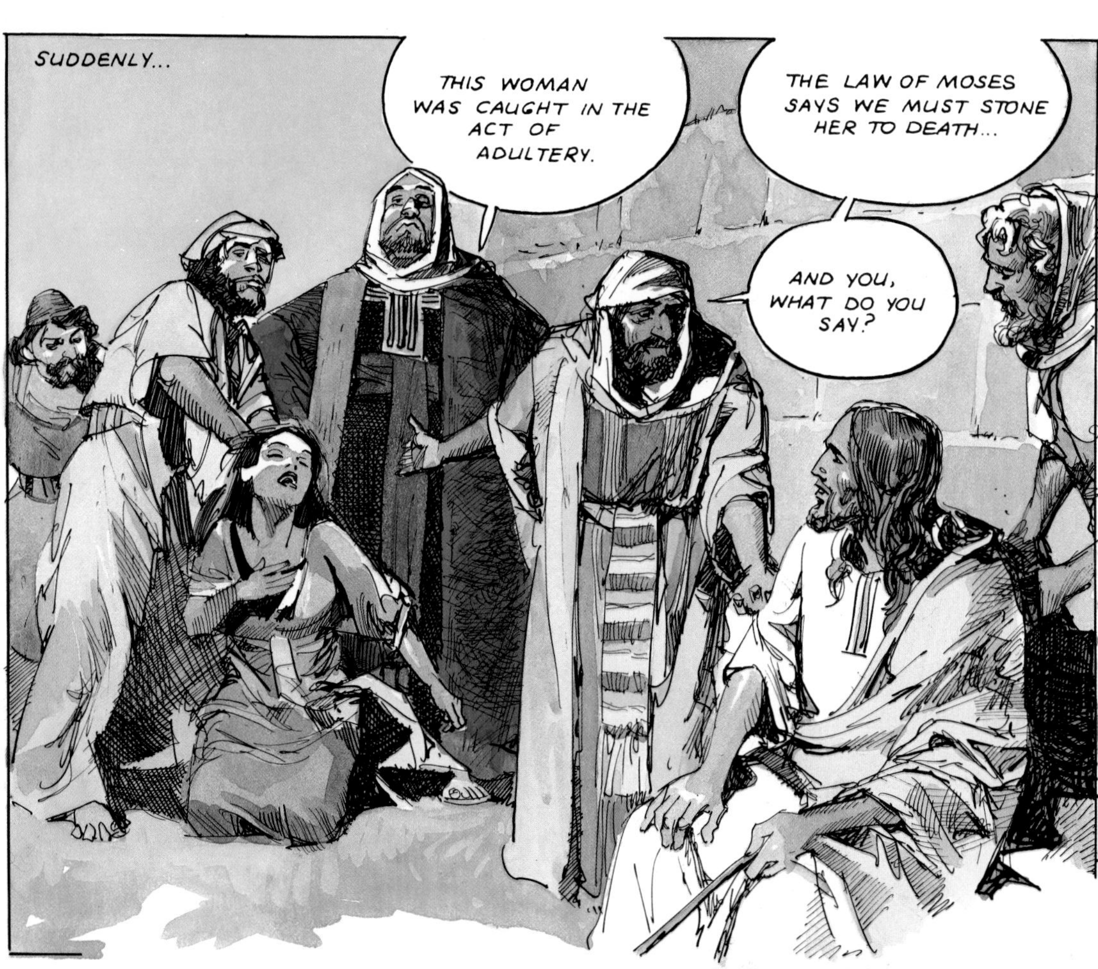
SUDDENLY...
THIS WOMAN WAS CAUGHT IN THE ACT OF ADULTERY.
THE LAW OF MOSES SAYS WE MUST STONE HER TO DEATH...
AND YOU, WHAT DO YOU SAY?

LET HIM WHO'S NEVER SINNED THROW THE FIRST STONE!

E BY ONE THE PHARISEES ALKED AWAY, STARTING TH THE OLDEST.
WOMAN, WHERE ARE YOUR ACCUSERS? DID NO ONE CONDEMN YOU?
NO, LORD.

I DON'T CONDEMN YOU EITHER. GO, AND DON'T SIN AGAIN.

TWO MONTHS PASSED. JESUS WENT TO THE TEMPLE FOR THE FESTIVAL OF DEDICATION.
HOW LONG ARE YOU GOING TO KEEP US WONDERING ABOUT YOU?
IF YOU ARE THE CHRIST, SAY SO PLAINLY.
I'VE TOLD YOU, BUT YOU DON'T BELIEVE ME...

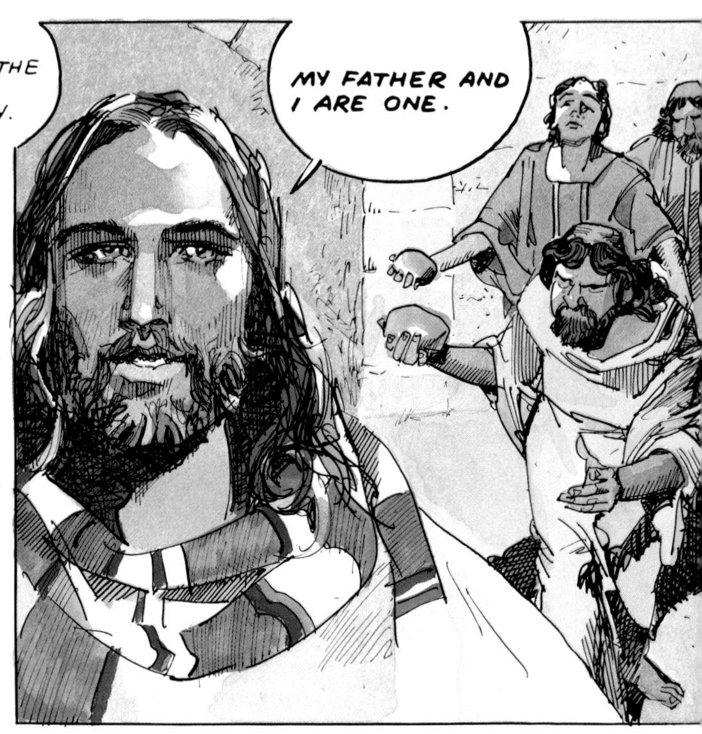
MY FATHER AND I ARE ONE.

I'VE SHOWN YOU MANY GOOD WORKS FROM MY FATHER. FOR WHICH ONE DO YOU WANT TO STONE ME?
IT'S NOT FOR ANY GOOD WORK THAT WE WANT TO STONE YOU...
...BUT FOR BLASPHEMY... YOU, A MERE MAN YOU MAKE YOURSELF GOD!

STONING IN THE HOUSE OF GOD! YOU'RE MAD!
AND JESUS MADE HIS ESCAPE.

THEN HE LEFT JERUSALEM AND WENT ACROSS THE JORDAN.

WHILE JESUS WAS WALKING THROUGH A VILLAGE, A GROUP OF CHILDREN RAN TO HIM. THE DISCIPLES CHASED THEM AWAY.
NOW, YOU CHILDREN, STAND BACK!
WHY CHASE THEM AWAY? LET THE LITTLE ONES COME TO ME...
THE KINGDOM OF GOD'S FOR THEM AND THOSE LIKE THEM!
URTHER ON...
MASTER! WHAT MUST I DO TO HAVE ETERNAL LIFE?
IF YOU WANT TO HAVE LIFE, KEEP THE COMMANDMENTS!
I'VE DONE THAT... WHAT MORE MUST I DO?

IF YOU WANT TO BE PERFECT, GO AND SELL EVERYTHING YOU HAVE AND GIVE THE MONEY TO THE POOR; THEN FOLLOW ME...
I TELL YOU AGAIN: IT'S EASIER FOR A CAMEL TO GO THROUGH THE EYE OF A NEEDLE THAN FOR A RICH PERSON TO ENTER THE KINGDOM OF GOD.
THEN WHO CAN BE SAVED?

THINGS THAT ARE IMPOSSIBLE FOR PEOPLE ARE POSSIBLE FOR GOD!

!?
THERE, SEE!

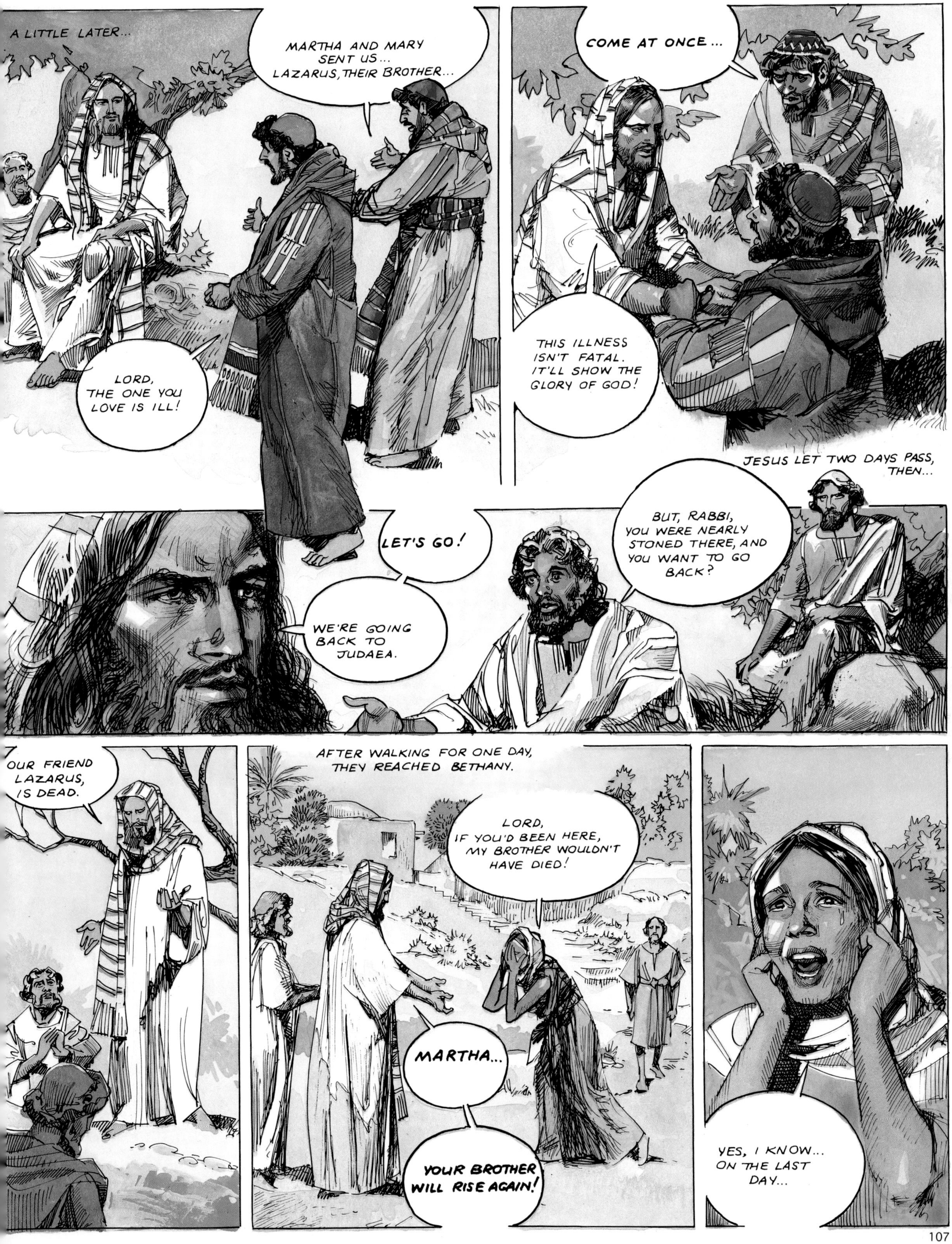

A LITTLE LATER...

LORD, THE ONE YOU LOVE IS ILL!

MARTHA AND MARY SENT US... LAZARUS, THEIR BROTHER...

COME AT ONCE...

THIS ILLNESS ISN'T FATAL. IT'LL SHOW THE GLORY OF GOD!

JESUS LET TWO DAYS PASS, THEN...

WE'RE GOING BACK TO JUDAEA.

BUT, RABBI, YOU WERE NEARLY STONED THERE, AND YOU WANT TO GO BACK?

LET'S GO!

I AM THE RESURRECTION AND THE LIFE. WHOEVER BELIEVES IN ME WILL LIVE, EVEN IF HE DIES.
I'LL TAKE YOU TO THE PLACE WHERE HE'S BURIED.

HE GAVE SIGHT TO THE BLIND. COULDN'T HE HAVE STOPPED LAZARUS FROM DYING?
FOLLOW ME, LORD. HE'S HERE.
THEN HE CAN'T BE THE MESSIAH!
JESUS TOLD THEM TO ROLL BACK THE STONE.

FATHER, I THANK YOU FOR LISTENING TO ME!

LAZARUS! COME OUT!

UNWRAP HIM, AND LET HIM GO HOME!
BECAUSE OF THIS, MANY JEWS BELIEVED IN JESUS.

IN JERUSALEM THE PRIESTS AND THE PHARISEES MET WITH THE JEWISH COUNCIL.

IF WE LET HIM GO ON LIKE THIS, EVERYONE WILL END UP BELIEVING IN HIM!
IT WOULD BE BETTER FOR ONE MAN TO DIE, RATHER THAN A WHOLE NATION.
ROME WILL ACCUSE US...
...OF REBELLION, AND DESTROY OUR TEMPLE AND OUR NATION.

JESUS WENT AWAY TO THE NEAR-BY VILLAGE CALLED EPHRAIM, THEN TO JERICHO.

I HEAR A NOISE. WHAT'S HAPPENING?

JESUS OF NAZARETH'S COMING ...

JESUS, SON OF DAVID, HAVE PITY ON ME!

JESUS! BLESS MY SON!

OVER HERE, MASTER!

WHAT DO YOU WANT ME TO DO FOR YOU?
LORD, GIVE ME BACK MY SIGHT.

SEE! YOUR FAITH HAS SAVED YOU!
BARTIMAEUS WAS HEALED IMMEDIATELY, AND BEGAN TO FOLLOW JESUS.

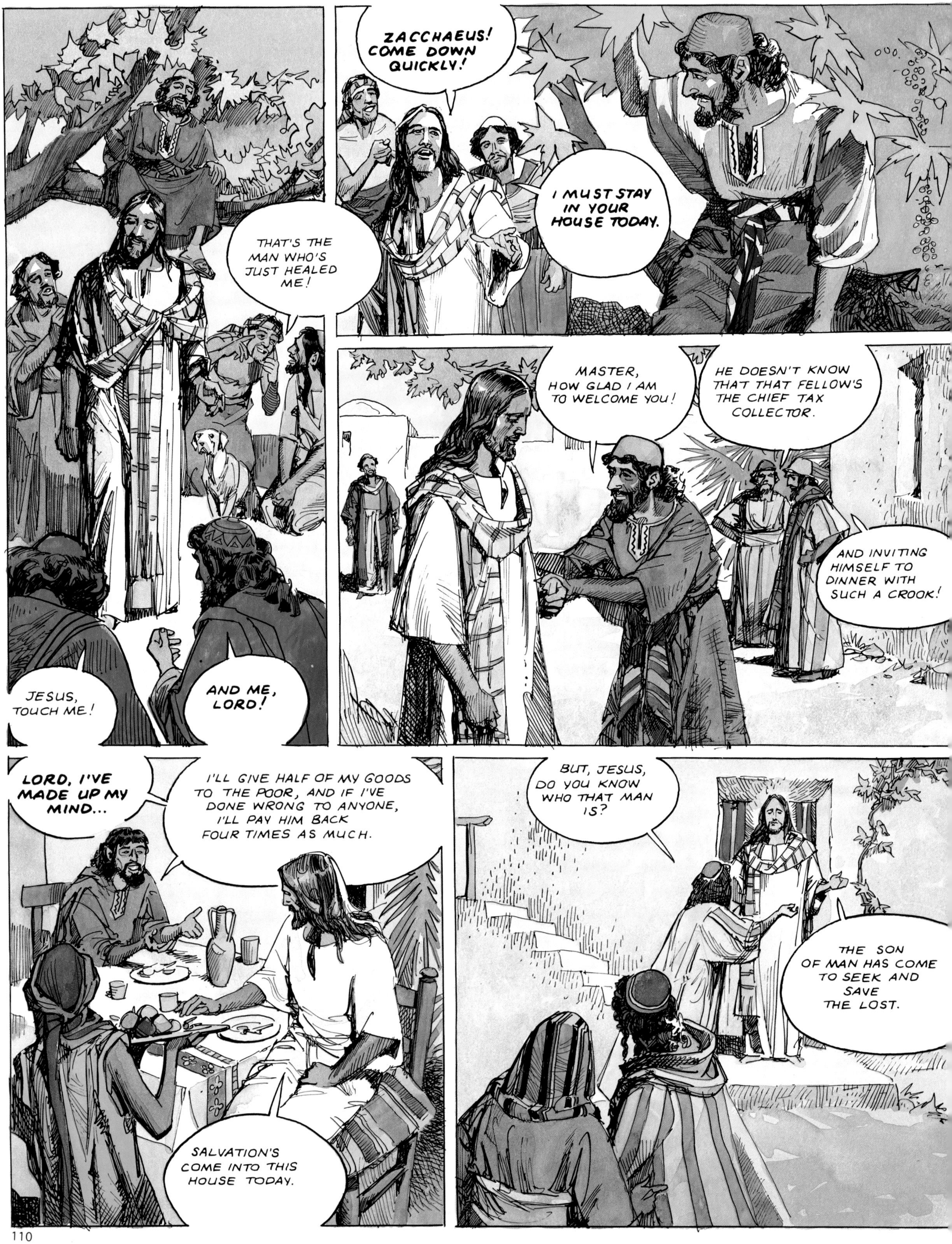

THAT'S THE MAN WHO'S JUST HEALED ME!

JESUS, TOUCH ME!

AND ME, LORD!

ZACCHAEUS! COME DOWN QUICKLY!

I MUST STAY IN YOUR HOUSE TODAY.

MASTER, HOW GLAD I AM TO WELCOME YOU!

HE DOESN'T KNOW THAT THAT FELLOW'S THE CHIEF TAX COLLECTOR.

AND INVITING HIMSELF TO DINNER WITH SUCH A CROOK!

SOON JESUS LEFT JERICHO FOR JERUSALEM.

IN A FEW DAYS THE SON OF MAN WILL BE HANDED OVER TO THE PRIESTS AND THE SCRIBES, WHO'LL PUT HIM TO DEATH.

IN SIGHT OF BETHANY...

GO INTO THE ILLAGE, WHERE YOU'LL FIND A DONKEY. UNTIE T, AND BRING IT HERE.

HOW DID HE KNOW THE DONKEY WAS THERE, AND THAT ITS OWNER WOULD GIVE IT TO US?

I DON'T KNOW, BUT THE LORD NEEDS IT!

LET'S GO TO JERUSALEM...

IT'S JESUS! THE ONE WHO RAISED LAZARUS!
BLESSED BE THE SON OF DAVID!

JESUS! JESUS!
BLESSED BE THE MESSENGER OF GOD!
GIVE ME A PALM! WE'LL GREET HIM LIKE A KING!

JERUSALEM! YOU'LL SOON BE DESTROYED BY YOUR ENEMIES, BECAUSE YOU DIDN'T REALIZE THE TIME WHEN GOD CAME TO SAVE YOU!

HOSANNA! SON OF DAVID! HOSANNA IN THE HIGHEST HEAVEN!

JESUS CAME TO THE OUTER COURT OF THE TEMPLE WHERE THE TRADERS WERE BUSY...

BUT... WHAT ARE YOU DOING?
IT IS WRITTEN:
MY HOUSE WILL BE A HOUSE OF PRAYER, BUT YOU'VE MADE IT A DEN OF ROBBERS!

WO DAYS LATER JESUS WENT BACK TO HE TEMPLE AND TAUGHT THERE.
HAVE YOU NEVER READ IN THE SCRIPTURES, THE STONE THE BUILDERS THREW AWAY HAS BECOME THE MOST IMPORTANT OF ALL?

THOSE WHO FALL ON THIS STONE WILL BE BROKEN, AND THOSE ON WHOM IT FALLS WILL BE CRUSHED!

WOE TO YOU, YOU SCRIBES AND PHARISEES! YOU HYPOCRITES! YOU DON'T GO INTO THE KINGDOM OF HEAVEN AND YOU STOP OTHERS FROM GOING IN!

WE MUST ARREST HIM!
NO, NOT HERE! THE PEOPLE THINK HE'S A PROPHET.

YOUR HOUSE WILL BE DESERTED! FROM NOW ON YOU WON'T SEE ME ANY MORE UNTIL THE DAY YOU'LL SAY 'BLESSED IS THE ONE WHO COMES IN THE NAME OF THE LORD!'

AS FOR THIS TEMPLE, NOT ONE STONE WILL BE LEFT ON ANOTHER.

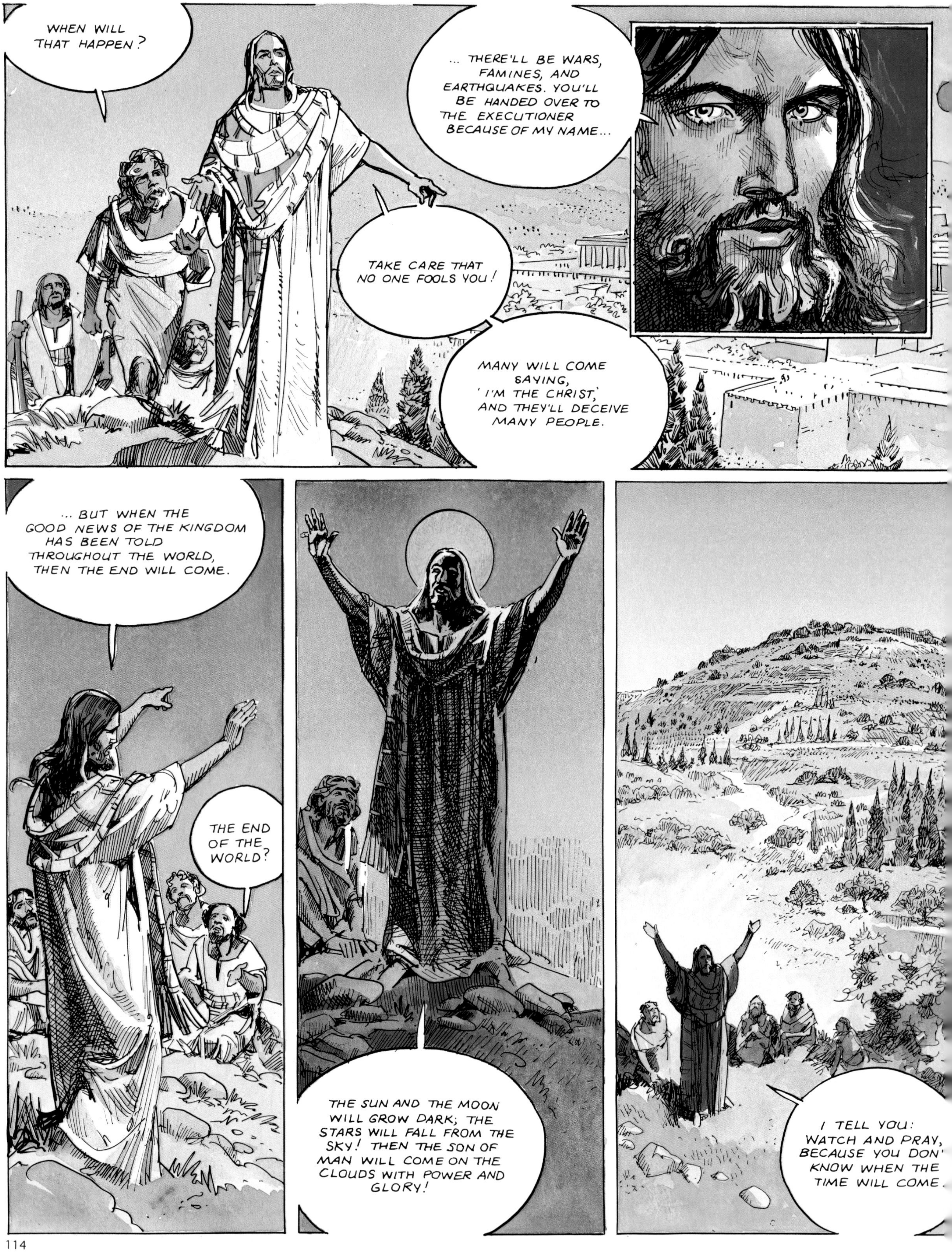

WHEN WILL THAT HAPPEN?

... THERE'LL BE WARS, FAMINES, AND EARTHQUAKES. YOU'LL BE HANDED OVER TO THE EXECUTIONER BECAUSE OF MY NAME...

TAKE CARE THAT NO ONE FOOLS YOU!

MANY WILL COME SAYING, 'I'M THE CHRIST,' AND THEY'LL DECEIVE MANY PEOPLE.

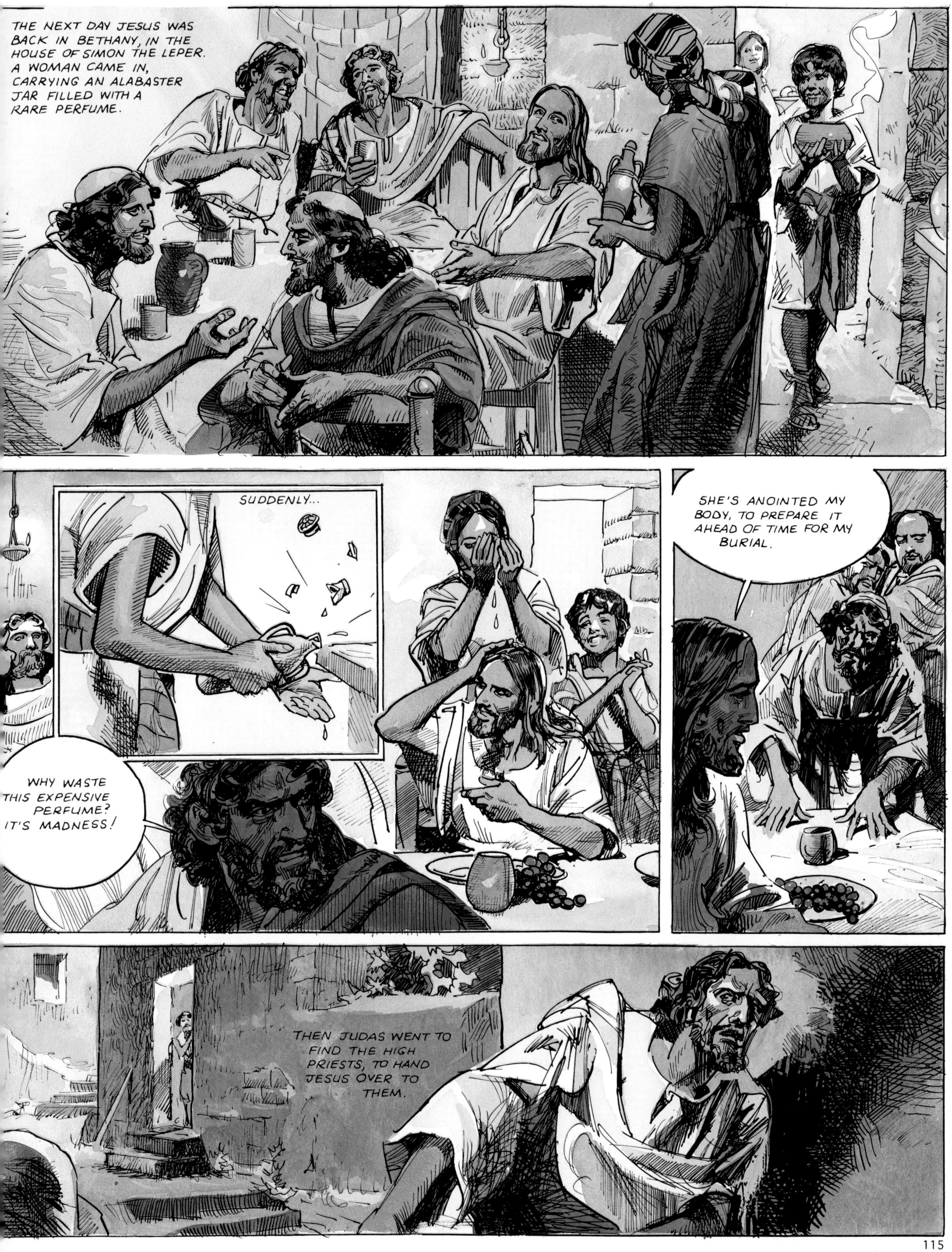

THE NEXT DAY JESUS WAS BACK IN BETHANY, IN THE HOUSE OF SIMON THE LEPER. A WOMAN CAME IN, CARRYING AN ALABASTER JAR FILLED WITH A RARE PERFUME.

SUDDENLY...
WHY WASTE THIS EXPENSIVE PERFUME? IT'S MADNESS!

SHE'S ANOINTED MY BODY, TO PREPARE IT AHEAD OF TIME FOR MY BURIAL.

THEN JUDAS WENT TO FIND THE HIGH PRIESTS, TO HAND JESUS OVER TO THEM.

THE PASSION

COME! EVERYTHING'S READY.

SOON IT WAS THE FEAST OF UNLEAVENED BREAD, WHEN THE JEWS CELEBRATED THE PASSOVER. JESUS SENT TWO DISCIPLES INTO JERUSALEM TO GET THE FESTIVAL MEAL READY. WHEN THEY RETURNED...

SCENARIO: Etienne DAHLER
DRAWING: Pierre FRISANO

IT'S HERE, IN THE UPPER ROOM.
I'VE SO LOOKED FORWARD TO CELEBRATING THIS PASSOVER WITH YOU.

AS YOU SEE, MASTER, NOTHING'S MISSING.
...NOTHING EXCEPT THE LAMB...
IT'S ROASTING DOWNSTAIRS.

THEN JESUS SAT DOWN AT THE TABLE WITH HIS DISCIPLES.
YOU ARE BLESSED, LORD OUR GOD, KING OF THE UNIVERSE, WHO CREATED THE FRUIT OF THE VINE.
THEN, AFTER WASHING HIS HANDS AS A SIGN OF CLEANSING, JESUS GAVE EACH OF THEM HERBS SOAKED IN VINEGAR.
MAY THE BITTERNESS OF THESE HERBS REMIND US OF THE TASTE OF SLAVERY AND SIN.
THEN JESUS RAISED THE UNLEAVENED BREAD, LIKE THE BREAD OF THE ANCESTORS WHEN THEY LEFT EGYPT...
...AND TAUGHT HIS DISCIPLES FROM THE STORY OF THE EXODUS.
AFTER THAT...
BRING ME A BASIN OF WATER.
BUT, LORD, A CUP'S ENOUGH TO WASH THE HANDS!
YOU, WASHING MY FEET?
YOU'LL UNDER-STAND SOON, PETER.

AFTER WASHING THE DISCIPLES' FEET, JESUS SAT DOWN AGAIN AT THE TABLE.
I'VE SET YOU AN EXAMPLE. YOU MUST DO WHAT I'VE DONE.
LOVE ONE ANOTHER, AS I'VE LOVED YOU.
THERE'S NO GREATER LOVE THAN THIS: TO GIVE YOUR LIFE FOR THOSE YOU LOVE.
JUDAS! THE THING YOU'VE DECIDED TO DO...
DO IT QUICKLY!
JESUS HANDED JUDAS A PIECE OF BREAD. HE TOOK IT, THEN HE WENT OUT.
I AM THE VINE AND MY FATHER IS THE GARDENER. HE CUTS OFF EACH BRANCH THAT DOESN'T BEAR FRUIT.

WHILE JUDAS WAS ON HIS WAY TO THE PRIESTS IN THE TEMPLE, IN THE UPPER ROOM THE PASSOVER MEAL WENT ON.
TAKE, THIS IS MY BODY.
RABBI, THIS IS THE BREAD OUR FATHERS ATE IN THE DESERT...
... AND THEY'RE DEAD! BUT WHOEVER EATS THIS BREAD WILL LIVE FOR EVER.
AT THE END OF THE MEAL, JESUS BLESSED THE LAST CUP AND GAVE IT TO THEM.
DRINK THIS, ALL OF YOU, FOR THIS IS MY BLOOD, THE BLOOD OF THE COVENANT, POURED OUT FOR YOU.
THAT'S THE FIRST TIME HE'S TAKEN THE FIFTH CUP - THE MESSIAH'S CUP!
AND SAID IT'S HIS BLOOD!
SIMON, THE SHEPHERD WILL BE KILLED, AND THE SHEEP WILL BE SCATTERED...
LORD, I'LL GO WITH YOU TO THE END.
I TELL YOU, PETER, THE COCK WON'T CROW UNTIL YOU'VE SAID THREE TIMES YOU DON'T KNOW ME.

THEN THEY ALL FOLLOWED JESUS TO THE GARDEN OF GETHSEMENE, AT THE FOOT OF THE MOUNT OF OLIVES.
SIT HERE...
PETER, JAMES AND JOHN, COME WITH ME.
MY SOUL'S SAD-EVEN TO DEATH. STAY HERE, AND KEEP WATCH WITH ME!
ABBA... FATHER... EVERYTHING'S POSSIBLE FOR YOU... TAKE THIS CUP AWAY FROM ME.
...FATHER... NOT WHAT I WANT... BUT WHAT YOU WANT.
LONG HOURS PASSED, AND THE TIRED DISCIPLES SLEPT.

IT HAPPENED AGAIN A SECOND TIME. IN SPITE OF THE MASTER'S APPEAL, THE DISCIPLES SLEPT.
WAKE UP, SIMON!
COULDN'T YOU PRAY WITH ME FOR ONE HOUR?
FORGIVE ME, MASTER, BUT I COULDN'T FIGHT IT OFF...
WHEN JESUS CAME BACK TO THEM THE THIRD TIME...
YOU CAN SLEEP NOW...
THE TIME'S COME. THE SON OF MAN'S BEING HANDED OVER TO SINFUL MEN.
THE MAN I KISS, THAT'S THE ONE!
ARREST HIM AND TAKE HIM AWAY!
GREETINGS, RABBI!
SO, JUDAS, THIS IS HOW YOU BETRAY ME!

PETER PUSHED BETWEEN THEM...
KEEP BACK!
THAT'S ENOUGH!
YOU COME TO ME WITH WEAPONS AND STICKS...
... WHEN I WAS AMONG YOU DAY AFTER DAY, TEACHING IN THE TEMPLE.
THE HOUR OF THE POWERS OF DARKNESS!
JOHN, WHAT DO THEY WANT WITH HIM?
PETER, YOU KNOW VERY WELL THAT HIS ENEMIES WANT TO ARREST HIM AND STONE HIM.

THEY FIRSTLY TOOK JESUS TO THE HOUSE OF ANNAS, FATHER-IN-LAW OF THE HIGH PRIEST CAIAPHAS.
YOU, THERE!
GO AND TELL YOUR MASTER THAT THE MAN'S HERE!
JOHN WAS WELL KNOWN IN ANNAS' HOUSE, AND HAD NO PROBLEM GETTING INSIDE. HE SENT SOMEONE TO GET PETER, WHO'D STAYED OUTSIDE.
BUT AREN'T YOU A FOLLOWER OF THE MAN THEY'VE JUST ARRESTED?
I DON'T KNOW WHAT YOU'RE TALKING ABOUT!
WHY ARE YOU SO OFTEN WITH PEOPLE WHO LEAD A BAD LIFE ...
...IS IT YOUR TEACHING THAT ATTRACTS THEM?
JESUS DID NOT REPLY.
PERHAPS YOU'D LIKE TO ENLIGHTEN ME ON CERTAIN MATTERS?
ASK THOSE WHO HAVE LISTENED TO ME! I'VE SAID NOTHING IN SECRET.
IS THAT HOW YOU SPEAK TO A HIGH PRIEST?

ANNAS THEN SENT JESUS, HIS HANDS STILL BOUND, TO CAIAPHAS, THE HIGH PRIEST THAT YEAR.
IT MUST BE IMPORTANT, TO BE DISTURBING THE HIGH PRIEST AT THIS HOUR!
GO IN QUICKLY! THEY'RE WAITING FOR YOU!
HAVE YOU NOTHING TO SAY IN YOUR DEFENCE?
I HOPE YOU'LL EXPLAIN YOURSELF TO THE **SANHEDRIN*** IN THE MORNING.
* The Jewish council.
MEANWHILE KEEP HIM LOCKED UP!
SAVE ME, MY GOD! THE WATER IS UP TO MY NECK. IT IS FOR YOUR SAKE I HAVE BEEN INSULTED. I HAVE BECOME A STRANGER TO MY BROTHERS.
MY DEVOTION TO YOUR TEMPLE BURNS IN ME LIKE A FIRE; THE INSULTS WHICH ARE HURLED AT YOU FALL ON ME.
Psalm 69

PETER JOINED A GROUP IN THE COURTYARD OF CAIAPHAS' HOUSE...
WHAT A COLD NIGHT!
BUT...
...WHAT'S GOING TO HAPPEN TO JESUS?
BUT YOU? WEREN'T YOU ONE OF HIS DISCIPLES?
I? NO, NOT I!
I WAS IN THE GARDEN WHEN THEY ARRESTED HIM... I COULD SWEAR I SAW YOU THERE!
THAT'S A LIE! I WASN'T THERE!
JUST THEN THE COCK CROWED... AND PETER BEGAN TO WEEP.

AT DAWN JESUS WAS BROUGHT BEFORE THE SANHEDRIN.*
*71 elders, priests and scribes.
MY FRIEND, YOU HAVE BEFORE YOU THE ENTIRE SANHEDRIN. IS THAT ENOUGH TO MAKE YOU SPEAK?

THEY GAVE ALL SORTS OF FALSE EVIDENCE...

I HEARD HIM SAY HE'D REBUILD THE TEMPLE IN THREE DAYS!

NO! HE SAID 'A TEMPLE' NOT 'THE TEMPLE'!

SILENCE!

CAIAPHAS, HOW CAN YOU JUDGE...

...A MAN ON SUCH LIES?
VERY WELL, MASTER NICODEMUS, I'M GOING TO PUT HIM A QUESTION SO TERRIBLE... I HARDLY DARE SPEAK IT...

ON YOUR OATH, BY THE LIVING GOD... TELL US: ARE YOU THE CHRIST, THE SON OF THE MOST HIGH?
I AM!

YOU HEARD...
FROM HIS OWN MOUTH...
BLASPHEMY!

DO WE NEED ANY MORE WITNESSES? THIS MAN DESERVES TO DIE!
JESUS ADDED...
YOU'LL SEE THE SON OF MAN SITTING AT THE RIGHT OF THE ALMIGHTY, AND COMING ON THE CLOUDS OF HEAVEN!
TELL US WHO HIT YOU?
NOW, THEN, PROPHET!
SO THEY TOOK JESUS BEFORE THE ROMAN GOVERNOR.
ROMAN LAW DOESN'T ALLOW US TO EXECUTE SOMEONE!
PILATE, THE GOVERNOR, CAN DO IT INSTEAD OF US. HE'S HERE IN JERUSALEM FOR THE PASSOVER.
THE PRIESTS OF THE SANHEDRIN ARE HERE WITH A PRISONER FOR YOU TO JUDGE.
LET THEM JUDGE HIM THEMSELVES, THEY HAVE THE AUTHORITY!
BUT...
... THEY SAY HE DESERVES TO DIE!
VERY WELL, I'LL HEAR THE CASE.
VERY SOON, IN THE FORT ANTONIA...

HERE'S THE ACCUSED!
AND WHERE ARE THE OTHERS?
THEY WON'T COME INSIDE. THAT WOULD MAKE THEM UNCLEAN FOR THE PASSOVER.
WE MUST RESPECT THEIR CUSTOMS.
WHAT'S THIS MAN ACCUSED OF?
HE STIRS THE PEOPLE UP AGAINST CAESAR!
HE CLAIMS TO BE KING OF THE JEWS!
WELL, ARE YOU THE KING OF THE JEWS?
DO YOU YOURSELF SAY THIS, OR HAVE OTHERS SAID IT TO YOU ABOUT ME?
AM I A JEW?
WELL? WHAT HAVE YOU DONE?

MY KINGDOM'S NOT OF THIS WORLD.
SO YOU ARE A KING!
I AM... AND I CAME INTO THE WORLD TO WITNESS TO THE TRUTH.
WHAT'S TRUTH?
HE'S NOTHING MORE THAN A FANATIC!
THEN WHY ARE THEY HUNTING HIM DOWN?
I FIND THIS MAN NOT GUILTY.
DON'T YOU KNOW HOW HE'S STIRRED UP ALL GALILEE?
IS HE A GALILEAN?
YES, FROM NAZARETH.
PERFECT!
HEROD ANTIPAS* IS IN JERUSALEM FOR PASSOVER...
LET HIM DEAL WITH JESUS. HE RULES OVER THAT REGION.
*Tetrarch: ruler.

JESUS WAS TAKEN TO HEROD'S PALACE. HE GAVE NO ANSWER TO ALL HIS QUESTIONS.
HE'S PLAYING THE FOOL WITH US! SEND HIM BACK TO PILATE!
TO MAKE FUN OF HIM, THEY DRESSED HIM IN A FINE ROBE.
GET THE CROWD TO GATHER OUTSIDE THE FORT AND SHOUT, 'DEATH TO JESUS!'
WE'LL SEE TO IT!
PILATE, THE CROWD'S GETTING TENSE. THEY'RE WAITING FOR YOU TO FOLLOW CUSTOM AND RELEASE A PRISONER.
LET'S WIN BOTH WAYS, AND BE RID OF THIS JESUS.
MY FRIENDS, I'M GOING TO RELEASE THE KING OF THE JEWS.
NO! NOT HIM!
NO! BAR-AB-BAS!
BAR-AB-BAS!
BAR-AB-BAS! BAR-AB-BAS!
BAR-ABBAS WAS A BANDIT ALREADY CONDEMNED.

PILATE! YOU HEAR THE CROWD? YOU MUST MAKE UP YOUR MIND ABOUT THIS JESUS!
I SENTENCE HIM TO BE WHIPPED...
MEANWHILE, IN THE COURTYARD OF FORT ANTONIA THE SOLDIERS PASSED THE TIME...
YOU'VE WON!
NOW CHOOSE YOUR KING!
HAVE THIS ONE! GET YOUR WHIPS!
THERE, MY KING'S ALREADY FOUND!
GAIUS, YOU'RE ALWAYS LUCKY!
TIE THE ROPE SHORT SO HE'LL STAND UP LONGER.

AFTER A LONG TIME ...
STOP! THAT'S ENOUGH!
WHAT ARE YOU DOING?
WAIT, I HAVEN'T CROWNED MY KING YET!
I, GAIUS, CROWN YOU KING OF THE JEWS!
LEAVE HIM! PILATE'S WAITING FOR HIM.
I'VE HAD HIM WHIPPED. THAT'S QUITE ENOUGH.
SHOW HIM TO US!
HERE'S THE MAN!
CRUCIF HIM!
HE MUST DI
HE SAYS HE'S THE SON OF GOD!

WHERE HAVE YOU COME FROM?
YOU DON'T ANSWER ME? DON'T YOU KNOW THAT I'VE THE POWER TO CRUCIFY YOU OR TO LET YOU GO?
YOU'D HAVE NO POWER OVER ME IF IT HADN'T BEEN GIVEN YOU FROM ABOVE.
PILATE, YOU'VE GOT TO DO SOMETHING. THEY'RE SHOUTING... IF YOU RELEASE HIM, YOU WON'T BE CAESAR'S FRIEND!
I'M COMING. THE PEOPLE WILL DECIDE.
HERE'S YOUR KING!
RELEASE BAR-ABBAS!
CRUCIFY HIM!
CRUCIFY HIM!
IT SHALL BE SO!
BUT KNOW THIS: I'M INNOCENT OF THE BLOOD OF THIS GOOD MAN.
MY CHILD!
MARY, THE MOTHER OF JESUS, AND JOHN WERE IN THE CROWD.

HURRY UP! WE'VE GOT TO BE DONE BY SUNSET, AND THERE ARE TWO OTHERS TO BE EXECUTED AS WELL!
HE'S IN A BAD WAY! WILL HE LAST TO THE END?

THEN THE ROAD OF THE CROSS BEGAN, LEADING THE CONDEMNED MEN THROUGH THE STREETS TO THE PLACE OF EXECUTION.
STAND BACK! LET THEM PASS!

EXHAUSTED BY THE WHIPPING, JESUS FELL.
YOU THERE,* CARRY THE CROSS FOR HIM.
IF HE DOESN'T GET HELP, HE'LL DIE ON THE WAY!

*Simon of Cyrene.

WOMEN OF JERUSALEM, DON'T CRY FOR ME! CRY FOR YOURSELVES AND YOUR CHILDREN!
COME ON, MOVE!

THEY CAME AT LAST TO THE PLACE CALLED GOLGOTHA.
FATHER... FORGIVE THEM, THEY DON'T KNOW WHAT THEY'RE DOING...
IESVS NAZARENVS REX IVDÆORVM
HERE, SHARE OUT HIS CLOTHES!
THE TUNIC! DRAW LOTS FOR THAT!
DON'T COME NEAR! STAY WITH THE OTHERS!
LEAVE HER! SHE'S HIS MOTHER!
HEY! IF YOU ARE THE SON OF GOD, COME DOWN FROM THE CROSS!
YES, COME DOWN RIGHT NOW!
HE SAVED OTHERS, BUT HE CAN DO NOTHING FOR HIMSELF!
ABOUT MIDDAY DARKNESS COVERED THE WHOLE LAND.
AND, LEARNING THAT JESUS HAD BEEN CONDEMNED, JUDAS TOOK HIS OWN LIFE.

IESVS NAZARENVS REX IVDÆORVM
AT ABOUT THE NINTH HOUR...*
*3 o'clock.
JESUS! REMEMBER ME WHEN YOU COME INTO YOUR KINGDOM!
I TELL YOU: TODAY YOU'LL BE WITH ME IN PARADISE.
ELI! ELI! LAMA SABACH-THANI...
HE'S CALLING FOR ELIJAH!
NO, THEY'RE WORDS FROM A PSALM...
MY GOD, MY GOD, WHY HAVE YOU ABANDONED ME?
THEN, SEEING HIS MOTHER AND JOHN, THE DISCIPLE HE LOVED, HE SAID...
MOTHER, THERE'S YOUR SON... JOHN, THERE'S YOUR MOTHER...
IT IS ACCOM-PLISHED!
AND, BOWING HIS HEAD, HE DIED.
AT THAT MOMENT THE CURTAIN IN THE TEMPLE WAS TORN IN HALF FROM TOP TO BOTTOM...
THAT MAN WAS TRULY THE SON OF GOD!

BECAUSE THEY DIDN'T WANT THE BODIES TO REMAIN ON THE CROSSES THROUGHOUT THE SABBATH, THE JEWS WENT TO PILATE.
CAN YOU GIVE THE ORDER FOR THE CRUCIFIED MEN TO BE FINISHED OFF, SO THAT THEY CAN BE BURIED BEFORE SUNSET?
I KNOW WHAT I HAVE TO DO!
TAKE YOUR LANCE, AND MAKE SURE HE'S DEAD.
NOT NECESSARY! HE'S ALREADY DEAD.
THE SOLDIER PIERCED JESUS' SIDE, AND BLOOD AND WATER POURED OUT.
WITH PILATE'S PERMISSION, JOSEPH OF ARIMATHEA AND NICODEMUS TOOK CARE OF THE BODY OF JESUS.
IT'S NEARLY THE SABBATH! WE HAVEN'T THE TIME TO WASH THE BODY AND ANOINT IT...
WRAP HIM IN THIS LINEN SHEET...
... AND LAY HIM IN THIS NEW TOMB.
AFTER THE SABBATH THE WOMEN WILL COME BACK TO ANOINT THE BODY.
HELP ME ROLL THE STONE IN FRONT OF THE TOMB.

THE SAME EVENING, WHEN MARY AND SOME OF THE DISCIPLES WERE PRESENT, JOHN READ THE PSALM JESUS HAD BEGUN TO RECITE ON THE CROSS.
OUR ANCESTORS PUT THEIR TRUST IN YOU. THEY CALLED TO YOU AND ESCAPED FROM DANGER.
MY STRENGTH, COME QUICKLY TO MY RESCUE. I WILL TELL MY PEOPLE WHAT YOU HAVE DONE...
(Psalm 22)
WHEN THE SABBATH WAS OVER, MARY, SALOME, AND MARY OF MAGDALA WENT TO THE TOMB EARLY IN THE MORNING, CARRYING SPICES.
BUT WHO'LL HELP US ROLL THE STONE BACK?
COME, MARY; WE'LL SEE WHEN WE GET THERE.
LOOK ... THE STONE...
QUICK! LET'S GO IN!
EMPTY!

AS SOON AS THE SABBATH ENDED, MARY OF MAGDALA, MARY THE MOTHER OF JAMES AND JESUS, AND SALOME WENT TO THE TOMB TO ANOINT THE BODY OF JESUS. BUT THE TOMB WAS OPEN, AND...

SOMEONE'S TAKEN THE LORD'S BODY AWAY!

WHOEVER WOULD DO SUCH A THING?

THE RISEN CHRIST

SCENARIO: Etienne DAHLER
DRAWING: Carlo MARCELLO

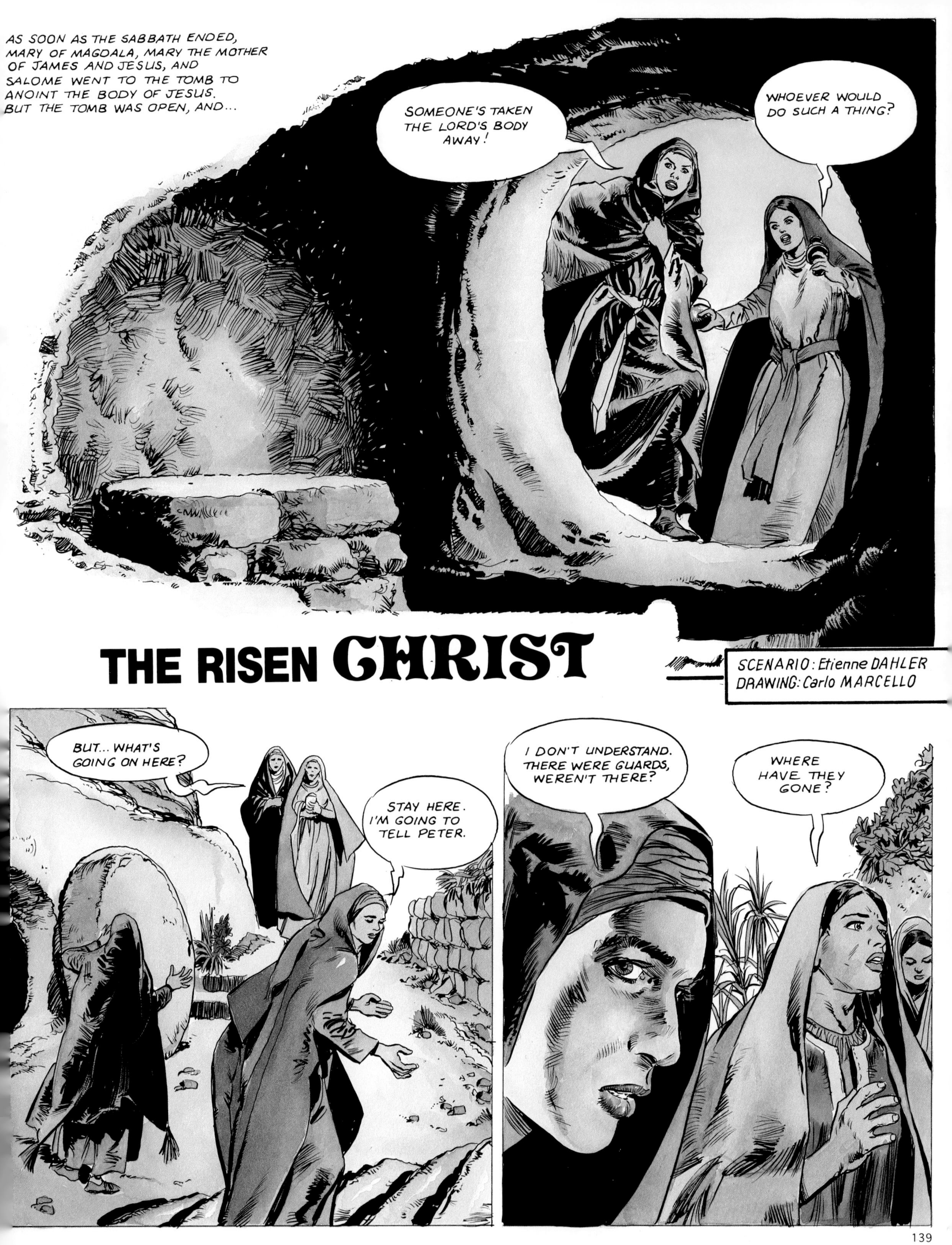

MARY, ARE YOU SURE?
IF YOU DON'T BELIEVE ME, GO AND SEE FOR YOURSELF!
SO PETER AND JOHN, WHO WERE IN THE UPPER ROOM WITH THE OTHER DISCIPLES, RAN TO THE TOMB.
AMAZING! ...EXACTLY AS SHE SAID!
PETER WENT IN FIRST...
JOHN, LOOK HERE!
?

PETER, WHAT ON EARTH'S HAPPENED?
I DON'T KNOW... I CAN'T UNDERSTAND IT.

WHILE PETER AND JOHN WENT BACK TO THE UPPER ROOM...

...MARY OF MAGDALA WENT BACK TO THE TOMB...

SUDDENLY...

LADY, WHY ARE YOU CRYING?

THEY'VE TAKEN MY LORD AWAY, AND I DON'T KNOW WHERE THEY'VE PUT HIM!
WHOM ARE YOU LOOKING FOR?

IF YOU'VE TAKEN HIM AWAY, TELL ME WHERE YOU'VE PUT HIM!

MARY...

RABBONI!

DON'T HOLD ONTO ME! GO AND TELL MY BROTHERS THAT I'M GOING TO MY FATHER AND YOUR FATHER.

MARY OF MAGDALA RAN TO THE UPPER ROOM TO TELL THE DISCIPLES THE NEWS. THOMAS WAS THERE TOO.

I'VE SEEN THE LORD!

THAT'S IMPOSSIBLE!

SOON THE OTHER WOMEN ARRIVED ...
WE'VE JUST MET THE LORD IN THE STREET!
COME ON! YOU'RE SEEING THINGS!

AFTER ALL THAT'S HAPPENED TO US, WE'RE SO TIRED THAT WE'RE IMAGINING ALL SORTS OF THINGS.

HE NEWS QUICKLY REACHED THE HIGH PRIESTS...
SPREAD THE RUMOUR THAT HIS DISCIPLES STOLE HIS BODY WHILE THE GUARDS WERE ASLEEP.
WHAT ELSE COULD HAVE HAPPENED?

THAT AFTERNOON, TWO DISCIPLES LEFT JERUSALEM, ON THE WAY TO EMMAUS...
LIFE GOES ON AS IF NOTHING'S HAPPENED!
ALL THE SAME, THE WOMEN'S STORIES TROUBLE ME.

JESUS JOINED THEM ON THE ROAD, BUT THEY DIDN'T RECOGNIZE HIM.
WHAT ARE YOU TALKING ABOUT?

DON'T YOU KNOW WHAT'S JUST HAPPENED IN JERUSALEM?
WHAT?
JESUS... OF NAZARETH...

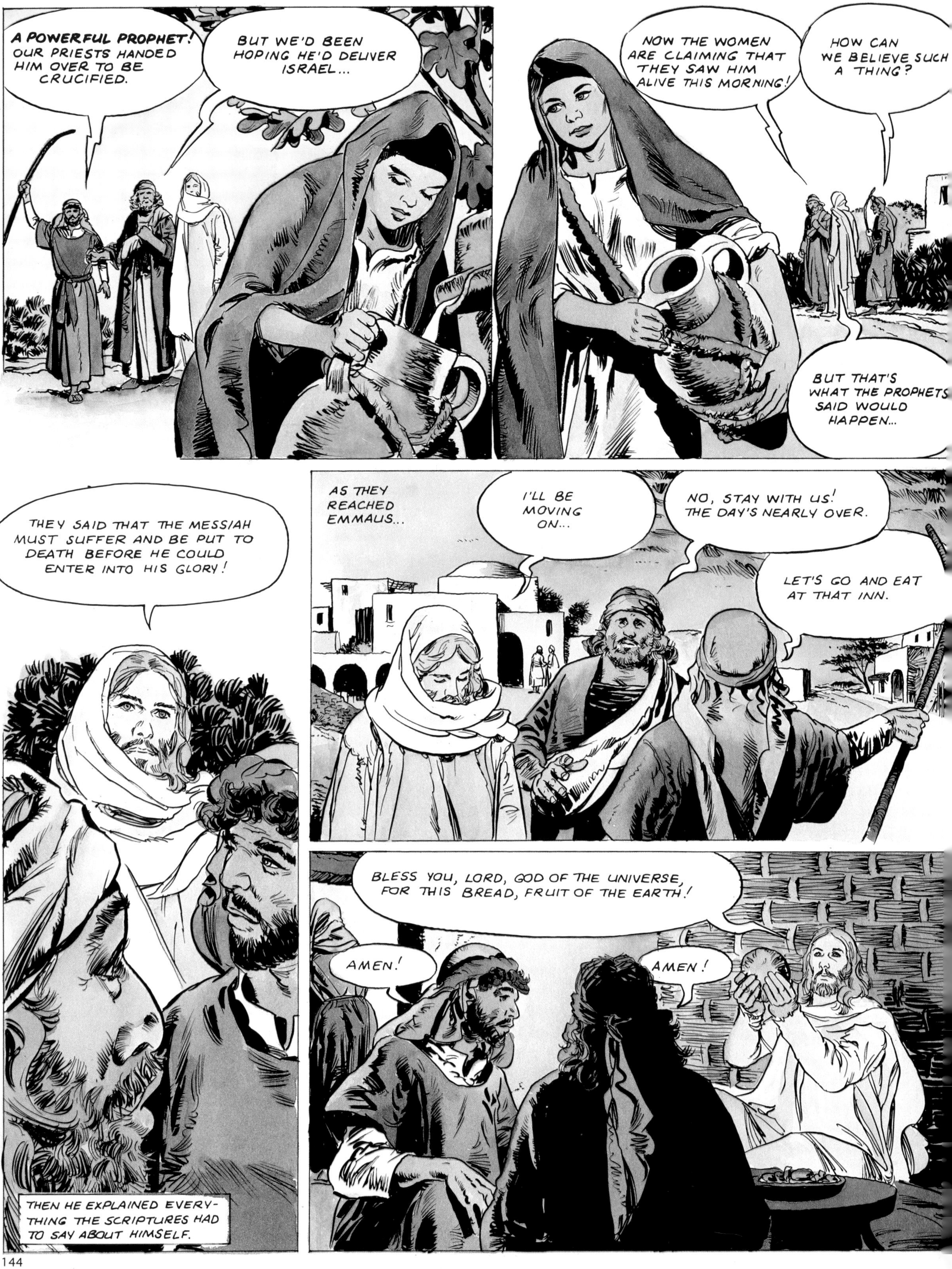

A POWERFUL PROPHET! OUR PRIESTS HANDED HIM OVER TO BE CRUCIFIED.
BUT WE'D BEEN HOPING HE'D DELIVER ISRAEL...
NOW THE WOMEN ARE CLAIMING THAT THEY SAW HIM ALIVE THIS MORNING!
HOW CAN WE BELIEVE SUCH A THING?
BUT THAT'S WHAT THE PROPHETS SAID WOULD HAPPEN...

THEY SAID THAT THE MESSIAH MUST SUFFER AND BE PUT TO DEATH BEFORE HE COULD ENTER INTO HIS GLORY!

TAKE SOME, AND EAT IT!
JESUS!
JESUS!
HE'S ALIVE!
THE WOMEN WERE TELLING THE TRUTH!
THEY HURRIED STRAIGHT BACK TO JERUSALEM.
THEY'LL NEVER BELIEVE US!
MATTHEW WELCOMED THEM INTO THE UPPER ROOM.
CLEOPAS, THE LORD'S RISEN! HE'S APPEARED TO SIMON PETER!
TO HIM TOO?
PETER, WE CAME SPECIALLY TO TELL YOU THAT WE MET HIM ON THE ROAD TO EMMAUS!
PRAISE THE LORD FOR SUCH WONDERFUL THINGS!

SUDDENLY JESUS WAS THERE WITH THEM.
PEACE BE WITH YOU!
LOOK... I'M REALLY ALIVE!
AS THE FATHER SENT ME, I ALSO SEND YOU...
THEN HE DISAPPEARED...
THE NEXT DAY...
IT'S REALLY TRUE, THOMAS! AFTER YOU LEFT, THE LORD CAME TO US.
HE EVEN SHOWED US THE MARKS OF HIS WOUNDS.
UNTIL I CAN TOUCH THEM, I WON'T BELIEVE IT!
A WEEK LATER THE DISCIPLES WERE TOGETHER, AND JESUS APPEARED TO THEM AGAIN.
THOMAS, STRETCH OUT YOUR HAND AND TOUCH MY SIDE.
MY LORD AND MY GOD!

JERUSALEM WAS FULL OF RUMOURS.

THEY'RE SPYING ON US. TWO MEN FOLLOWED ME THIS MORNING.
IT'S NOT SAFE HERE ANY LONGER. LET'S GO BACK TO GALILEE.

ONE EVENING PETER DECIDED TO GO FISHING. BUT THAT NIGHT...

NOT A SINGLE FISH! JOHN, I'VE NEVER SEEN ANYTHING LIKE IT.
BUT, PETER, REMEMBER THE MARVELLOUS CATCH...

HEY, THERE! HAVE YOU CAUGHT ANYTHING?
NO!
THROW OUT THE NET ON THE RIGHT SIDE OF THE BOAT!

HELP ME!
THE NET'S GOING TO BREAK!
PETER, IT'S THE LORD! I'M SURE IT IS!

PETER!
LET'S FOLLOW HIM IN THE BOAT.

BRING SOME OF THE FISH YOU'VE JUST CAUGHT.

NOW COME AND HAVE BREAKFAST.

WHEN THEY'D EATEN, JESUS TOOK SIMON PETER ON ONE SIDE, AND ASKED HIM THE SAME QUESTION THREE TIMES:

AND THREE TIMES PETER GAVE THE SAME ANSWER.

SIMON, DO YOU LOVE ME?

LORD, YOU KNOW EVERYTHING. YOU KNOW I LOVE YOU.

THEN FEED MY SHEEP.

A FEW DAYS LATER THE ELEVEN WENT TO A MOUNTAIN IN GALILEE, WHERE JESUS HAD TOLD THEM TO GO.
JOHN, DO YOU KNOW IF THE MASTER WILL STILL BE WITH US FOR A LONG TIME?
I DON'T THINK SO, PHILIP.
THERE HE IS!
GO! TEACH ALL THE NATIONS; BAPTIZE THEM IN THE NAME OF THE FATHER, AND THE SON, AND THE HOLY SPIRIT.
AND I WILL BE WITH YOU, TO THE END OF TIME.
BUT, LORD...

I WONDER WHAT'S GOING TO HAPPEN. HE SENDS US OUT, BUT AT THE SAME TIME HE STAYS WITH US...
YOU KNOW IT'S DIFFICULT FOR US TO UNDERSTAND...

BUT, PETER, WHY DID THE MASTER SAY WE MUST GO BACK TO JERUSALEM?
BECAUSE THE FEAST OF SHAVUOTH* IS COMING, AND WE MUST GO TO JERUSALEM FOR IT.

* Pentecost, 50 days after Passover.

A LITTLE WHILE LATER...
WE'LL LEAVE EARLY TOMORROW, AND GO THROUGH THE JORDAN VALLEY.

JEWS FROM EVERY COUNTRY WENT UP TO JERUSALEM TO CELEBRATE THE GIVING OF THE TORAH TO MOSES.

NOT FAR FROM THE HOLY CITY...
FOLLOW ME! YOUR MASTER'S WAITING FOR YOU

MY FRIENDS, IN A LITTLE WHILE THE WORLD WON'T SEE ME ANY MORE, BECAUSE I'M GOING TO THE FATHER...
EVERYTHING YOU ASK IN MY NAME, I'LL DO FOR YOU, AND I'LL PRAY THE FATHER TO SEND YOU THE SPIRIT OF TRUTH.
AT LAST YOU'RE TALKING PLAINLY! NOW WE KNOW THAT YOU CAME FROM GOD.
REMEMBER: THE SERVANT'S NOT GREATER THAN THE MASTER. IF THEY PERSECUTED ME, THEY'LL PERSECUTE YOU TOO.
LORD, WHAT MUST WE DO? WHERE MUST WE GO?
STAY IN JERUSALEM UNTIL YOU RECEIVE POWER FROM HEAVEN.
NOW I WANT TO BLESS YOU.

BE MY WITNESSES–IN JERUSALEM, IN ALL OF JUDAEA, IN SAMARIA, AND RIGHT OUT TO THE ENDS OF THE EARTH.
AFTER SAYING THIS, HE WAS LIFTED INTO THE SKY...
... AND HE DISAPPEARED FROM THEIR SIGHT.
THERE ARE MANY OTHER THINGS THAT JESUS DID. IF THEY WERE ALL WRITTEN DOWN ONE BY ONE, I SUPPOSE THAT THE WHOLE WORLD COULD NOT HOLD THE BOOKS THAT WOULD BE WRITTEN.
- EPILOGUE TO THE GOSPEL OF JOHN.

AFTER JESUS HAD ASCENDED TO HEAVEN, PETER TURNED TO HIS BROTHER-DISCIPLES.
LET'S DO AS THE MASTER SAID, AND GO BACK TO THE UPPER ROOM.

SO THE DISCIPLES AND MARY, JESUS' MOTHER, GATHERED IN THE UPPER ROOM.
LET'S PRAY AND GET READY TO RECEIVE WHAT THE LORD PROMISED US.

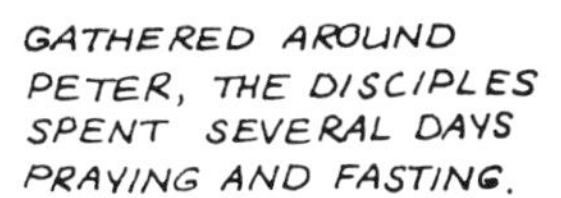
GATHERED AROUND PETER, THE DISCIPLES SPENT SEVERAL DAYS PRAYING AND FASTING.

BROTHERS, JUDAS WAS ONE OF US AND SHARED OUR WORK, BEFORE HE BETRAYED JESUS. NOW SOMEBODY MUST TAKE HIS PLACE...

...ONE WHO'S BEEN WITH US FROM THE BEGINNING.

WE PROPOSE JOSEPH JUSTUS...
...AND WE PROPOSE MATTHIAS.

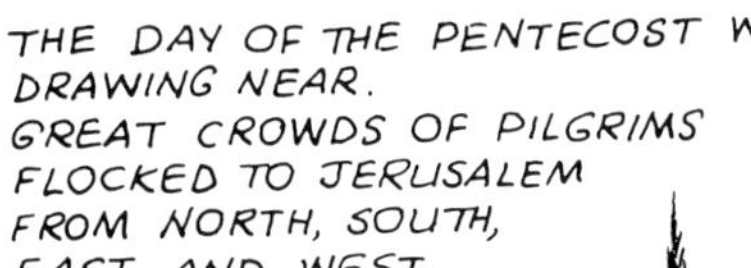

THE DAY OF THE PENTECOST WAS DRAWING NEAR.
GREAT CROWDS OF PILGRIMS FLOCKED TO JERUSALEM FROM NORTH, SOUTH, EAST AND WEST.

I WAS GLAD
WHEN THEY SAID TO ME,
'LET US GO TO THE
LORD'S HOUSE.'
AND NOW WE
ARE HERE,
STANDING INSIDE THE
GATES OF JERUSALEM.

– Psalm 122

ON THE DAY OF THE PENTECOST THEY WERE ALL TOGETHER IN THE SAME PLACE TO CELEBRATE THE GIVING OF THE LAW ON SINAI.
SUDDENLY THERE WAS A NOISE FROM THE SKY, LIKE A STRONG WIND BLOWING AND...
. THEY WERE ALL ILLED WITH THE OLY SPIRIT.
PRAISE AND GLORY TO YOU, LORD!
OUR GOD, HOW BLESSED YOU ARE!
THE GOD OF THE UNIVERSE BE PRAISED!
... AND EACH ONE BEGAN TO SPEAK IN A DIFFERENT LANGUAGE.

YOU HEAR THAT? WHAT'S GOING ON?
YES, IT'S LIKE A GREAT WIND... MAKING MUSIC...
HURRY UP! COME WITH US!
IT'S THE DISCIPLES OF JESUS OF NAZARETH UP THERE.
BUT I CAN HEAR THEM SINGING IN MY OWN LANGUAGE!
I TOO! I'M FROM EGYPT!
I ALSO UNDERSTAND... AND I'M GREEK!
IT'S A MIRACLE!
COME ON! THOSE MEN ARE FULL OF GOOD WINE - THAT'S ALL!
THERE THEY ARE!

THEN PETER SPOKE.
LISTEN TO ME, ALL OF YOU! SOME PEOPLE SAY WE'RE DRUNK. BE SERIOUS: IT'S ONLY THE THIRD HOUR*...
* 9 o'clock a.m.

REMEMBER WHAT THE PROPHET JOEL SAID: IN THE LAST DAYS I WILL POUR OUT MY SPIRIT ON EVERYONE...

...YOUR SONS AND DAUGHTERS WILL HAVE VISIONS; YOUR OLD MEN WILL DREAM DREAMS...'

WELL, I'M TELLING YOU THAT THIS PROPHECY'S BEING FULFILLED TODAY.

AND JOHN ADDED...
KNOW THIS, BROTHERS: JESUS OF NAZARETH, WHO WAS CRUCIFIED, HAS REALLY RISEN FROM THE DEAD!

DAVID WAS TALKING ABOUT HIM WHEN HE SAID: 'YOU WILL NOT LEAVE ME IN THE WORLD OF THE DEAD'.

AND JAMES...
YES, THIS JESUS IS ALIVE, AND WE'RE THE WITNESSES! HE'S THE CHRIST YOU CRUCIFIED!

MANY IN THE CROWD WERE DEEPLY TROUBLED BY WHAT THEY HEARD.
THESE MEN ARE TELLING THE TRUTH. YOU CAN SEE BY THEIR FACES!
YOU'RE RIGHT; THEY'RE MEN OF GOD.

AND PETER REPLIED...

BROTHERS, WHAT MUST WE DO?

EACH OF YOU MUST TURN TO GOD, BE BAPTIZED IN THE NAME OF JESUS CHRIST, AND THEN YOU TOO WILL RECEIVE THE HOLY SPIRIT.

JOHN, IN HIS TURN...

JOHN THE BAPTIST SAID, 'I BAPTIZE YOU WITH WATER, BUT THE ONE WHO COMES AFTER ME WILL BAPTIZE YOU WITH THE HOLY SPIRIT.'

WANT TO BE BAPTIZED, I AND MY WHOLE FAMILY!
SO DO I!
AND I! MAY GOD FORGIVE ME FOR NOT RECOGNIZING HIS MESSIAH!
THEN THE APOSTLES WENT DOWN INTO THE CROWD, TO BAPTIZE THOSE WHO ASKED FOR IT...
...AFTER THAT THEY LAID HANDS ON THEM.
YOUR SINS ARE FORGIVEN.
ON THE DAY OF THE PENTECOST IN JERUSALEM THE CHURCH WAS BORN.

WHAT A JOY TO SEE THE HEARTS OF SO MANY PEOPLE TURNING TO THE LORD!
PETER, WHAT ARE WE GOING TO DO WITH THIS CROWD THAT WANTS TO JOIN US?
WE WILL SHOW THEM THE WAY.
TOGETHER WITH THE APOSTLES, THE NEW FOLLOWERS OF JESUS WENT EVERY DAY TO THE TEMPLE.
ASK AND YOU WILL RECEIVE, SEEK AND YOU WILL FIND, KNOCK AND THE DOOR WILL BE OPENED TO YOU, THE LORD SAID.
IN THE EVENING THEY MET AT SOMEONE'S HOUSE TO LISTEN TO THE APOSTLES' TEACHING...
...TO BREAK BREAD, AND TO PRAISE GOD.
THIS IS MY BODY, GIVEN FOR YOU. DO THIS IN MEMORY OF ME.

THE BELIEVERS' INFLUENCE GRADUALLY SPREAD.
DAVID, I'VE SOMETHING IMPORTANT TO TELL YOU. I WENT TO CHRIST'S DISCIPLES...
YOU? YOU'RE BETRAYING YOUR BROTHERS!
NO, DAVID. THEY'RE HONOURABLE MEN. THEY GO TO THE TEMPLE 3 TIMES A DAY TO PRAY...
...AND LOVE REALLY UNITES THEM!
THE BELIEVERS SHARED THEIR BELONGINGS WITH ONE ANOTHER.
HOW WONDERFUL, HOW PLEASANT, FOR GOD'S PEOPLE TO LIVE TOGETHER IN HARMONY! (Psalm 133)

IN FRONT OF YOU ALL, WHO ARE HIS DISCIPLES, I ACKNOWLEDGE THAT JESUS OF NAZARETH IS TRULY THE MESSIAH FORETOLD BY THE PROPHETS.
EVERY DAY MANY CONVERTS JOINED PETER AND THE OTHER APOSTLES.
SCENARIO: Etienne DAHLER
DRAWING: Carlo MARCELLO
PETER AND THE JERUSALEM CHURCH
BE BAPTIZED IN THE NAME OF JESUS CHRIST, AND YOU'LL BECOME PART OF OUR COMMUNITY.
THE WORD 'COMMUNITY'* WAS OFTEN USED TO DESCRIBE JESUS' DISCIPLES, BECAUSE THEY MET TOGETHER SO REGULARLY.
*In Greek, ekklesia, meaning 'assembly' and so 'church'.

ONE DAY IN JERUSALEM, WHEN PETER AND JOHN WERE GOING TO THE TEMPLE...

HAVE PITY ON A POOR LAME MAN!

I HAVE NO GOLD OR SILVER, BUT WHAT I DO HAVE I GIVE YOU!

IN THE NAME OF JESUS CHRIST OF NAZARETH GET UP AND WALK!

THE LAME MAN JUMPED TO HIS FEET...
I'M HEALED! I CAN STAND UP!
THEN COME WITH US, AND GIVE THANKS TO GOD.

OVER THERE... ISN'T THAT THE BEGGAR FROM THE BEAUTIFUL GATE?
IT CERTAINLY IS, BUT HE'S WALKING!
UNBELIEVABLE! LET'S GO AND SEE!

PETER, EVERYBODY'S FOLLOWING US. YOU MUST SPEAK TO THEM.

FELLOW ISRAELITES, WHY ARE YOU SURPRISED AT THIS? DO YOU THINK IT WAS BY OUR OWN POWER THAT WE MADE THIS MAN WALK?

KNOW THAT JESUS OF NAZARETH, WHOM YOU HANDED OVER TO BE KILLED, WAS RAISED BY THE GOD OF OUR FATHERS.

WHAT DO YOU MEAN?
IT'S TRUE; WE'RE THE WITNESSES...

AND THIS MAN'S BEEN HEALED IN THE NAME OF JESUS!
THAT'S RIGHT!

TURN BACK TO GOD! BECAUSE IT WAS FIRST OF ALL FOR YOU THAT HE SENT HIS SERVANT.
YOU'D BETTER GO AND ALERT THE COMMANDER OF THE TEMPLE GUARD, BEFORE THESE TWO CAUSE ANY TROUBLE.
RIGHT!

HE EVEN SAID THAT JESUS IS ALIVE AND STILL DOING THINGS.
THAT'S MORE THAN ENOUGH TO HAVE THEM ARRESTED!
MOSHE, ASSEMBLE THE GUARD!

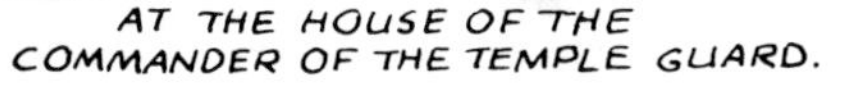

AT THE HOUSE OF THE COMMANDER OF THE TEMPLE GUARD.

MAKE WAY!

THAT'S ENOUGH! I'M ARRESTING YOU!

MANY OF THOSE WHO WERE THERE BELIEVED IN JESUS AND JOINED THE APOSTLES.

THE NEXT MORNING PETER AND JOHN APPEARED BEFORE THE SANHEDRIN. CAIAPHAS QUESTIONED THEM.

BY WHOSE POWER OR IN WHOSE NAME DID YOU DO THIS?

IN THE NAME OF JESUS CHRIST OF NAZARETH, WHOM YOU CRUCIFIED AND GOD RAISED FROM THE DEAD.

HE'S THE STONE YOU BUILDERS THREW AWAY, BUT NOW IT'S BECOME THE MOST IMPORTANT OF ALL!

TAKE THE ACCUSED OUTSIDE.

THEY'RE SO SURE OF THEMSELVES – THAT'S WHAT BOTHERS ME.
AND EVERYBODY KNOWS THERE'S BEEN A MIRACLE!
WE MUST DO ALL WE CAN TO KEEP THIS FROM SPREADING ANY FURTHER AMONG THE PEOPLE.

THEN THE COUNCIL CALLED PETER AND JOHN BACK.
WE FORBID YOU EVER AGAIN TO SPEAK OR ACT IN THAT NAME!
WHAT'S RIGHT IN GOD'S SIGHT? TO OBEY YOU, OR TO OBEY HIM?
ENOUGH! WE'LL HAVE NO MORE OF THIS JESUS!
THEN PETER AND JOHN WERE RELEASED.
GOD BE PRAISED!
YES, PRAISE HIM! HE GAVE US THE STRENGTH TO STAND FIRM.
BACK WITH THE OTHER BELIEVERS, THEY TOLD THEM EVERYTHING THAT HAD HAPPENED. THEN JAMES SAID...
BROTHERS, LET'S THANK GOD FOR ALL THESE WONDERFUL THINGS...
...LORD, GIVE YOUR SERVANTS THE STRENGTH TO SPEAK YOUR WORD BOLDLY.
AMEN!
STRETCH OUT YOUR HAND TO HEAL, AND MAY THERE BE SIGNS AND MIRACLES IN THE NAME OF YOUR HOLY SERVANT JESUS!
AMEN!

A LITTLE LATER PETER WAS PREACHING...

THE LORD JESUS SAID TO THE RICH YOUNG MAN, 'IF YOU WANT TO FOLLOW ME, SELL ALL YOU HAVE AND GIVE IT TO THE POOR...'

IT WOULD BE A GOOD THING IF THERE WERE NO RICH OR POOR AMONG US, BUT WE ALL SHARED EVERYTHING...

VERY SOON, IN FRONT OF MATTHEW, WHO KEPT THE RECORD...

MY NAME'S HANANIEL. I'VE SOLD MY HOUSE, AND HERE'S THE MONEY.

I'M JOSEPH. HERE'S WHAT I GOT FOR MY FIELD.

ALL BROTHERS! THIS IS THE KINGDOM OF GOD!

AT THAT TIME...
I'M A WIDOW, WITH FOUR LITTLE ONES...
HERE, THIS WILL HELP YOU.
DO YOU REMEMBER THE WORDS OF ISAIAH? 'THE WOLF WILL LIVE WITH THE LAMB; THE PANTHER WILL SLEEP WITH THE KID...'
WHY DO YOU SAY THAT?
WELL, SOME OF US WERE REAL WOLVES, AND OTHERS, LIKE YOU, REAL LAMBS... **NOW WE ALL LIVE TOGETHER!**
YOU'RE RIGHT!
AND THE PROPHET ALSO SAID: 'THAT DAY THE DESCENDANT OF JESSE WILL BE LIKE A BANNER FOR THE NATIONS, AND EVERYONE WILL TURN TO HIM.'

ONE DAY A MAN CALLED ANANIAS CAME TO PETER.
I'VE SOLD MY PROPERTY. HERE'S THE MONEY.
ANANIAS, YOU'RE LYING! YOU'VE KEPT PART OF THE MONEY FOR YOURSELF!
NO ONE FORCED YOU TO SELL YOUR PROPERTY. AND ONCE IT WAS SOLD, THE MONEY WAS YOURS TO DO WITH AS YOU LIKED...
YOU'VE NOT LIED TO MEN - YOU'VE LIED TO GOD!
BUT...
TAKE HIS BODY AWAY.
THERE'S NOTHING HIDDEN THAT WON'T BE MADE KNOWN, NO SECRET THAT WON'T SEE THE LIGHT OF DAY.

ANANIAS AND HIS WIFE SAPPHIRA HAD ACTUALLY AGREED TO HIDE PART OF THE MONEY. ABOUT 3 HOURS LATER SAPPHIRA CAME TO PETER.

YOUR HUSBAND BROUGHT US THIS MONEY. IS IT THE FULL AMOUNT YOU GOT FOR SELLING YOUR FIELD?
THAT'S RIGHT; IT'S ALL THERE.

YOU BOTH PLOTTED TO DECEIVE THE LORD! THE MEN WHO BURIED YOUR HUSBAND WILL CARRY YOU OUT TOO!

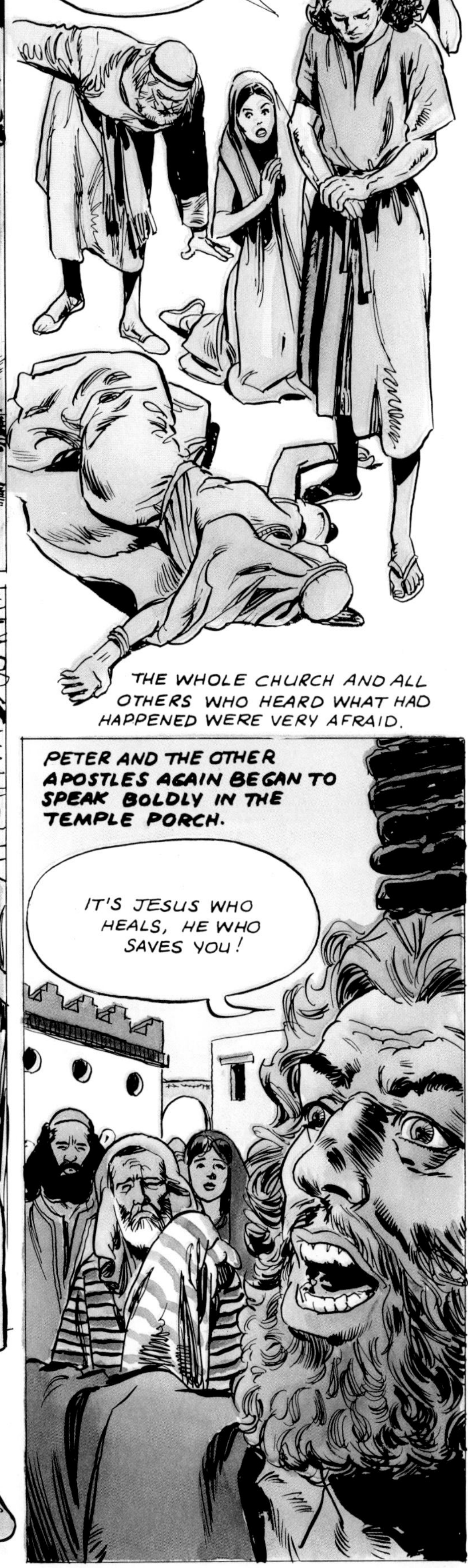

THE MASTER SAID THAT ALL SINS WILL BE FORGIVEN, BUT THOSE WHO SIN AGAINST THE HOLY SPIRIT WON'T BE FORGIVEN.
THE WHOLE CHURCH AND ALL OTHERS WHO HEARD WHAT HAD HAPPENED WERE VERY AFRAID.
PETER AND THE OTHER APOSTLES AGAIN BEGAN TO SPEAK BOLDLY IN THE TEMPLE PORCH.
IT'S JESUS WHO HEALS, HE WHO SAVES YOU!

EVERY DAY THE APOSTLES BECAME MORE FAMOUS.

LORD, HAVE MERCY ON OUR SICK BROTHER!

I CAN SEE! I CAN SEE!

AT THE SAME TIME, IN THE HOME OF CAIAPHAS...
THEY'VE STARTED AGAIN!
ARREST THEM!

THE APOSTLES WERE THROWN INTO PRISON, BUT THAT SAME NIGHT...
GO AND STAND IN THE TEMPLE, AND CARRY ON SPEAKING TO THE PEOPLE.

LOOK! THE DOORS ARE OPEN!
THERE'LL BE TROUBLE IN THE MORNING!

THE NEXT DAY, WHEN THE SANHEDRIN CONVENED...
THE NAZARENE DISCIPLES HAVE ESCAPED!
BUT WE FOUND ALL THE DOORS SHUT, AND THE GUARDS HEARD AND SAW NOTHING.
THEY MUST HAVE FRIENDS INSIDE THE PRISON! I DEMAND AN INVESTIGATION!

SUDDENLY A TEMPLE GUARD CAME TO SPEAK TO CAIAPHAS, THE HIGH PRIEST.
THE MEN YOU PUT IN PRISON YESTERDAY ARE TEACHING IN THE TEMPLE.
BRING THEM HERE... BUT DON'T USE FORCE ON THEM!
THE APOSTLES APPEARED AGAIN BEFORE THE SANHEDRIN.
WE FORBADE YOU TO SPEAK IN THE NAME OF THAT... GALILEAN! NOW YOU'VE FILLED JERUSALEM WITH YOUR TEACHING, AND YOU PUBLICLY ACCUSE US OF KILLING THAT MAN!
WE MUST OBEY GOD RATHER THAN MEN!
GOD RAISED JESUS, WHOM YOU CRUCIFIED, AND MADE HIM THE SAVIOUR...
...SO THAT ISRAEL WOULD TURN BACK TO GOD AND BE FORGIVEN FOR HER SINS.
THIS IS CRAZY! CAIAPHAS, SILENCE THEM!
KILL THEM! HAVE THEM PUT TO DEATH NOW!
SEEING THE WAY THINGS WERE GOING, CAIAPHAS HAD THE APOSTLES TAKEN FROM THE ROOM.
FRIENDS, LET'S KEEP CALM! RABBI GAMALIEL WANTS TO SPEAK.

DON'T TAKE ANY FURTHER ACTION AGAINST THESE MEN. IF WHAT THEY'RE SAYING AND DOING IS ONLY SOMETHING HUMAN, IT WILL COME TO NOTHING...

...BUT IF IT COMES FROM GOD, YOU'LL NEVER DESTROY IT... TAKE CARE THAT YOU DON'T FIND YOURSELVES FIGHTING AGAINST GOD!

RABBI GAMALIEL, YOU'VE SAID A WISE THING. I AGREE.
SO DO I!
AND I!
GOOD! BRING BACK THE ACCUSED.

YOU'RE CONDEMNED TO BE WHIPPED... AND - FOR THE LAST TIME - WE ORDER YOU NEVER AGAIN TO SPEAK IN THE NAME OF JESUS.

AFTER THE WHIPPING, THE APOSTLES WERE SET FREE.
THIS TIME THEY WERE SHAKEN. I THINK THEY'LL LEAVE US IN PEACE.
THE APOSTLES WENT ON PREACHING THE GOOD NEWS ABOUT JESUS CHRIST WITH EVEN MORE VIGOUR.

THE NUMBER OF CONVERTS KEPT GROWING... WHICH CAUSED CERTAIN PROBLEMS...
THIS CAN'T GO ON! I MUST TALK TO PETER!
QUITE SO! HERE HE IS...
WELL, WHAT'S GOING ON?
PETER, WHEN THE SUPPLIES ARE HANDED OUT EACH DAY, THE WIDOWS OF THE HELLENES* ARE BEING NEGLECTED.
* Greek-speaking Jews.
I MUST ADMIT THAT ALL THOSE IN CHARGE OF SERVING THE TABLES ARE HEBREWS*, AND SOMETIMES PEOPLE AREN'T TREATED FAIRLY...
WE MUST ORGANIZE THINGS DIFFERENTLY, SO THAT THAT DOESN'T HAPPEN AGAIN.
* Palestinian Jews, speaking Aramaic.
PETER CALLED THE APOSTLES TOGETHER...
WE CAN'T DO EVERYTHING OURSELVES OR BE EVERYWHERE AT ONCE!
I THINK WE SHOULD STICK TO THE PREACHING.
I AGREE. I SUGGEST THAT THE MEETING CHOOSES 7 BROTHERS WHO'LL BE IN CHARGE OF SERVING THE TABLES.
HERE ARE THE 7 BROTHERS WHO WERE ELECTED: STEPHEN, PHILIP, PROCHORUS, TIMON, PARMENAS AND NICOLAUS.

THE APOSTLES AGREED WITH THE MEN CHOSEN BY THE MEETING, AND LAID HANDS ON THEM.
BE LIKE THE MASTER, WHO DIDN'T COME TO BE SERVED, BUT TO SERVE.

EACH DAY MORE AND MORE PEOPLE BECAME DISCIPLES.
WE'RE A GROUP OF LEVITES; WE WANT TO BE BAPTIZED.
YES, WE BELIEVE THAT JESUS IS THE MESSIAH.

SOON A YOUNG RABBI, A COUNCILLOR OF THE SANHEDRIN, WENT TO CAIAPHAS, THE HIGH PRIEST.
THE NAZARENES ARE A REAL THREAT TO OUR RELIGION. HOW CAN YOU ALLOW THEM TO ACT FREELY?
WE FOLLOWED GAMALIEL'S ADVICE. NO DOUBT WE WERE WRONG!

EVERYBODY CAN SEE THAT THIS MOVEMENT'S BEEN ALLOWED TO LAST TOO LONG!
AND... WHAT EXACTLY DO YOU SUGGEST, **SAUL OF TARSUS?**

ARREST THEIR LEADERS AND PUT THEM TO DEATH!

LITTLE LATER, IN HE ROOM WHERE HE SANHEDRIN ET, CAIAPHAS...
THE NAZARENES TAKE NO NOTICE OF OUR ORDERS, SO WE'LL HAVE TO TAKE ANOTHER LINE OF ACTION.
SAUL OF TARSUS, THE SANHEDRIN APPOINTS YOU CHIEF INVESTIGATOR, WITH FULL POWERS TO BUILD UP THE CASE AGAINST THE NAZARENES AND PROSECUTE THEM IN THIS COURT.
FIRST THING THE NEXT MORNING, SAUL...
I WANT TO KNOW EVERYTHING: THE NAMES OF THE LEADERS, WHERE AND HOW THEY ACT, WHO SUPPORTS THEM... EVERYTHING! HURRY!
THE INVESTIGATION WENT AHEAD QUICKLY...
MOSES WAS TAUGHT THE WISDOM OF THE EGYPTIANS, AND HE WAS STRONG IN WORDS AND DEEDS.
THAT'S STEPHEN SPEAKING. HE'S TERRIFIC! HE KNOWS ALL THE SCRIPTURES BY HEART, AS WELL AS THE WORDS OF THE WISE.
HM... DOES HE COME HERE OFTEN?
YES, EVERY SABBATH. DURING THE WEEK YOU'LL FIND HIM ALL OVER JERUSALEM, TEACHING AND HEALING THE SICK.

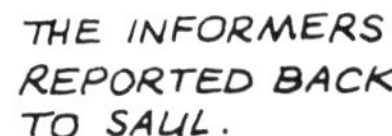

THE INFORMERS REPORTED BACK TO SAUL.

THAT STEPHEN'S A TROUBLE-MAKER. EVERYONE LISTENS TO HIM AS IF HE'S AN EXPERT.
PERFECT! I'LL DEAL WITH IT!

A FEW DAYS LATER, WHILE STEPHEN WAS PREACHING IN THE SYNAGOGUE...
HE SHOULD SHUT UP! THAT MAN'S BLASPHEMING AGAINST MOSES AND GOD!
THAT JESUS WAS NOTHING BUT A DECEIVER, A BANDIT!
NO, LET HIM SPEAK!

TAKE YOUR HANDS OFF THIS UPRIGHT MAN!
AN UPRIGHT MAN? WHO BETRAYS THE LAW AND THE PROPHETS?
SEIZE HIM, AND TAKE HIM BEFORE THE SANHEDRIN!

THE REST OF YOU GO HOME, IF YOU DON'T WANT THE SAME TO HAPPEN TO YOU!

VERY SOON, BEFORE THE SANHEDRIN, IN THE PRESENCE OF CAIAPHAS...

LET THE TRIAL BEGIN! BRING IN THE WITNESSES...

THIS MAN SPOKE AGAINST THE HOLY TEMPLE AND AGAINST THE LAW.
I HEARD HIM SAY THAT JESUS THE NAZARENE WOULD DESTROY THE TEMPLE AND CHANGE THE TRADITIONS MOSES GAVE US.
HE SAID THAT JESUS IS THE MESSIAH AND THAT HE WOULD COME BACK TO SET UP HIS KINGDOM.
STEPHEN, IS THIS TRUE?
STEPHEN BEGAN TO SPEAK. HE OUTLINED THE WHOLE HISTORY OF ISRAEL...
YOU STUBBORN PEOPLE, WILL YOU ALWAYS RESIST THE HOLY SPIRIT? WAS THERE ANY PROPHET YOUR FATHERS DIDN'T PERSECUTE?
AND WHEN THE RIGHTEOUS ONE CAME, YOU MURDERED HIM!
SILENCE!
THAT'S ENOUGH! HIS WORDS CONDEMN HIM!
PUT HIM TO DEATH!
I SEE HEAVEN OPENED, AND THE SON OF MAN STANDING AT GOD'S RIGHT HAND.
EVERYONE OF THEM STORMED AND SHOUTED AT HIM.

CAIAPHAS READ THE COURT'S SENTENCE...

BEING FOUND GUILTY OF BLASPHEMY AND OF LEADING THE ISRAELITES ASTRAY FROM THE RIGHT PATH, STEPHEN IS CONDEMNED TO BE STONED TO DEATH.

YOU HERETIC! YOU'RE WORSE THAN A PAGAN!
YOU'LL GO STRAIGHT TO THE FIRES OF GEHENNAH!
MAKE WAY!

THEY TOOK STEPHEN TO THE PLACE OF STONING.

THROW HIM IN!

LORD JESUS, RECEIVE MY SPIRIT.
LET THE WITNESSES THROW THE FIRST STONES.

LORD, DON'T HOLD THIS SIN AGAINST THEM!
AND NOW LET THE OTHER PEOPLE COME FORWARD.

VERY SOON STEPHEN WAS DEAD.
STOP!
AT THE SAME TIME, AMONG THE DISCIPLES...
THIS IS SURELY JUST THE BEGINNING. THAT SAUL'S MAD!
OUR BROTHERS, ESPECIALLY THE GREEK-SPEAKERS, MUST LEAVE JERUSALEM AND GO ELSEWHERE.
SAUL ACTED SO QUICKLY THAT SOME OF THE BELIEVERS DIDN'T MANAGE TO GET AWAY.
THROW THEM ALL INTO PRISON!
AS FOR THE OTHERS, THEY SPREAD THE FAITH IN JESUS CHRIST.
PHILIP, HERE ARE SOME SAMARITANS WANTING TO BE BAPTIZED. WHAT SHALL WE DO?
BAPTIZE THEM! THEN GO BACK TO JERUSALEM, AND ASK SOME OF THE APOSTLES TO JOIN US.
PETER! JOHN! IT'S SO GOOD TO SEE YOU AGAIN!
PHILIP! GOD BE PRAISED!

THE HARVEST'S GREAT! MANY HEARTS ARE OPENING TO THE LORD!

THAT SAME EVENING PETER PRAYED...
LORD, SEND YOUR SPIRIT, AS YOU PROMISED, TO ACT POWERFULLY AMONG OUR BROTHERS.

PETER AND JOHN STAYED IN SAMARIA FOR A WHILE, PREACHING ABOUT JESUS CHRIST THE SAVIOUR, AND HEALING THE SICK. THEN THEY WENT BACK TO JERUSALEM.

IT'S VERY STRANGE! THE JEWS REJECT THE MESSIAH, AND THE SAMARITANS WELCOME HIM!
JOHN, I BELIEVE THIS IS ONLY THE FIRST OF MANY SURPRISES...

THIS IS WHAT HAPPENED NEXT TO PHILIP, ONE OF THE 7 DEACONS.

GET UP, PHILIP, AND GO SOUTH TO THE ROAD BETWEEN JERUSALEM AND GAZA!

PHILIP GOT UP STRAIGHT AWAY AND WENT.

WHEN HE REACHED THAT ROAD...

GO AND MEET THAT CHARIOT.

DO YOU UNDERSTAND WHAT YOU'RE READING?
HOW CAN I UNDERSTAND IF THERE'S NO ONE TO EXPLAIN IT? IF YOU CAN HELP ME, COME UP AND SIT BESIDE ME.
I'M THE MINISTER IN CHARGE OF THE QUEEN OF ETHIOPIA'S TREASURY, AND I'VE BEEN ON A PILGRIMAGE TO JERUSALEM, BECAUSE I'VE ADOPTED THE JEWISH RELIGION.
AND YOU'RE TRYING TO UNDERSTAND THE SCRIPTURES?
YES, I WAS READING THE BOOK OF THE PROPHET ISAIAH.
LIKE A LAMB LED AWAY TO BE SLAUGHTERED, LIKE A EWE DUMB BEFORE HER SHEARERS, HE NEVER SAID A WORD.
'...HE WAS HUMILIATED, AND JUSTICE WAS DENIED HIM. NO ONE WILL BE ABLE TO TELL ABOUT HIS DESCENDANTS, BECAUSE HIS LIFE ON EARTH HAS COME TO AN END.'
IS THE PROPHET SPEAKING ABOUT HIMSELF, OR ABOUT SOMEONE ELSE?
THEN, STARTING WITH THAT PASSAGE, PHILIP TOLD THE ETHIOPIAN THE GOOD NEWS ABOUT JESUS.
HERE'S SOME WATER. WHAT'S TO STOP ME FROM BEING BAPTIZED?
NOTHING, IF YOU BELIEVE WITH ALL YOUR HEART.

THE ETHIOPIAN ORDERED THE CHARIOT TO STOP, AND THE TWO MEN GOT DOWN.

I BAPTIZE YOU IN THE NAME OF JESUS.

SUDDENLY...
BUT... WHERE'S HE GONE?
HE'S VANISHED!

PRAISE THE LORD! HE SENT THAT MAN TO ME!

THE ETHIOPIAN WENT BACK TO HIS COUNTRY, PROCLAIMING THE MESSAGE OF CHRIST WHEREVER HE WENT.

THE PERSECUTION OF THE COMMUNITY IN JERUSALEM WAS BEGINNING TO BEAR ITS FIRST FRUITS.

THE FIRST PERSECUTION AGAINST JESUS' FOLLOWERS CLAIMED MANY VICTIMS.
THOSE WHO MANAGED TO ESCAPE, WENT ON SPREADING THE GOOD NEWS.
THE SANHEDRIN APPOINTED SAUL, WHO HAD AGREED TO STEPHEN'S MURDER, TO DIRECT THE PERSECUTIONS.

THERE! JERUSALEM HAS BEEN RID OF THE NAZARENES...

YES, SAUL, BUT THE RING-LEADERS HAVE ESCAPED! YOU MUST HUNT THEM DOWN!

DO YOU KNOW WHERE THEY'RE HIDING?

YES, CAIAPHAS. IN JOPPA AND SAMARIA AND ANTIOCH, BUT ESPECIALLY IN DAMASCUS.

PETER AND PAUL

THE GOOD NEWS IS TOLD TO THE PAGANS

THEY'VE BEEN PREACHING THEIR MESSAGE IN MANY SYNAGOGUES...
FROM TOMORROW, SAUL, YOU'LL HAVE FULL AUTHORITY TO ARREST THEM AND BRING THEM HERE FOR TRIAL.

CAIAPHAS, DO YOU THINK WE'LL BE ABLE TO CONTROL THE SITUATION?
I HOPE SO. AT ANY RATE, SAUL IS THE MAN WE NEED!

SCENARIO: Etienne DAHLER
DRAWING: Carlo MARCELLO

SAUL AND HIS ESCORT IMMEDIATELY LEFT JERUSALEM FOR DAMASCUS.
AFTER A DIFFICULT JOURNEY OF SEVERAL DAYS...
...THE LITTLE GROUP STOPPED TO REST BEFORE REACHING DAMASCUS.
WE'LL RIDE ON AGAIN TONIGHT. I WANT TO GET TO DAMAS-CUS AS EARLY AS POSSIBLE.
IF SAUL GIVES THEM AS HARD A TIME AS HE GIVES US, THERE'LL SOON BE NO MORE NAZARENES!
WITH A MAN LIKE THAT THERE'S NO HOPE OF TAKING THINGS EASY!
THAT NIGHT SAUL COULDN'T SLEEP.
I'LL BREAK THAT NAZARENE SECT!
SETTING OFF LONG BEFORE SUNRISE, THE RIDERS SOON SAW THE CITY.
DAMASCUS!
LET'S GO!

SUDDENLY SAUL FELL TO THE GROUND AND HEARD A VOICE...
SAUL! SAUL! WHY ARE YOU PERSECUTING ME?
I AM JESUS, THE ONE YOU ARE PERSECUTING.
WHAT'S HAPPENING?
WHO ARE YOU, LORD?
GET UP! GO INTO THE CITY. YOU'LL BE TOLD WHAT TO DO.

SAUL! WHAT'S WRONG? ARE YOU HURT?
NO, BUT I CAN'T SEE... I'M BLIND!
WE ALL HEARD THE VOICE... BUT... THERE WAS NO ONE THERE.
OH, YES... THERE **WAS** SOMEBODY THERE!
GET UP BEHIND ME. WE'LL RIDE SLOWLY.
SIR, WHAT AN HONOUR FOR ME... THAT A MAN LIKE YOU...
THAT'S ENOUGH! TAKE ME TO A ROOM, AND LEAVE ME ALONE!
IN DAMASCUS...
WE'VE ARRIVED. NOW, SAUL, YOU'LL BE ABLE TO REST.
SAUL STAYED LIKE THAT FOR THREE DAYS; HE ATE AND DRANK NOTHING.

IN DAMASCUS THERE WAS A DISCIPLE OF JESUS NAMED ANANIAS. HE CAME TO SEE SAUL.
SAUL, MY BROTHER, THE LORD JESUS, WHO APPEARED TO YOU ON THE ROAD, HAS SENT ME SO THAT YOU CAN GET YOUR SIGHT BACK, AND BE FILLED WITH THE HOLY SPIRIT.
THE LORD SAYS, 'YOU'RE THE ONE I'VE CHOSEN TO MAKE MY NAME KNOWN TO PAGANS, TO KINGS, AND TO THE PEOPLE OF ISRAEL.'
I'M HEALED... I CAN SEE AGAIN!
THEN SAUL, ANANIAS, AND SEVERAL DISCIPLES WENT TO A PLACE NEAR THE CITY.
SAUL, I BAPTIZE YOU IN THE NAME OF JESUS.
FROM NOW ON YOU'LL BE CALLED PAUL, BECAUSE TODAY YOU'VE BECOME A NEW MAN.
BROTHERS, I WANT TO LIVE AND WORK WITH YOU.

PAUL SPENT SEVERAL DAYS WITH THE DISCIPLES, BUT THEN...

I CAN'T GO ON HIDING FOR EVER... I MUST GO AND TELL OTHERS WHAT HAS HAPPENED TO ME.

YES, PAUL, EVEN IF THAT WILL BE DANGEROUS FOR YOU!

THE NEXT SABBATH, IN THE SYNAGOGUE IN DAMASCUS...

THE MESSIAH APPEARED TO ME ON THE ROAD. HE IS JESUS, THE ONE THEY CALL THE NAZARENE.

BUT... ISN'T THAT SAUL OF TARSUS, THE SANHEDRIN'S AGENT... SAYING THESE THINGS?

INCREDIBLE! EVEN HE HAS BEEN LED ASTRAY BY THAT SECT!

THAT SAME NIGHT THE ELDERS OF THE SYNAGOGUE MET.

WE MUST LET JERUSALEM KNOW STRAIGHT AWAY WHAT IS GOING ON HERE!

BUT ONE THING IS FOR SURE: SAUL MUST DIE! THE SANHEDRIN CAN'T DO ANYTHING ELSE!

THE NEXT DAY...
PAUL, YOU MUST LEAVE DAMASCUS. YOU'RE PUTTING YOURSELF AND US IN DANGER.
BUT HOW? THE JEWS HAVE POSTED ARMED GROUPS TO WATCH THE CITY GATES AROUND THE CLOCK.
WE WILL FIND A WAY...

AND THAT IS HOW PAUL ESCAPED FROM HIS ENEMIES.

PAUL DIDN'T HESITATE. HE DECIDED TO GO BACK TO JERUSALEM.
IN A FEW DAYS I'LL BE WITH THE APOSTLES... I'LL BE ABLE TO HEAR EVERYTHING THE MASTER TAUGHT THEM.
BUT IN JERUSALEM PEOPLE WERE SUSPICIOUS OF HIM.
MY FRIENDS, LET ME...
IT IS SAUL OF TARSUS!
SPLIT UP!
THEY STILL THINK I'M PERSECUTING THEM...
A LITTLE LATER...
PAUL!
BARNABAS! THE LORD HAS SENT YOU!
THE APOSTLES WANT NOTHING TO DO WITH ME... THEY ALL DISTRUST ME... YOU WERE IN DAMASCUS... HELP ME!
BUT HOW?

EARLY THE NEXT DAY, BARNABAS...
PETER, THIS IS SAUL, CALLED PAUL SINCE HIS BAPTISM. YOU CAN TRUST HIM. IN DAMASCUS I MYSELF HEARD HIM PREACHING IN THE NAME OF JESUS.
IN THAT CASE, PAUL, YOU'RE ONE OF US. GOD BE PRAISED!
FROM THAT DAY PAUL DIDN'T LEAVE THE APOSTLES, AND HE STARTED PREACHING POWERFULLY IN THE SYNAGOGUES. BUT HIS ENEMIES STILL WANTED TO KILL HIM.
SON OF SATAN! FIRST HE BETRAYS US, THEN HE MOCKS US!
THINGS HAPPENED VERY QUICKLY.
PAUL, THE SANHEDRIN HAVE PAID MEN TO KILL YOU. YOU MUST LEAVE JERUSALEM.
VERY WELL! I'LL GO BACK TO TARSUS AND STAY THERE, UNTIL THEY'VE FORGOTTEN ABOUT ME.
THE CHRISTIANS WENT AS FAR AS CAESAREA WITH PAUL.
GOD PROTECT YOU!
BARNABAS, PRAY FOR ME!
THE SANHEDRIN WAS SATISFIED BECAUSE PAUL HAD GONE. THE YOUNG CHURCH LIVED IN PEACE FOR A WHILE.

URING THAT TIME
ETER BEGAN
'SITING THE OTHER
ONGREGATIONS IN THAT
REA. HE WAS AT LYDDA...
WE'VE COME FROM JOPPA.* TABITHA HAS JUST DIED...
YOU KNOW HOW MUCH SHE DID, AND HOW EVERYONE LOOKED UP TO HER...
VERY WELL! I'LL GO WITH YOU, AND WE'LL PRAY FOR HER.
* Now called JAFFA.
T JOPPA, IN THE
PPER ROOM WHERE
HE DEAD WOMAN LAY...
LOOK AT HER LOVELY WORK... HOW SAD IT IS!
EVERYONE LEAVE THE ROOM!
PETER STAYED ALONE, AND AFTER PRAYING FOR A LONG TIME...
TABITHA! GET UP!
THEN TABITHA OPENED HER EYES, AND SAT UP...
THE WHOLE TOWN HEARD THE NEWS, AND MANY BELIEVED IN THE LORD.

PETER STAYED ON AT JOPPA, WITH A MAN CALLED SIMON. ONE MIDDAY, WHILE HE WAS PRAYING...
PETER! GET UP! KILL AND EAT!
NEVER, LORD! I'VE NEVER EATEN ANYTHING FORBIDDEN OR UNCLEAN.
WHAT GOD SAYS IS CLEAN YOU MUSTN'T CALL UNCLEAN!
PETER WAS STILL WONDERING WHAT THIS VISION COULD MEAN...
HEY! SIMON LIVES HERE, DOESN'T HE?
WE'RE LOOKING FOR SOMEBODY CALLED PETER...
I'M PETER. WHAT DO YOU WANT?

AN ANGEL OF THE LORD TOLD OUR MASTER TO INVITE YOU TO HIS HOUSE, SO THAT HE CAN HEAR WHAT YOU HAVE TO SAY...
VERY WELL! COME IN, AND WE'LL TALK ABOUT IT WHILE WE EAT.
WHO IS YOUR MASTER?
CENTURION CORNELIUS OF THE CAESAREA GARRISON. HE IS A GOOD MAN WHO WORSHIPS GOD.
EVERYONE KNOWS HOW KIND-HEARTED AND GENEROUS HE IS.
SIMON, TOMORROW MORNING I'LL BE GOING TO CAESAREA WITH OUR FRIENDS.
BUT, PETER, HOW CAN YOU EAT WITH PAGANS?
YESTERDAY I COULDN'T HAVE DONE IT, BUT TODAY...
AND EARLY THE NEXT DAY PETER LEFT FOR CAESAREA...

WHEN THEY REACHED CAESAREA, CORNELIUS MET PETER AND KNELT DOWN IN FRONT OF HIM.
SIR!
GET UP! I'M ONLY A HUMAN BEING LIKE OTHER PEOPLE.
I'VE ASKED MY FAMILY AND FRIENDS TO COME...
YOU KNOW THAT A JEW ISN'T ALLOWED TO GO INTO A PAGAN'S HOUSE ... BUT THE LORD HAS SHOWN ME THAT I MUSTN'T THINK OF ANY-BODY AS UNCLEAN.
EVERYONE HAS COME TO HEAR WHAT THE LORD WANTS YOU TO TELL US.
NOW I KNOW THAT GOD DOESN'T REJECT ANYBODY, BUT HE ACCEPTS EVERYONE WHO WORSHIPS HIM.
YOU KNOW HE SENT HIS WORD TO ISRAEL, THE GOSPEL OF PEACE THAT JESUS CHRIST BROUGHT.
YOU KNOW THAT JESUS WAS REJECTED AND PUT TO DEATH. BUT WE ARE WITNES-SES THAT GOD RAISED HIM AND THAT HE IS ALIVE.

PETER WAS STILL SPEAKING, WHEN THE HOLY SPIRIT CAME DOWN ON ALL THOSE WHO WERE LISTENING.

PETER! EVEN THE PAGANS RECEIVE THE HOLY SPIRIT!
SO LET US NOT SET A LIMIT TO GOD'S WORK ANY LONGER... LET THEM ALL BE BAPTIZED!

PETER STAYED IN CAESAREA FOR A FEW DAYS, THEN HE SET OFF BACK TO JERUSALEM.

THESE WORDS WHICH THE LORD SPOKE WERE ALSO FULFILLED AT CAESAREA:

ACK IN JERUSALEM SOME OF THE ELIEVERS CRITICIZED PETER.

IS IT TRUE? YOU ATE WITH PAGANS?
IT IS TRUE. I EVEN PRAYED WITH THEM AND BAPTIZED THEM.

AND TO CALM THEM DOWN, PETER HAD TO EXPLAIN HOW THE LORD HAD LED HIM TO DO THESE THINGS.

SOON AFTERWARDS...
PETER, THERE IS A BROTHER FROM ANTIOCH WITH INCREDIBLE NEWS.
BRING HIM IN STRAIGHTAWAY.
WE'RE LISTENING, BROTHER.
HAVE YOU HEARD THAT IN ANTIOCH MANY PAGANS— AND JEWS TOO— HAVE ACCEPTED THE WORD OF THE LORD?
BUT WHO TOOK THEM THE GOOD NEWS?
TRADERS AND TRAVELLERS FROM JUDAEA, CYPRUS, AND PHOENICIA...
LET'S REJOICE!
THIS IS GOD'S DOING, NOT OURS! ONE OF US MUST GO TO ANTIOCH TO HELP THESE NEW BROTHERS.
THEY CHOSE BARNABAS, WHO CAME FROM CYPRUS.

THERE IS ANTIOCH! AFTER ROME IT IS THE BIGGEST CITY IN THE EMPIRE.
500 000 PEOPLE LIVE THERE.
BARNABAS MADE CONTACT WITH THE CHURCH IN ANTIOCH.
DO YOU KNOW WHAT THE PEOPLE HERE CALL US?
NO, I DON'T.
CHRISTIANOI... CHRISTIANS... CHRIST'S PEOPLE!
BE PROUD OF IT! NOW YOU BEAR THE NAME OF THE LORD HIMSELF!
WEEK AFTER WEEK BARNABAS ENCOURAGED THE NEW BROTHERS TO REMAIN FAITHFUL TO THE LORD, AND THE ANTIOCH CHURCH GREW. BUT ONE DAY...
BARNABAS, YOU MUST HAVE SOMEONE TO HELP YOU. THE WORK HAS BECOME TOO HEAVY FOR ONE MAN.
IN JERUSALEM, PERHAPS...
NO! I KNOW THE MAN WE NEED...
PAUL!
SO BARNABAS SET OFF FOR TARSUS TO GET PAUL.

IN A WEAVER'S SHOP IN TARSUS...
PAUL, ANTIOCH NEEDS YOU. I BEG YOU: YOU MUST COME.
BARNABAS, THIS IS THE SIGN I'VE BEEN WAITING FOR! I'M WITH YOU!

ON THE WAY BARNABAS TOLD PAUL THE WONDERFUL THINGS THE LORD HAD BEEN DOING IN ANTIOCH. AT LAST THEY ARRIVED...

THERE, PAUL! THERE IS ANTIOCH!
MAY GOD HELP US TO MAKE HIS CHURCH STRONG.

SO, PAUL, HERE YOU ARE AT LAST! WHAT A BLESSING!

EVER SINCE BARNABAS LEFT WE HAVE BEEN PRAYING THAT YOU WOULD AGREE TO JOIN US.

WHAT ARE YOU THINKING ABOUT, PAUL?

WE'VE NEVER MET BEFORE, AND WE'RE ALREADY BROTHERS!

AND THE LORD WILL GIVE YOU MANY MORE!

PAUL'S POWERFUL PREACHING HELPED MANY PEOPLE TO BELIEVE, AND THE CHRISTIANS REGULARLY MET TOGETHER FOR THE AGAPÉ.*

THE SAME NIGHT THAT HE WAS BETRAYED, THE LORD TOOK BREAD, AND AFTER GIVING THANKS, HE BLESSED IT AND SAID:
TAKE THIS, THIS IS MY BODY WHICH IS GIVEN FOR YOU.

* The Christian love-meal, repeating the Last Supper.

PAUL HAD BEEN IN ANTIOCH FOR A YEAR, WHEN ONE NIGHT, DURING A MEETING...
THIS IS WHAT THE LORD SAYS: A GREAT FAMINE* IS COMING; IT WILL RAVAGE JUDAEA, AND YOUR BROTHERS WILL LOSE EVERYTHING.
THAT IS AGABUS, A PROPHET FROM JERUSALEM...

WE MUST LISTEN TO HIM. LET'S START COLLECTING MONEY RIGHT NOW TO HELP OUR BROTHERS.

WITHIN A FEW MONTHS THE FAMINE HAD BECOME VERY SEVERE...
PAUL AND BARNABAS, WE'VE DECIDED THAT YOU TWO SHOULD TAKE WHAT WE'VE COLLECTED TO JERUSALEM.
RIGHT YOU ARE!

*This famine broke out between AD 46 and 48, during the reign of the Emperor Claudius.

A LITTLE LATER THE TRAVELLERS LEFT FOR SELEUCIA, WHERE THEY TOOK SHIP FOR JOPPA.
IN SPITE OF THE FAMINE, I'LL BE GLAD TO SEE JERUSALEM AGAIN!
BUT WHAT IS WAITING FOR US THERE?

IN JERUSALEM, KING HEROD AGRIPPA I, WHO HAD BEEN MADE KING SEVERAL YEARS BEFORE BY THE EMPEROR CLAUDIUS, WANTED TO GAIN THE SUPPORT OF THE PIOUS JEWS.
THEY DEMAND THE HEADS OF SOME OF THE NAZARENES! LET IT BE DONE!
THEY'VE ARRESTED JAMES, JOHN'S BROTHER!
A FEW HOURS LATER HE WAS BEHEADED.
SOON AFTERWARDS, PETER WAS ALSO ARRESTED.
PUT A STRONG GUARD ON THAT ONE! I'LL TRY HIS CASE AFTER PASSOVER.
BUT THE NIGHT BEFORE PETER WAS TO APPEAR BEFORE HEROD...
PETER, GET UP!

PUT ON YOUR SANDALS, PICK UP YOUR CLOAK, AND FOLLOW ME!

THE LORD SENT HIS ANGEL TO RELEASE ME FROM HEROD'S CLUTCHES...

THEN PETER RAN TO THE HOUSE OF MARY, MARK'S MOTHER. MANY BELIEVERS HAD GATHERED THERE TO PRAY, WHEN SUDDENLY...

SOMEBODY IS KNOCKING AT THE DOOR!
I'LL GO!

PETER TOLD THEM HOW HE HAD JUST BEEN SET FREE. HE HAD SOMETHING TO EAT. THEN...

*James, the brother of Jesus, the leader of the Church in Jerusalem.

A FEW DAYS LATER, PAUL AND BARNABAS REACHED JERUSALEM, AND JAMES WELCOMED THEM.

WHEN THEY HAD FINISHED THEIR BUSINESS IN JERUSALEM, PAUL AND BARNABAS WENT BACK TO ANTIOCH. JOHN MARK WENT WITH THEM.
YES, MARK, LEAVING JERUSALEM IS HARD, BUT WE MUST GO ON SPREADING THE GOOD NEWS IN ANTIOCH!
BARNABAS AND MARK, LET'S GO!
IN ANTIOCH, A YEAR LATER...
THE LORD HAS BLESSED THE CHURCH IN ANTIOCH... IT HAS PROPHETS AND WISE PEOPLE...
YES, BUT WHAT ABOUT THE COUNTRIES ALL AROUND? THE GOOD NEWS MUST BE TAKEN TO THEM, TOO!
LET'S PRAY AND FAST BEFORE WE DECIDE ABOUT THAT.
THE WHOLE CONGREGATION AGREED THAT PAUL AND BARNABAS SHOULD GO TO SPREAD THE GOOD NEWS.
LORD, GIVE YOUR SERVANTS YOUR STRENGTH TO TELL PEOPLE ABOUT YOUR KINGDOM WHEREVER THEY GO.
AMEN!
VERY SOON THEY SET SAIL FOR CYPRUS.
PAUL, I'M SO HAPPY TO SEE MY COUNTRY AGAIN!
THIS TIME WE DON'T NEED A GUIDE!
LEAVING THE SHIP AT SALAMIS, THEY PREACHED THE WORD OF GOD IN THE SYNAGOGUES. THEN THEY WENT ON TO PAPHOS.
SALAMIS
CYPRUS
PAPHOS

SERGIUS PAULUS, THE GOVERNOR OF THE ISLAND, LIVED IN PAPHOS. AFTER HEARING THE APOSTLES SPEAK, HE INVITED THEM TO EAT WITH HIM.
WE CAN'T GO AND EAT WITH THIS PAGAN!
BUT WE KNOW PETER SPENT MANY DAYS IN A CENTURION'S HOME...
MARK, WE MUST GRASP EVERY OPPORTUNITY GOD GIVES US TO TELL PEOPLE ABOUT HIS SALVATION.
PAUL SPOKE AT LENGTH ABOUT CHRIST'S LIFE AND TEACHING, BUT THERE WAS A JEWISH MAGICIAN WHO KEPT ON CONTRADICTING HIM.
JESUS IS TRULY THE SON OF GOD...
OH, COME ON! ANY MAGICIAN COULD DO WHAT HE DID!
YOU SON OF THE DEVIL! STOP TWISTING GOD'S TRUTH!
THE LORD'S HAND IS ON YOU... AND THERE - YOU'RE BLIND!
AAAH!
THERE! THE MAGICIAN IS DEPRIVED OF THE LIGHT OF THE SUN! BUT DON'T WORRY, HE'LL GET HIS SIGHT BACK.
PAUL, YOUR GOD REALLY LIVES!

VERY SOON IT WAS TIME TO THINK OF LEAVING THE ISLAND OF CYPRUS.
LET'S FIND A BOAT FOR PERGA. FROM THERE WE'LL BE ABLE TO REACH PAMPHYLIA AND PHRYGIA AND CILICIA...
I'M WITH YOU, PAUL.
PAUL, BARNABAS, I'M LEAVING YOU AT PERGA; I'M GOING BACK TO JERUSALEM.
MARK! WHAT'S GOING ON?
ARE YOU LEAVING US IN THE MIDDLE OF THE JOURNEY? BUT YOU WOULD LEARN SUCH A LOT WITH US...
WHEN THEY REACHED PERGA...
MARK, ARE YOU STICKING TO YOUR DECISION?
YES, FORGIVE ME... BUT I CAN'T FOLLOW YOU...
GO, THEN – AND GOD GO WITH YOU...
WELL, BARNABAS, DO WE PRESS ON?
YES, PAUL. LET'S GO FURTHER!

PAUL

PAUL'S JOURNEYS

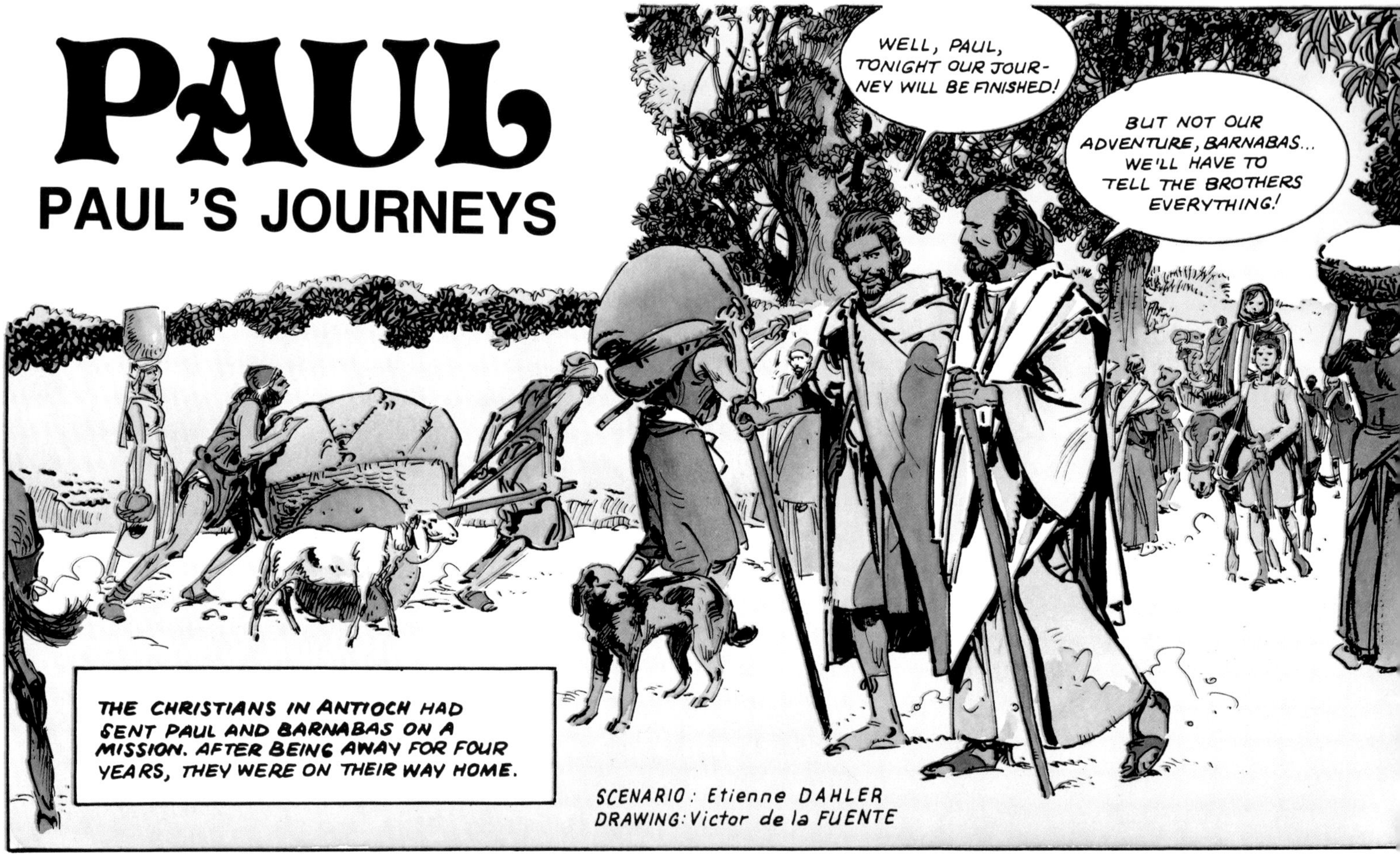

WELL, PAUL, TONIGHT OUR JOURNEY WILL BE FINISHED!

BUT NOT OUR ADVENTURE, BARNABAS... WE'LL HAVE TO TELL THE BROTHERS EVERYTHING!

THE CHRISTIANS IN ANTIOCH HAD SENT PAUL AND BARNABAS ON A MISSION. AFTER BEING AWAY FOR FOUR YEARS, THEY WERE ON THEIR WAY HOME.

SCENARIO: Etienne DAHLER
DRAWING: Victor de la FUENTE

AFTER MEETING THE CONGREGATION, PAUL AND BARNABAS WERE NOT ALLOWED TO REST... EVERYONE WANTED TO HEAR THEIR STORY. SO BARNABAS TOLD THEM...

AFTER WE HAD PARTED FROM JOHN MARK AT PERGA, WE SET OFF FOR ANTIOCH IN PISIDIA.

THERE WE FOUND WORK WITH A JEWISH WEAVER, AND ON THE SABBATH PAUL PREACHED THE GOOD NEWS IN THE SYNAGOGUE...

SO UNDERSTAND THIS, MY BROTHERS: WHEN GOD RAISED JESUS TO LIFE AGAIN, HE FULFILLED FOR US THE PROMISE HE HAD MADE TO OUR FATHERS.

PAUL'S WORDS WERE SO ASTONISHING THAT THE NEXT SABBATH THE SYNAGOGUE WAS FULL TO OVERFLOWING.

THEN SOME OF THE JEWS BECAME VERY ANGRY AND TRIED TO STOP PAUL.

YOU'RE TRYING TO MAKE US LEAVE THE FAITH OF OUR FATHERS! IT'S THE DEVIL SPEAKING!
I HAD TO SPEAK GOD'S WORD TO YOU FIRST...

...BUT SINCE YOU REJECT IT, WE'LL TURN TO THE PAGANS!
PAUL, YOU'LL PAY FOR THAT INSULT!

AFTER THAT WE WERE ABLE TO CONTINUE OUR MISSION AMONG THE PEOPLE WHO WEREN'T JEWS FOR SEVERAL MONTHS... MANY WERE WON FOR CHRIST.

BUT THEN THE JEWS BEGAN TO PERSECUTE PAUL AND BARNABAS, AND THEY HAD TO LEAVE ANTIOCH IN PISIDIA.
WHERE SHOULD WE GO, PAUL? TO ICONIUM, THE NEXT TOWN?
VERY WELL! OFF WE GO TO ICONIUM!
AFTER TRAVELLING ABOUT 120 KILOMETRES...
PAUL, I THINK THAT'S THE PLACE...
ICONIUM! MAY GOD BLESS YOU!
AND ICONIUM **WAS** BLESSED! THE FIRST BELIEVERS WERE QUICKLY ORGANIZED INTO A CONGREGATION, BUT THEN WE JUST ESCAPED BEING STONED!
AT FIRST PAUL AND BARNABAS TOOK REFUGE IN LYSTRA, BUT, AFTER PAUL HAD HEALED A LAME MAN, THE PEOPLE OF THE TOWN THOUGHT THE TWO OF THEM WERE GODS.
IT IS HERMES!
IT IS ZEUS!
THE GODS HAVE COME BACK!
ONLY WITH GREAT DIFFICULTY DID THE APOSTLES MANAGE TO STOP THE TOWNSPEOPLE FROM OFFERING THEM A SACRIFICE...
A LITTLE WHILE LATER THINGS BECAME MORE SERIOUS...
PAUL! HURRY!

STIRRED UP BY MESSENGERS FROM ANTIOCH IN PISIDIA, THE JEWS STONED PAUL AND LEFT HIM FOR DEAD.

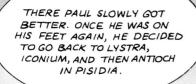

WELL?
HE IS STILL BREATHING...
TAKE HIM TO MY HOUSE!

THE NEXT DAY, AT FIRST LIGHT...
TIMOTHY, LOOK AFTER THIS LITTLE GROUP OF CHRISTIANS...
I'LL DO MY BEST, PAUL.
LET'S GO ON TO DERBE!

THERE PAUL SLOWLY GOT BETTER. ONCE HE WAS ON HIS FEET AGAIN, HE DECIDED TO GO BACK TO LYSTRA, ICONIUM, AND THEN ANTIOCH IN PISIDIA.

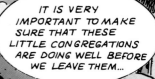

IT IS VERY IMPORTANT TO MAKE SURE THAT THESE LITTLE CONGREGATIONS ARE DOING WELL BEFORE WE LEAVE THEM...

AS BARNABAS HAS TOLD YOU SO WELL... I BELIEVE THAT THROUGH ALL THESE DIFFICULTIES...

...THE LORD HAS HELPED US TO OPEN THE DOOR TO PAGANS, SO THAT THEY TOO CAN BELIEVE IN HIM.

AFTER THIS REPORT A SERIOUS DEBATE BEGAN AMONG THE CHRISTIANS IN ANTIOCH.

I SAY THAT PEOPLE WHO AREN'T CIRCUMCISED CAN'T BE SAVED!
YOU'RE RIGHT! PERHAPS PAUL AND BARNABAS ARE GOING TOO FAST.
FOR MY PART, I TRUST THEM...
I SUGGEST WE REFER THE MATTER TO THE APOSTLES IN JERUSALEM.

SOON THE TWO MISSIONARIES HAD TO EXPLAIN THEIR VIEWS ON THIS SUBJECT.

BROTHERS, WHAT IS THE SENSE IN ASKING A PAGAN TO BE CIRCUMCISED AFTER HE HAS BEEN BAPTIZED?
SO, PAUL, YOU'RE THROWING OUT THE LAW OF MOSES?
YOU YOURSELF SAID THAT CHRIST DID NOT COME TO DO AWAY WITH THE LAW, BUT TO FULFIL IT!

PAUL, THIS IS A PROBLEM THAT MUST BE SOLVED...
AND WHO IS GOING TO DO IT?

SO PAUL, BARNABAS, AND SEVERAL OTHERS SET OUT FOR THE HOLY CITY.

THEY WENT THROUGH PHOENICIA, THEN SAMARIA, AND AT LAST...
BARNABAS, THE LORD IS GOOD! I DIDN'T THINK I'D SEE JERUSALEM AGAIN SO SOON.

HE APOSTLES WELCOMED THEM
TH OPEN ARMS. THEN THEY
ERE ABLE TO POSE THE QUESTION.
PETER, IT IS OBVIOUS: THE LAW OF MOSES MUST BE OBEYED!
WE MUST THINK ABOUT IT VERY CAREFULLY, BEFORE WE COME TO A DICISION.

BROTHERS, WE'RE SAVED BY GRACE, NOT BY CIRCUM-CISION! THE PAGANS RECEIVE THE HOLY SPIRIT IN THE SAME WAY AS WE DO. I'VE FOUND THAT OUT MYSELF.
ND PETER BEGAN TO SPEAK...

I THINK WE SHOULD SIMPLY ASK BELIEVERS WHO AREN'T JEWS NOT TO HAVE ANYTHING TO DO WITH IDOLS, NOT TO EAT MEAT WHICH CONTAINS BLOOD, AND NOT TO LIVE IMMORAL LIVES.
EVERYONE AGREED WITH JAMES'S SUGGESTION.

SOON THE MESSENGERS FROM ANTIOCH RETURNED HOME. JUDAS AND SILAS WENT WITH THEM, CARRYING A LETTER TO THE LOCAL CONGREGATION.

GOD PROTECT YOU, PAUL, TRAVELLER FOR CHRIST!

WHEN THEY REACHED ANTIOCH, JUDAS READ THE MESSAGE FROM THE CHURCH IN JERUSALEM.
IT SEEMS RIGHT NOT TO ASK ANY MORE OF YOU THAN THAT YOU DON'T EAT MEAT SACRIFICED TO IDOLS, OR MEAT THAT CONTAINS BLOOD, AND THAT YOU DON'T LIVE IMMORAL LIVES.

I BELIEVE WE'VE TAKEN AN IMPORTANT STEP TODAY.

NOW THE GOOD NEWS CAN BE SPREAD TO THE ENDS OF THE EARTH!

A LITTLE WHILE LATER JUDAS WENT BACK TO JERUSALEM, WHILE SILAS DECIDED TO STAY IN ANTIOCH.

GOODBYE, JUDAS.

I THINK IT IS TIME FOR US TO TAKE TO THE ROAD AGAIN TOO.

WHAT ARE YOU THINKING ABOUT, PAUL?

I'M ANXIOUS ABOUT THE BROTHERS IN THE DIFFERENT PLACES; THEY'RE STILL VERY YOUNG IN THE FAITH.
GOOD! I'LL COME WITH YOU... BUT ONLY IF MARK COMES TOO...
MARK? NO! THAT IS IMPOSSIBLE! HE'LL TURN BACK AGAIN THE FIRST TIME WE FACE A PROBLEM!
THEN, PAUL, I'LL NOT GO WITH YOU EITHER...

PLEASE YOURSELF, BARNABAS! I'M SURE I'VE ONLY TO ASK SILAS AND HE'LL GO WITH ME.
YOU'RE RIGHT, PAUL!

PAUL, I HAVEN'T YET TOLD YOU THAT I'M A ROMAN CITIZEN.
SO AM I! IT IS USEFUL FOR GETTING OUT OF TIGHT CORNERS!
PAUL AND SILAS SET OUT FOR SYRIA AND THEN CILICIA...

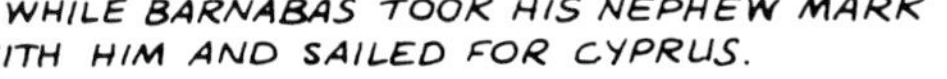
WHILE BARNABAS TOOK HIS NEPHEW MARK WITH HIM AND SAILED FOR CYPRUS.

TIMOTHY! GOD BE PRAISED!
PAUL! I KNEW YOU WOULD COME BACK!
AFTER TARSUS AND DERBE, THE TWO TRAVELLERS ARRIVED AT LYSTRA.

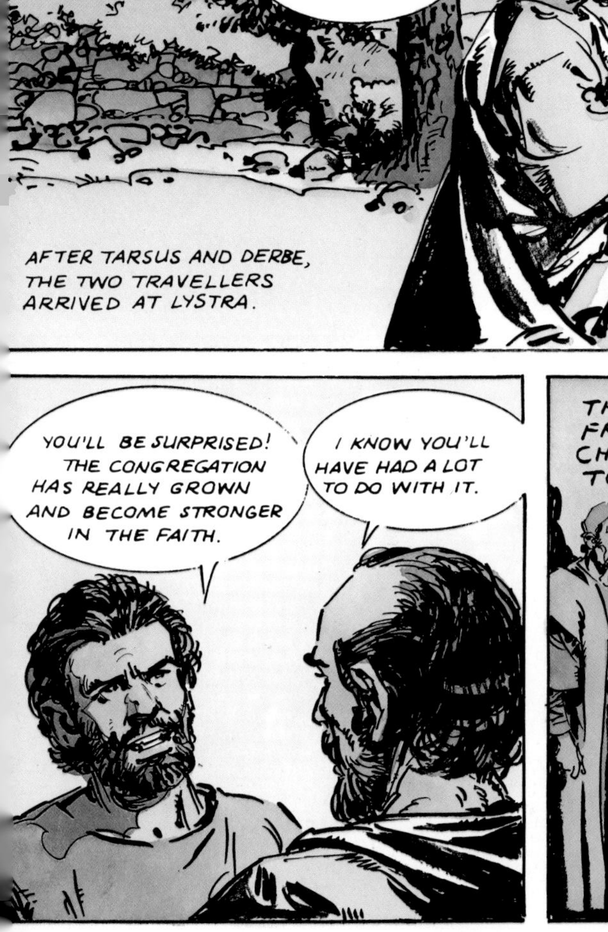
YOU'LL BE SURPRISED! THE CONGREGATION HAS REALLY GROWN AND BECOME STRONGER IN THE FAITH.
I KNOW YOU'LL HAVE HAD A LOT TO DO WITH IT.

THAT SAME EVENING, IN FRONT OF THE WHOLE CHURCH GATHERED TOGETHER...
TIMOTHY, MAY THE HOLY SPIRIT GIVE YOU STRENGTH AND AUTHORITY!

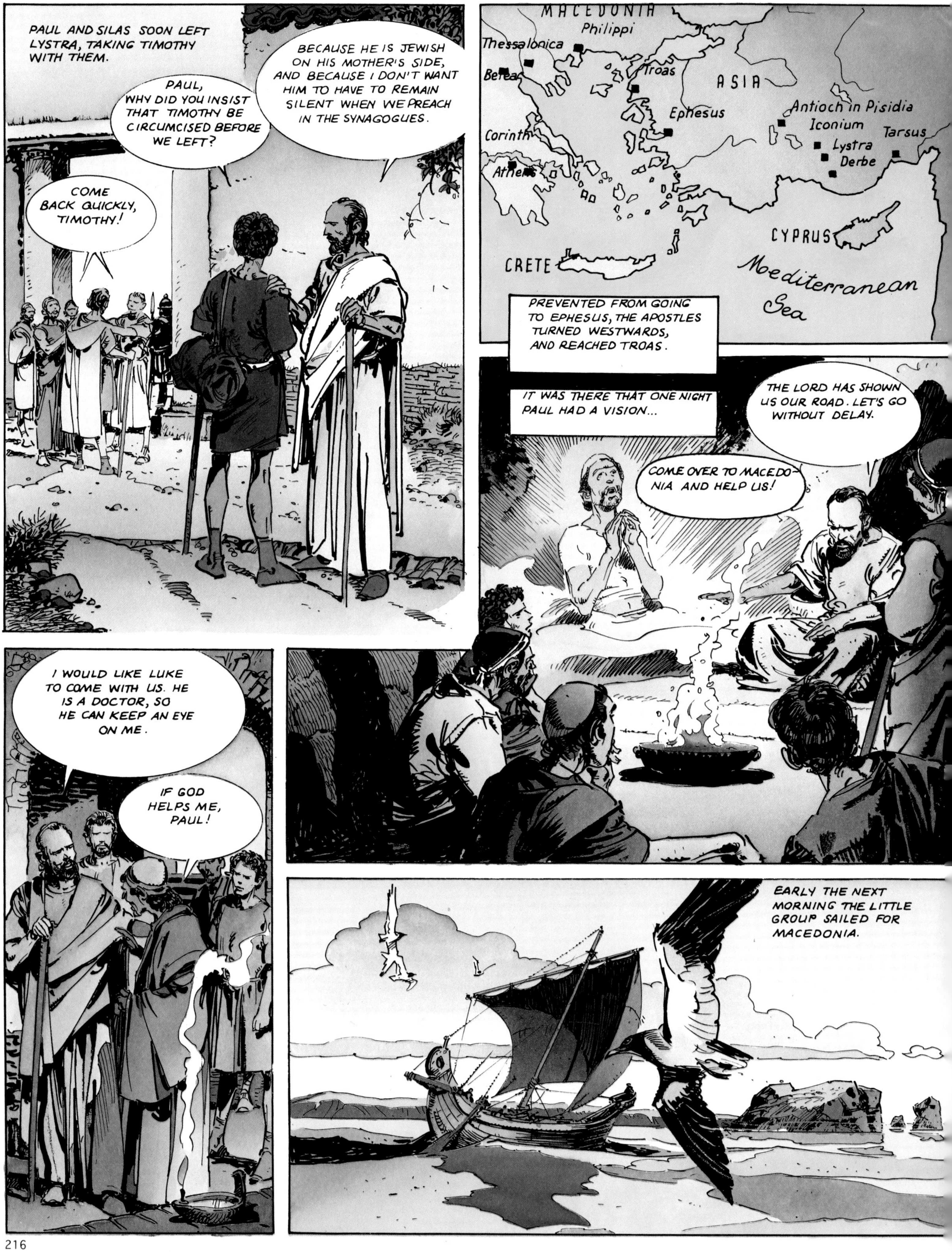

MACEDONIA
Philippi
Thessalonica
Berea
Troas
ASIA
Ephesus
Antioch in Pisidia
Iconium
Tarsus
Corinth
Lystra
Derbe
Athens
CYPRUS
CRETE
Mediterranean Sea

PREVENTED FROM GOING TO EPHESUS, THE APOSTLES TURNED WESTWARDS, AND REACHED TROAS.

IT WAS THERE THAT ONE NIGHT PAUL HAD A VISION...

COME OVER TO MACEDONIA AND HELP US!

THE LORD HAS SHOWN US OUR ROAD. LET'S GO WITHOUT DELAY.

A DAY OR TWO LATER THEY REACHED PHILIPPI.
LUKE, I DON'T KNOW ROME, BUT THIS TOWN MUST BE LIKE IT!
IT CERTAINLY IS, JUDGING BY THE NUMBER OF ROMANS LIVING HERE.
CAN YOU TELL ME WHERE THE SYNAGOGUE IS?
THERE ISN'T ONE, MY FRIEND! THE FEW JEWS WHO LIVE HERE MEET FOR PRAYER ON THE BANKS OF THE GANGITES.
ON THE SABBATH PAUL TRIED TO MAKE CONTACT WITH THE LITTLE JEWISH COMMUNITY.
THERE! THAT MUST BE THEM!
BUT... ARE THERE NO MEN AMONG YOU?
NO! WE'RE ONLY FOUR JEWESSES WHO WORSHIP GOD.
WE MUST SPEAK TO YOU.
AUL FIRST SPOKE ABOUT THE AIN EVENTS IN JEWISH HISTORY. THEN HE LD THEM ABOUT JESUS, THE MESSIAH, HO DIED AND ROSE AGAIN.
I'M LYDIA. I COME FROM THYATIRA, AND I'M A TRADER IN PURPLE CLOTH... I WANT TO BE BAPTIZED.
LYDIA, WE MUST TALK MORE ABOUT IT. LET'S GO TO YOUR HOME.
AFTER THE MEETING ONE OF THE WOMEN WENT TO FIND PAUL.
BRING MY FRIENDS SOMETHING TO DRINK.
CERTAINLY, MISTRESS!
WHAT A LUXURIOUS HOME, LUKE!
YES, TIMOTHY. SHE HAS A LOT OF INFLUENCE...

A LITTLE WHILE LATER LYDIA AND ALL HER FAMILY WERE BAPTIZED...

IN THE NAME OF THE FATHER, THE SON, AND THE HOLY SPIRIT...
...AND HER HOME BECAME THE MEETING PLACE FOR THE NEW CHRISTIANS.

BUT THIS WAS QUICKLY FOLLOWED BY SOMETHING WHICH TOOK AWAY SOME OF THE SUCCESS OF PAUL'S MISSION TO PHILIPPI...

THESE MEN ARE SERVANTS OF THE MOST HIGH GOD. THEY TELL YOU HOW YOU CAN BE SAVED!

PAUL, DO SOMETHING! SHE HAS BEEN SHOUTING AFTER US FOR TWO DAYS NOW.

WHO IS SHE?

A POOR SLAVE - GIRL WHO FORETELLS THE FUTURE, AND THIS EARNS A LOT OF MONEY FOR HER MASTERS.

COME HERE!

UNCLEAN SPIRIT! IN THE NAME OF JESUS, I COMMAND YOU TO COME OUT OF THIS WOMAN!

THE YOUNG WOMAN WAS SET FREE, AND FROM THAT MOMENT SHE WAS NO LONGER ABLE TO TELL THE FUTURE... WHICH GREATLY UPSET HER MASTERS.
THOSE MEN WILL PAY ME FOR IT!

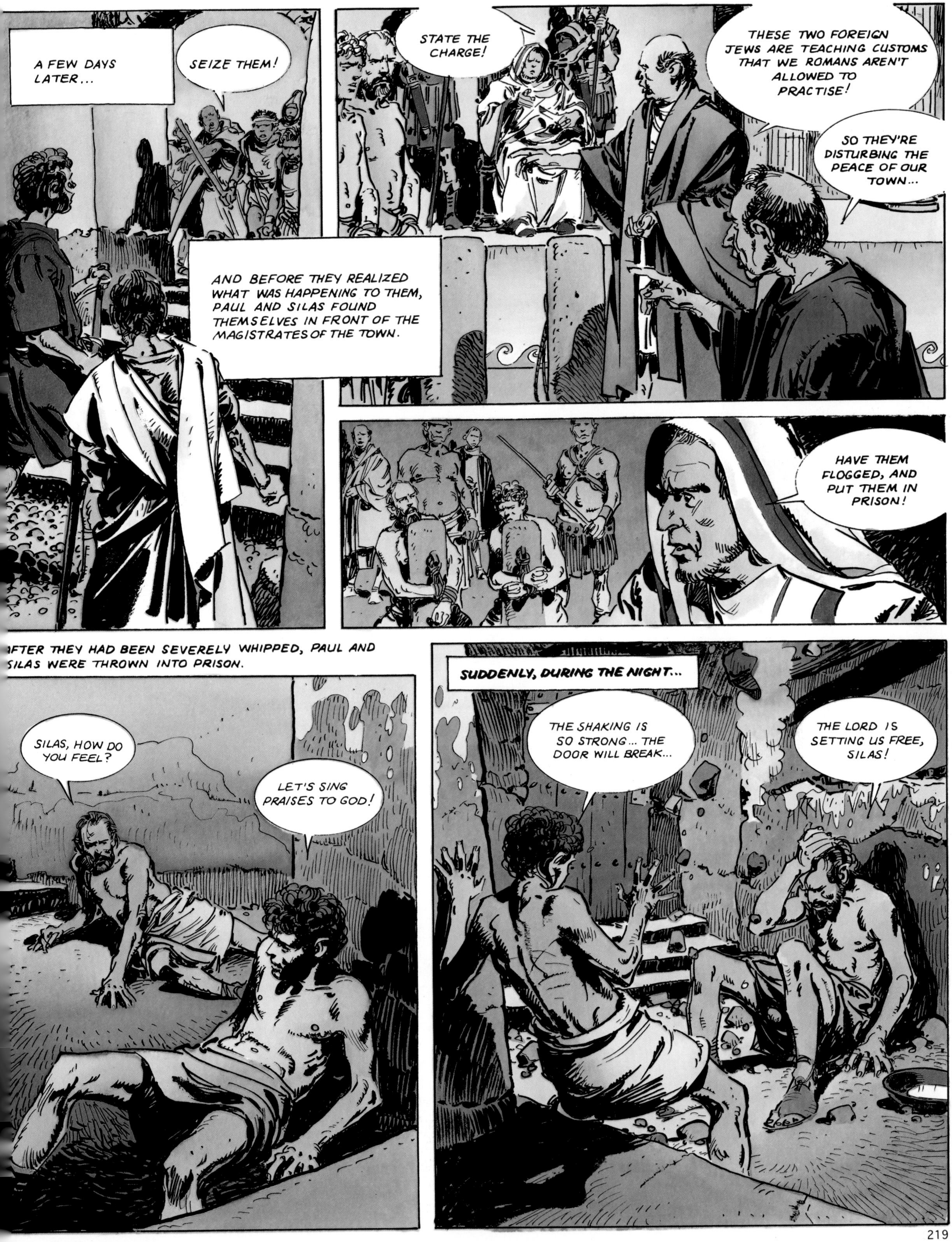

A FEW DAYS LATER...

SEIZE THEM!

AND BEFORE THEY REALIZED WHAT WAS HAPPENING TO THEM, PAUL AND SILAS FOUND THEMSELVES IN FRONT OF THE MAGISTRATES OF THE TOWN.

STATE THE CHARGE!

THESE TWO FOREIGN JEWS ARE TEACHING CUSTOMS THAT WE ROMANS AREN'T ALLOWED TO PRACTISE!

SO THEY'RE DISTURBING THE PEACE OF OUR TOWN...

HAVE THEM FLOGGED, AND PUT THEM IN PRISON!

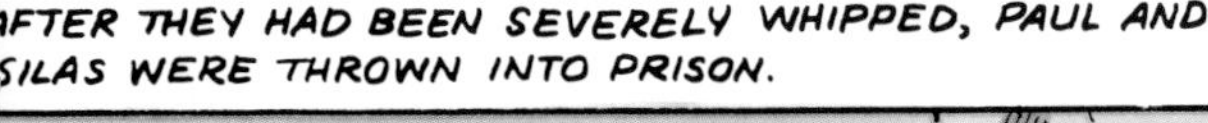

ALL THE DOORS OF THE PRISON FLEW OPEN, AND THE CHAINS FELL OFF THE PRISONERS...
NO! DON'T RUN AWAY!

WE MUST SEE TO THOSE WHO HAVE BEEN HURT... AND IF YOU STAY, YOU MAY BE PARDONED.

WHEN HE SAW WHAT HAD HAPPENED, THE JAILER WAS IN DESPAIR, AND WAS GOING TO KILL HIMSELF.

STOP! WE'RE ALL STILL HERE!

YOUR GOD LIVES!
LET HIM BE YOUR GOD TOO, BECAUSE HE SAVED YOU FROM DEATH...

AND THAT SAME NIGHT THE JAILER WAS BAPTIZED.

THE NEXT DAY EVERYBODY WAS SET FREE...
PAUL! SILAS! WHAT HAPPENED TO YOU?
NOTHING SURPRISING TO THOSE WHO WALK IN THE FOOTSTEPS OF CHRIST, TIMOTHY!
...AND A LITTLE LATER, LEAVING LUKE AT PHILIPPI, THE THREE MISSIONARIES WENT ON THEIR WAY.

AFTER WALKING FOR SEVERAL DAYS, THE THREE TRAVELLERS ARRIVED IN THESSALONICA, THE BIGGEST TOWN IN MACEDONIA.
WHAT IS YOUR PLAN, PAUL?
THE USUAL ONE, TIMOTHY. FIRST, TO MAKE CONTACT WITH THE JEWS, AND TO PREACH IN THE SYNAGOGUE. AFTER THAT... WE'LL SEE.

PAUL'S PREACHING MET WITH SOME SUCCESS...
THIS JESUS I'M TALKING ABOUT IS THE MESSIAH YOU'RE WAITING FOR!
THE ELDERS OF THE SYNAGOGUE TOOK NOTE OF WHAT WAS HAPPENING.

LET'S START A RIOT. THEN WE CAN ACCUSE THESE TRAITORS OF CAUSING IT!
THEY'RE STAYING WITH JASON. WE CAN ARREST THEM WITHOUT ANY DIFFICULTY.

AUL AND SILAS WERE WARNED IN TIME, AND HID. AT JASON'S HOME...

THEY'VE FLED!
THEN THAT IS TOO BAD FOR YOU, JASON! YOU'LL PAY FOR THEM!

JASON GOT OFF WITH A FINE. THE FOLLOWING NIGHT...
GO TO BEREA. YOU'LL BE SAFE THERE.

THE JEWS IN BEREA WELCOMED PAUL'S WORDS. A FEW MONTHS WENT BY...

PAUL, SOME JEWS FROM THESSALONICA ARRIVED THIS MORNING. THEY'RE STIRRING UP THE LOCAL PEOPLE AGAINST YOU.
THAT IS THE SIGN FOR ME TO LEAVE... SILAS AND TIMOTHY, YOU STAY HERE A LITTLE LONGER... I MUST GO...
WHERE TO, PAUL?

ATHENS!

SOME CHRISTIANS FROM BEREA WENT WITH PAUL. SOON THEY REACHED THE WONDERFUL CITY.

LIKE THE PHILOSOPHERS, PAUL WENT TO THE PUBLIC SQUARE EVERY DAY, TO TEACH HIS DOCTRINE.
... AND SO, ON THE THIRD DAY JESUS LEFT THE TOMB.
IN MANY WAYS A VERY STRANGE PHILOSOPHY!
HE IS FROM THE EAST! BUT SOME OF WHAT HE SAYS IS INTERESTING...
LET'S INVITE HIM TO EXPLAIN HIMSELF BEFORE THE MEETING OF THE AREOPAGUS.*

* A kind of council of wise men. It was this council which had condemned Socrate four centuries earlier.

A LITTLE LATER IN FRONT OF THE AREOPAGUS...
WE WANT TO KNOW WHAT THIS NEW TEACHING MEANS. EXPLAIN YOURSELF...
AS I WAS WALKING THROUGH YOUR CITY, I SAW AN ALTAR DEDICATED TO AN UNKNOWN GOD... WELL, IT IS THIS VERY GOD I'VE COME TO TALK ABOUT...

THEN PAUL GAVE THEM A LONG EXPLANATION OF THE GOD OF ISRAEL AND HIS MESSENGER JESUS.

HOW CAN YOU CLAIM THAT THE BODY MUST BE RAISED? ISN'T IT THE SOUL'S PRISON?
THAT IS ENOUGH! YOU MAY SPEAK TO US AGAIN ABOUT THIS ANOTHER DAY.
IT IS RIDICULOUS!
MANY DIDN'T WANT TO ACCEPT WHAT PAUL SAID, BUT A FEW BELIEVED AND BECAME CHRISTIANS. ONE OF THEM WAS DIONYSIUS, A MEMBER OF THE COUNCIL OF THE AREOPAGUS.

AUL DIDN'T STAY LONG IN ATHENS. HE WENT ON TO CORINTH, HE CAPITAL OF ACHAIA.
THIS IS THE MOST CORRUPT CITY IN THE WHOLE EMPIRE! DID YOU KNOW THAT THE TEMPLE OF APHRODITE HAS MORE THAN 1000 PROSTITUTES?
THERE MUST ALSO BE SOME GOOD PEOPLE HERE... I'LL KNOW HOW TO FIND THEM...
ΠΡΟΕΔΡ
PAUL FOUND LODGING WITH A JEWISH TENT-MAKER NAMED AQUILA. HE AND HIS WIFE PRISCILLA HAD FLED FROM ROME WHEN CLAUDIUS PUBLISHED HIS EDICT IN A D 49.
...THAT IS WHEN JESUS APPEARED TO ME ON THE ROAD AND ASKED, 'WHY ARE YOU PERSECUTING ME?'
IT IS INCREDIBLE!
GO ON, PAUL! TELL US MORE ABOUT HIM.
A FEW WEEKS LATER SILAS AND TIMOTHY ARRIVED FROM MACEDONIA.
THE CHRISTIANS IN THESSALONICA ARE DOING WELL IN SPITE OF THEIR DIFFICULTIES, BUT THEY NEED ENCOURAGEMENT.
EVEN SO, I CAN'T LEAVE CORINTH... I'LL WRITE TO THEM...
...DON'T PUT OUT THE SPIRIT'S FIRE... DON'T DESPISE WHAT IS PREACHED TO YOU... BUT TEST EVERYTHING, AND HOLD ON TO WHAT IS GOOD... KEEP YOURSELVES FROM EVERY KIND OF EVIL.
THAT IS HOW THE FIRST PARTS OF THE NEW TESTAMENT CAME TO BE WRITTEN.
...NOW LET'S GET ON WITH OUR MISSION IN THIS CITY!

IN CORINTH THE PREACHING OF THE THREE APOSTLES WAS MORE AND MORE SUCCESSFUL. SO THE JEWS BROUGHT PAUL BEFORE GALLIO, THE PROCONSUL.

THIS MAN IS TRYING TO GET THE PEOPLE TO SERVE GOD IN WAYS THAT ARE AGAINST OUR LAW.
THESE ARGUMENTS ABOUT DOCTRINE HAVE NOTHING TO DO WITH ME. I WON'T TRY THIS SORT OF CASE!

THE COURT IS ADJOURNED!

THEN THE ANGRY JEWS TURNED ON SOSTHENES, THE LEADER OF THE SYNAGOGUE...

THIS IS ALL YOUR FAULT! FOR MONTHS YOU ALLOWED HIM TO PREACH IN THE SYNAGOGUE!
YOU TRAITOR! YOU'RE ONE OF THEM!
THEY WERE SO ANGRY THAT THEY BEAT HIM WITH STICKS.

AFTER THAT PAUL STILL STAYED ON IN CORINTH, BRINGING MANY PEOPLE TO BE-LIEVE IN JESUS CHRIST. THEN IN THE SPRING OF THE YEAR 52...
SO, PAUL, YOU'VE DECIDED TO LEAVE?
I'VE BEEN HERE NEARLY A YEAR AND A HALF. OTHER PEOPLE ARE WAITING FOR ME... AND I'VE MADE A VOW... I MUST BE IN JERUSALEM BEFORE PASSOVER.
AT CENCHREAE, THE PORT OF CORINTH, PAUL SHAVED HIS HEAD, FOLLOWING NAZIRITE* CUSTOM. THEN HE SAILED FOR EPHESUS.
WHO WOULD HAVE THOUGHT THAT THE LORD COULD DO SUCH WONDERFUL THINGS IN A CITY LIKE THIS!
REMEMBER ONE THING, AQUILA: WHERE THERE ARE MANY SINS, THERE IS EVEN MORE GRACE!

* As long as his vow lasted, the Nazirite (a specially dedicated person) didn't cut his hair. When his vow ended, he had to shave his head, then go to the Temple in Jerusalem, to burn his hair on the altar and offer sacrifices.

MACEDONIA
ASIA
Antioch in Pisidia
Iconium
Lystra
Derbe
Tarsus
Ephesus
Antioch
CRETE
CYPRUS
Caesarea
Jerusalem
AUL DIDN'T STAY LONG IN EPHESUS,
HERE HE LEFT AQUILA AND PRISCILLA.
E HURRIED ON TO JERUSALEM.
WHEN HE HAD DONE WHAT THE LAW
AID DOWN ABOUT HIS VOW, HE
ETURNED TO ANTIOCH. HE SPENT
HE WINTER OF 52-53 THERE, THEN...
WHAT A LOVELY DAY! ...SPRING IS COMING...
THE BEST TIME OF THE YEAR TO TRAVEL...

YOU'RE OFF AGAIN, PAUL?
I MUST GO AND VISIT THE CHURCHES, AND I PROMISED THE CHRISTIANS IN EPHESUS I WOULD BE BACK...

ONCE AGAIN THE TIRELESS APOSTLE TOOK UP HIS PILGRIM STAFF: TARSUS, DERBE, LYSTRA, ICONIUM, ANTIOCH IN PISIDIA...

A YEAR LATER...

EPHESUS!

CRADLE OF PHILOSOPHY AND CITY OF ARTEMIS,* MAY YOU OPEN YOUR HEART TO THE LOVE OF CHRIST!

* Goddess of fertility.

PAUL STAYED IN EPHESUS FOR THREE YEARS. WITH THE HELP OF MANY DISCIPLES, HE SPREAD THE GOOD NEWS.

JESUS HAS FULFILLED EVERYTHING THE PROPHETS FORETOLD!

IN THE NAME OF JESUS, BE HEALED!

I GIVE UP ALL MY MAGIC!

BE BAPTIZED, AND THE SPIRIT WILL LIVE IN YOUR HEARTS!

I'LL SOON BE LEAVING EPHESUS FOR MACEDONIA AND ACHAIA. TIMOTHY AND ERASTUS MUST GO ON AHEAD... THE TIME IS GETTING SHORT!

THE SUCCESS OF THE CHRISTIANS HAD UPSET SOME OF THE WORKING PEO-PLE IN EPHESUS. ONE OF THEM WAS A SILVERSMITH NAMED DEMETRIUS...
THIS FELLOW PREACHES EVERYWHERE THAT OUR GODS AREN'T GODS AT ALL! NOW THERE ARE FAR FEWER PILGRIMS THIS YEAR...

...AND IF WE LET THIS GO ON, ONE OF THESE DAYS WE WON'T HAVE ANY WORK!
LET'S STIR UP THE CITY AGAINST HIM!

THE RIOT SPREAD THROUGHOUT THE CITY, AND EVERYBODY RUSHED TO THE THEATRE.
GREAT IS ARTEMIS OF EPHESUS!
THOSE TWO ARE COMPANIONS OF THE DECEIVER!
GLORY TO APOLLO!
KILL THEM!

THE CROWD WENT ON SHOUTING FOR SEVERAL HOURS. THEN THE TOWN CLERK STEPPED FORWARD.
CITIZENS OF EPHESUS! CALM DOWN! THESE MEN AREN'T GUILTY OF DISHONOURING ARTEMIS, OUR GREAT GODDESS! BUT, BECAUSE OF THIS UNLAWFUL GATHERING, WE RUN THE RISK THAT ROME WILL ACCUSE US OF A RIOT.
I ORDER YOU TO DISPERSE AND GO HOME!

THE RIOT MADE PAUL LEAVE EPHESUS ALL THE SOONER. SO HIS FRUITFUL STAY IN THE CITY ENDED. DURING THIS TIME, THE APOSTLE TO THE PAGANS HAD LAID THE FOUNDATION OF THE CHURCH IN EPHESUS, AND BY HIS LETTERS HAD ENCOURAGED THE CHRISTIANS IN CORINTH AND OTHER PLACES.

DURING THE SUMMER OF 57 PAUL VISITED THE CHURCHES IN PHILIPPI AND THESSALONICA. HE RETURNED TO CORINTH AT THE BEGINNING OF THE WINTER.

WE'VE NEEDED YOU BADLY TO BRING SOME ORDER BACK INTO THE CONGREGATION.
MY HEART IS SET ON TWO PLANS: TO GO TO JERUSALEM, AND THEN TO ROME... IF IT IS GOD'S WILL!

WRITE THIS: BROTHERS, I WANT YOU TO KNOW THAT MANY TIMES I'VE PLANNED TO VISIT YOU... BUT SO FAR I'VE BEEN PREVENTED FROM DOING SO...

... I MUST GO TO GREEKS AND BARBARIANS, TO THE WISE AS WELL AS THE IGNORANT. WHAT IS MORE, I'M VERY EAGER TO PREACH THE GOSPEL TO YOU IN ROME.

THE NEXT SPRING...

PAUL, I BEG YOU: DON'T TAKE THE SHIP TO CAESAREA! THERE ARE MANY JEWS THERE. SOMETHING WILL HAPPEN TO YOU.

VERY WELL! I'LL GO BY LAND. IF I'M NOT IN JERUSALEM BEFORE PASSOVER, I'LL BE THERE FOR PENTECOST!

MACEDONIA
Philippi
Troas
ASIA
Tarsus
Antioch
Ephesus
Corinth
Miletus
Athens
Mediterranean Sea
Jerusalem
IN ONE TOWN AFTER ANOTHER EACH CONGREGATION DID AS PAUL ASKED: IT CHOSE A BROTHER TO GO WITH HIM AND TAKE ITS OFFERING TO THE CHRISTIANS IN JERUSALEM.
A LITTLE LATER, AT TROAS...
THROUGH ALL MY TRAVELS I'VE BEEN AMAZED AT THE LOVING WAY IN WHICH THE LORD WATCHES OVER US, IN LITTLE THINGS AS WELL AS IN BIG THINGS...

SUDDENLY, WHILE PAUL WAS STILL PREACHING, A TEENAGER SITTING ON THE WINDOW-SILL FELL ASLEEP, AND...
EUTYCHUS!

HE'S DEAD!
LUKE BENT OVER THE BODY...

DON'T WORRY! HE'S STILL ALIVE!

NOTHING CAN SEPARATE US FROM THE LOVE OF CHRIST!

PAUL AND HIS COMPANIONS LEFT TROAS AND SET SAIL FOR JERUSALEM. THEY STOPPED AT MILETUS.
THE ELDERS OF THE CHURCH IN EPHESUS HAVE JUST ARRIVED.
THAT IS FINE, LUKE! LET'S TALK TO THEM BY THEMSELVES.

I DON'T KNOW WHAT WILL HAPPEN TO ME IN JERUSALEM, BUT IN EVERY TOWN THE HOLY SPIRIT HAS WARNED ME THAT TROUBLE IS WAITING FOR ME.

I'VE PREACHED THE KINGDOM OF GOD TO YOU. NOW YOU'LL NEVER SEE ME AGAIN.

AFTER AGAIN ENCOURAGING THE BROTHERS, PAUL SAID GOODBYE TO THEM.
GOD PROTECT YOU, PAUL!
ONE DAY HE'LL BRING US TOGETHER AGAIN, AND WIPE AWAY ALL OUR TEARS.

AFTER LANDING ON COS, ON RHODES, AND AT TYRE, AT LAST PAUL ONCE AGAIN WALKED ON THE BLESSED SOIL OF HIS FATHERS AND HIS LORD.

PAUL

from Jerusalem to Rome

I HOPE YOU'LL BE STAYING WITH US FOR SOME TIME, PAUL.
FOR A FEW DAYS, PHILIP... THE FEAST OF PENTECOST IS COMING, AND I'M STILL NOT IN JERUSALEM!
SCENARIO: Etienne DAHLER
DRAWING: Victor de LA FUENTE
AT THE END OF HIS THIRD VOYAGE, ON HIS WAY TO JERUSALEM, PAUL STOPPED AT CAESAREA. HE STAYED IN THE HOME OF PHILIP, ONE OF THE SEVEN DEACONS IN THE FIRST CHRISTIAN COMMUNITY.
PAUL! AGABUS IS HERE. HE HAS COME FROM JUDAEA TO SPEAK TO YOU.
AGABUS, THE PROPHET... WE MUST LISTEN TO HIM, LUKE.
CABUS CAME FORWARD, AND ASKED PAUL OR HIS BELT. THEN...
THE HOLY SPIRIT SAYS: THE OWNER OF THIS BELT WILL BE TIED UP LIKE THIS BY THE JEWS IN JERUSALEM, AND THEY'LL HAND HIM OVER TO THE PAGANS!
PAUL, DON'T GO TO JERUSALEM!
YOU SEE WHAT'S WAITING FOR YOU!
SO? I'M READY, NOT ONLY TO BE TIED UP IN JERUSALEM, BUT EVEN TO DIE FOR THE SAKE OF THE LORD JESUS.
AND A FEW DAYS LATER PAUL TOOK THE ROAD TO THE HOLY CITY.

THE DAY AFTER HE HAD ARRIVED IN JERUSALEM, PAUL WENT TO SEE JAMES AND THE LEADERS OF THE CHURCH.

GOD BE PRAISED FOR BRINGING YOU BACK TO US, PAUL!

BROTHERS, IT'S A JOY FOR US ALL TO BE WITH YOU AGAIN!

AND PAUL GAVE THEM A FULL ACCOUNT OF EVERYTHING THAT HAD HAPPENED TO HIM AMONG THE PAGANS. THEN JAMES SPOKE...

PAUL, I MUST TELL YOU THAT THERE'S A RUMOUR THAT YOU'RE ENCOURAGING THE JEWS TO TURN AWAY FROM THE LAW OF MOSES.
THAT'S NOT TRUE! ALL I SAY IS THAT THE PAGANS DON'T NEED TO BE CIRCUM-CISED. I'M JUST CARRYING OUT WHAT WE DECIDED HERE ALMOST 10 YEARS AGO.

YOU MUST SHOW EVERYONE THAT YOU ALSO KEEP THE LAW... FOUR OF US HAVE MADE A VOW...
YOU'RE NOT THE ONLY ONES!

I WAS INTENDING TO GO TO THE TEMPLE TOMORROW FOR THE SEVEN DAYS OF CLEANSING. I'LL GO WITH YOU.
PAUL, FORGIVE ME...

THE NEXT DAY...

WHEN THE 7 DAYS OF PRAYER AND FASTING WERE NEARLY OVER...
SAY, ISN'T THAT THE TRAITOR, SAUL OF TARSUS, OVER THERE?
YOU'RE RIGHT! I RECOGNIZE HIM!
LET'S STIR UP THE CROWD AGAINST HIM!

THAT'S THE FELLOW WHO ATTACKS OUR PEOPLE AND THE LAW!
GRAB HIM!

TRIBUNE! THERE'S A RIOT IN THE TEMPLE!
MUSTER THE MEN STRAIGHT AWAY!
KILL HIM!

THE ROMANS! RUN!
SCATTER!

... AND THE ROMAN SOLDIERS SEIZED PAUL.

TAKE HIM TO THE FORTRESS!

SO PAUL SPOKE TO THE CROWD IN HEBREW. HE TOLD THEM ABOUT HIS EARLY LIFE, THEN HOW HE BECAME A CHRISTIAN...

CENTURION, SINCE WHEN HAS IT BEEN LEGAL TO FLOG A ROMAN CITIZEN, WHOSE CASE HASN'T EVEN BEEN TRIED?

WHAT? ARE YOU A ROMAN?

HE SENT TO WARN LYSIAS, THE TRIBUNE, WHO SOON ARRIVED...

WELL, I WAS BORN ONE!

ROMAN CITIZEN! YOU KNOW, I HAD TO PAY A LOT OF MONEY TO BECOME ONE!

UNTIE HIM!

I WANT TO KNOW WHAT THE JEWS HAVE AGAINST THIS MAN! ORDER THE SANHEDRIN TO MEET AT ONCE!

AND A LITTLE LATER PAUL WAS BROUGHT BEFORE THAT COUNCIL.

PAUL KNEW VERY WELL THAT IN THE SANHEDRIN THE PHARISEES DISAGREED WITH THE SADDUCEES, SO HE WAS CLEVER IN THE WAY HE BEGAN HIS SPEECH.
BROTHERS, I'M A PHARISEE, THE SON OF A PHARISEE. AND I'M BEING JUDGED BECAUSE WE HOPE THAT THE DEAD WILL RISE AGAIN!
YOU HAVE TO BE A PHARISEE TO BELIEVE THAT NONSENSE!
WHAT A JOKE!
BE QUIET, YOU SADDUCEES! THIS MAN IS RIGHT!
THEY SHOUTED LOUDER, AND CAME TO BLOWS... THEN THE TRIBUNE...
BRING THE PRISONER TO ME BEFORE THEY TEAR HIM TO PIECES!
THE NEXT NIGHT THE LORD APPEARED TO PAUL.
BE BRAVE! YOU'VE WITNESSED FOR ME HERE IN JERUSALEM, AND YOU MUST DO SO IN ROME AS WELL.

BUT SEVERAL PHARISEES GOT TO HEAR OF THE PLOT. ONE OF THEM WAS PAUL'S BROTHER-IN-LAW...

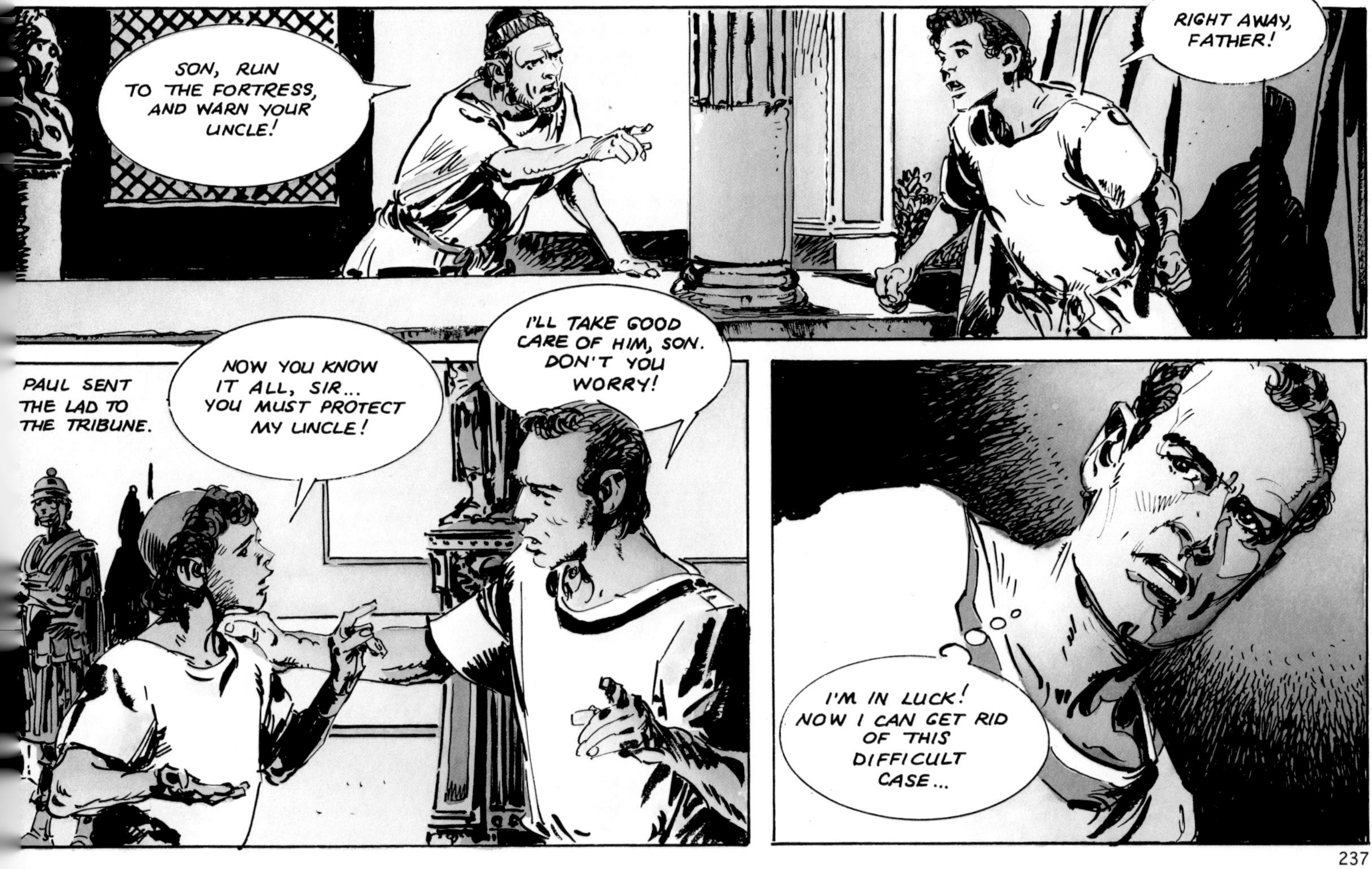

SON, RUN TO THE FORTRESS, AND WARN YOUR UNCLE!

RIGHT AWAY, FATHER!

PAUL SENT THE LAD TO THE TRIBUNE.

NOW YOU KNOW IT ALL, SIR... YOU MUST PROTECT MY UNCLE!

I'LL TAKE GOOD CARE OF HIM, SON. DON'T YOU WORRY!

I'M IN LUCK! NOW I CAN GET RID OF THIS DIFFICULT CASE...

I'VE DECIDED TO TRANSFER PAUL TO CAESAREA. FELIX THE PROCURATOR CAN DEAL WITH HIM. LEAVE TONIGHT, WITH 200 SOLDIERS, 70 CAVALRY, AND 200 ARCHERS!
FOR ONE PRISONER?
I'M AFRAID OF AN AMBUSH... DON'T FORGET THAT HE'S A ROMAN CITIZEN... HE MUST REACH CAESAREA SAFE AND SOUND.
SPQR
THE STRONG ESCORT LEFT FORT ANTONIA, TAKING A LETTER FROM TRIBUNE LYSIAS TO FELIX...
...I've found out that what this man is accused of has to do with the Jewish law, but he has done nothing to deserve death or to be imprisoned...
I was informed of a plot against him, so I am sending him to you. I have told his accusers that in future they must make their charges in front of you.
YOUR EXCELLENCY, WE'VE COME STRAIGHT FROM JERUSALEM. THIS LETTER IS ABOUT THE PRISONER.
I'LL HEAR YOUR CASE WHEN YOUR ACCUSERS ARRIVE.
FELIX KEPT PAUL IN THE PALACE.

FIVE DAYS LATER THE HIGH PRIEST ANANIAS, SEVERAL ELDERS, AND TERTULLUS, A LAWYER, CAME FROM JERUSALEM AND APPEARED BEFORE FELIX.

LET THE ACCUSERS BEGIN! I'M LISTENING, TERTULLUS!
MOST EXCELLENT FELIX, I SHALL BE BRIEF. THIS MAN IS A PEST! HE STARTS RIOTS AMONG THE JEWS ALL OVER THE WORLD. HE'S ONE OF THE LEADERS OF THE NAZARENE SECT...

...AND HE TRIED TO DEFILE THE TEMPLE!
IN OTHER WORDS, THREE CRIMES WHICH CARRY THE DEATH PENALTY IN ROMAN LAW: RABBLE-ROUSING, ILLEGAL RELIGION, AND DEFILING A HOLY PLACE!

PAUL, I WANT TO HEAR WHAT YOU HAVE TO SAY.
NOBLE FELIX, I ARRIVED IN JERUSALEM 12 DAYS AGO. I SPENT 6 OF THEM IN THE TEMPLE, AND 5 MORE IN PRISON! WHEN COULD I HAVE HAD TIME TO START A REVOLUTION AGAINST THE EMPIRE?

AND I SWEAR TO YOU: I WORSHIP THE GOD OF MY FATHERS. I BELIEVE THE LAW AND THE PROPHETS. LIKE MY BROTHERS, THE PHARISEES, I BELIEVE THAT THE DEAD WILL RISE AGAIN...
... FINALLY, I WENT TO THE TEMPLE TO FAST AND PRAY. IT WAS THEY WHO STARTED THE RIOT, NOT I!

THIS IS A DIFFICULT CASE. I SHALL RESERVE JUDGEMENT UNTIL THERE HAS BEEN A COMPLETE INQUIRY.

CENTURION, SEE THAT PAUL HAS ALL HE NEEDS! HE CAN SEE HIS FRIENDS WHENEVER HE LIKES!
WELL, PAUL?
FELIX DECIDED HE WOULD RATHER BURY THE CASE! SO, LUKE, I AM FORCED TO STAY IN CAESAREA!
ON SEVERAL OCCASIONS FELIX SENT FOR PAUL, TO LISTEN TO HIM. HE HOPED TO MAKE HIM UNDERSTAND THAT HE COULD BE SET FREE IF HE PAID A LOT OF MONEY. HE TALKED TO DRUSILLA HIS JEWISH WIFE, ABOUT THIS. BUT...
FELIX, YOU'RE FOOLING YOURSELF! PAUL WON'T DO THAT. HE'S WAITING FOR A PROPER TRIAL!
THEN, BELIEVE ME, HE'LL HAV TO WAIT A LON TIME!
PAUL, THIS CASE HAS BEEN DRAGGING ON FOR TWO YEARS! ISN'T THERE ANY WAY WE CAN FINISH IT?
I HEARD THIS MORNING THAT NERO IS GOING TO APPOINT A NEW GOVERNOR... PERHAPS, FELIX, THE MAN WHO FOLLOWS YOU WILL WANT TO SETTLE IT...
AS SOON AS HE ARRIVED, THE NEW GOVERNOR, FESTUS, WENT TO JERUSALEM. THE JEWS QUICKLY ASKED FOR A MEETING WITH HIM...
THE GOVERNOR BEFORE YOU SEEMS TO HAVE NEGLECTED A VERY IMPORTANT MATTER...
YES, PAUL HAS BEEN AWAITING TRIAL FOR TWO YEARS... HAVE HIM BROUGHT TO JERUSALEM, SO THAT...
I'M SORRY. PAUL IS BEING KEPT IN CAESAREA. HE MUST APPEAR BEFORE THE COURT THERE.

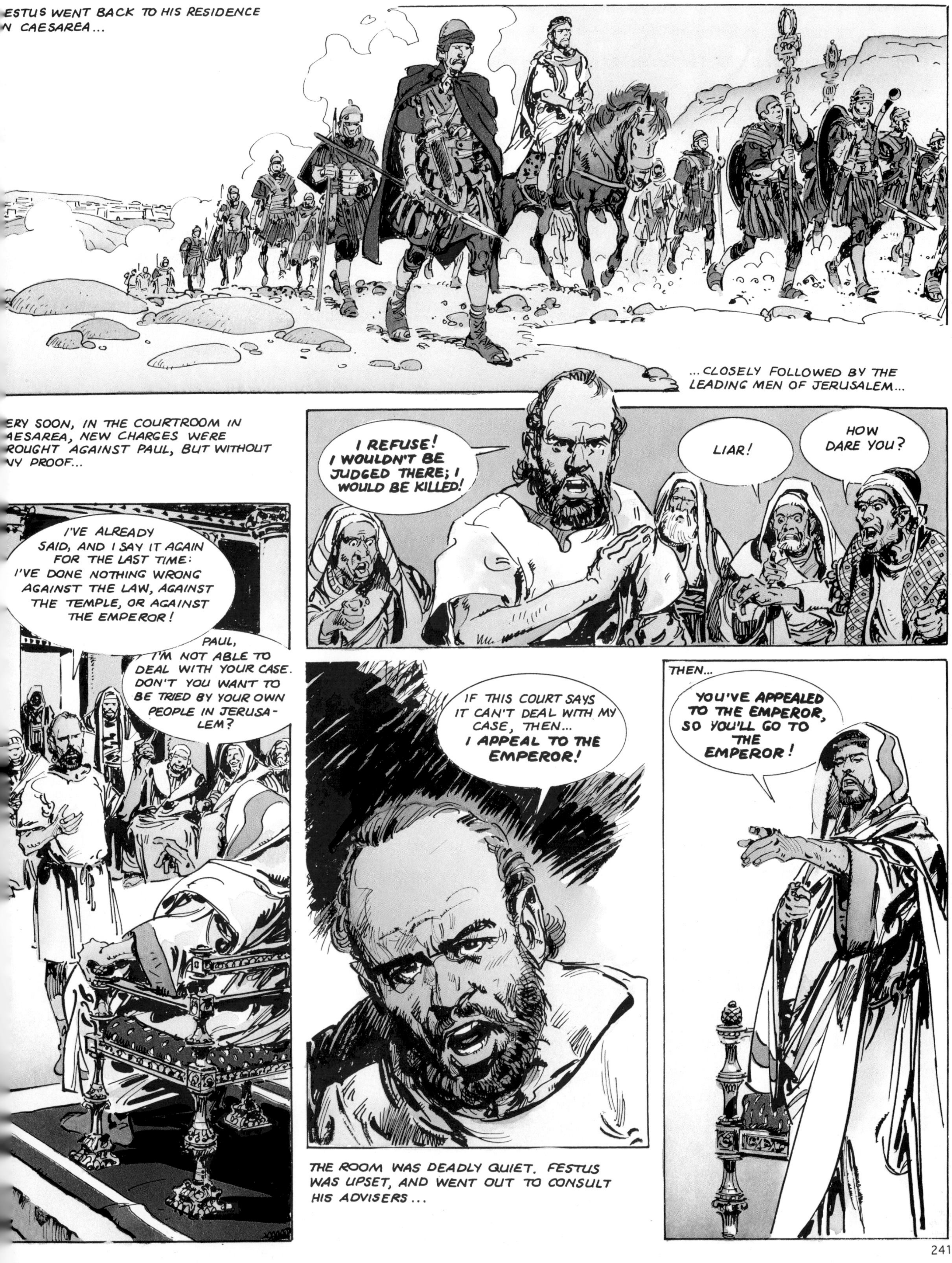

ESTUS WENT BACK TO HIS RESIDENCE
N CAESAREA...

...CLOSELY FOLLOWED BY THE
LEADING MEN OF JERUSALEM...

ERY SOON, IN THE COURTROOM IN
AESAREA, NEW CHARGES WERE
ROUGHT AGAINST PAUL, BUT WITHOUT
NY PROOF...

I'VE ALREADY SAID, AND I SAY IT AGAIN FOR THE LAST TIME: I'VE DONE NOTHING WRONG AGAINST THE LAW, AGAINST THE TEMPLE, OR AGAINST THE EMPEROR!

PAUL, I'M NOT ABLE TO DEAL WITH YOUR CASE. DON'T YOU WANT TO BE TRIED BY YOUR OWN PEOPLE IN JERUSA-LEM?

I REFUSE! I WOULDN'T BE JUDGED THERE; I WOULD BE KILLED!
LIAR!
HOW DARE YOU?

IF THIS COURT SAYS IT CAN'T DEAL WITH MY CASE, THEN... I APPEAL TO THE EMPEROR!

THE ROOM WAS DEADLY QUIET. FESTUS
WAS UPSET, AND WENT OUT TO CONSULT
HIS ADVISERS...

THEN...

YOU'VE APPEALED TO THE EMPEROR, SO YOU'LL GO TO THE EMPEROR!

A FEW DAYS LATER KING AGRIPPA II, GRANDSON OF HEROD THE GREAT, WHO NOW RULED OVER A SMALL REGION TO THE NORTH-EAST OF PALESTINE, CAME WITH HIS SISTER BERNICE, TO WELCOME THE NEW GOVERNOR.

EVER SINCE I GOT HERE, I'VE HAD TO DEAL WITH A PETTY AFFAIR THAT YOU WOULD BE INTERESTED TO HEAR ABOUT, AGRIPPA.
PLEASE, FESTUS, DON'T KEEP ME ON TENTERHOOKS ANY LONGER!

I WOULD VERY MUCH LIKE TO HEAR THIS FELLOW...
NO TROUBLE! I'VE ARRANGED A SPECIAL HEARING FOR TOMORROW...

NEXT DAY...

GUARDS! BRING IN THE EMPEROR'S PRISONER!

KING AGRIPPA, AND ALL HERE WITH US, THIS IS THE MAN WHO'LL SOON BE LEAVING FOR ROME.
I WANT YOUR ADVICE BEFORE WRITING TO THE EMPEROR ABOUT HIM.

PAUL, YOU MAY SPEAK IN YOUR DEFENCE.
I'M HAPPY TO DEFEND MYSELF BEFORE YOU, KING AGRIPPA, BECAUSE YOU KNOW ALL ABOUT THE JEWS' CUSTOMS AND QUARRELS.
THEN, IN A LONG SPEECH, PAUL TOLD OF HIS YOUTH, HIS EDUCATION, HOW HE HAD PERSECUTED THE CHRISTIANS, HIS CONVERSION, AND HIS MISSION.

AND HE ENDED BY SAYING...
MOSES AND THE PROPHETS TOLD US THAT THE MESSIAH WOULD SUFFER, AND THAT, AFTER HE HAD BEEN RAISED FROM THE DEAD, HE WOULD ANNOUNCE LIGHT TO THE JEWS AND TO THE PAGANS. I'M ONLY TESTIFYING THAT THEY SPOKE THE TRUTH.
PAUL, YOU'RE MAD! YOUR KNOWLEDGE IS MAKING YOU LOSE YOUR HEAD!

KING AGRIPPA, DO YOU BELIEVE THE PROPHETS? I KNOW YOU DO!
WHAT I KNOW IS THAT YOU'LL SOON MAKE ME A CHRISTIAN!
I PRAY THAT YOU'LL BECOME LIKE ME - EXCEPT FOR THESE CHAINS!

WELL, AGRIPPA? YOUR ADVICE?
YOU COULD HAVE RELEASED HIM IF HE HADN'T APPEALED TO THE EMPEROR.

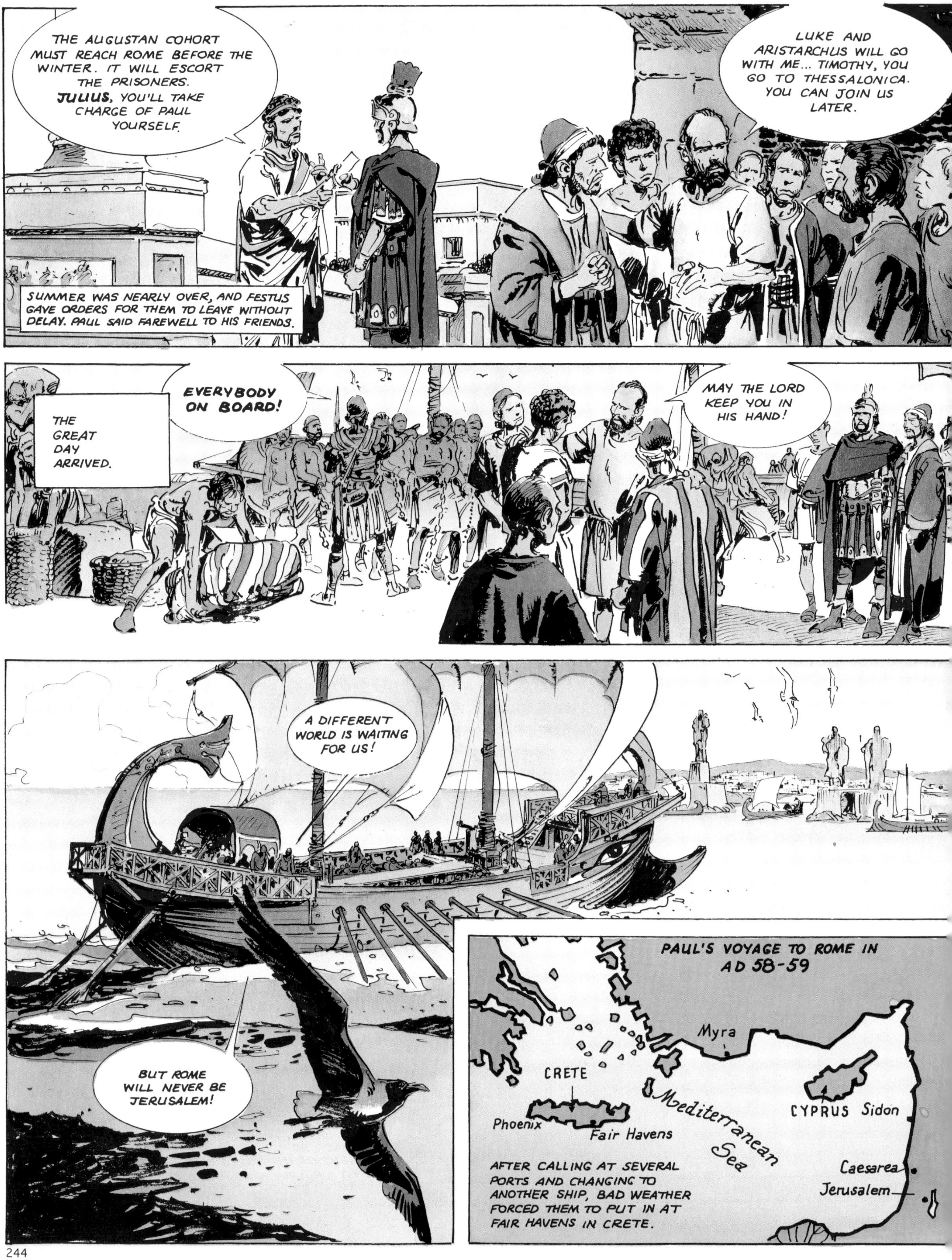

THE AUGUSTAN COHORT MUST REACH ROME BEFORE THE WINTER. IT WILL ESCORT THE PRISONERS. **JULIUS**, YOU'LL TAKE CHARGE OF PAUL YOURSELF.

LUKE AND ARISTARCHUS WILL GO WITH ME... TIMOTHY, YOU GO TO THESSALONICA. YOU CAN JOIN US LATER.

SUMMER WAS NEARLY OVER, AND FESTUS GAVE ORDERS FOR THEM TO LEAVE WITHOUT DELAY. PAUL SAID FAREWELL TO HIS FRIENDS.

THE GREAT DAY ARRIVED.

EVERYBODY ON BOARD!

MAY THE LORD KEEP YOU IN HIS HAND!

A DIFFERENT WORLD IS WAITING FOR US!

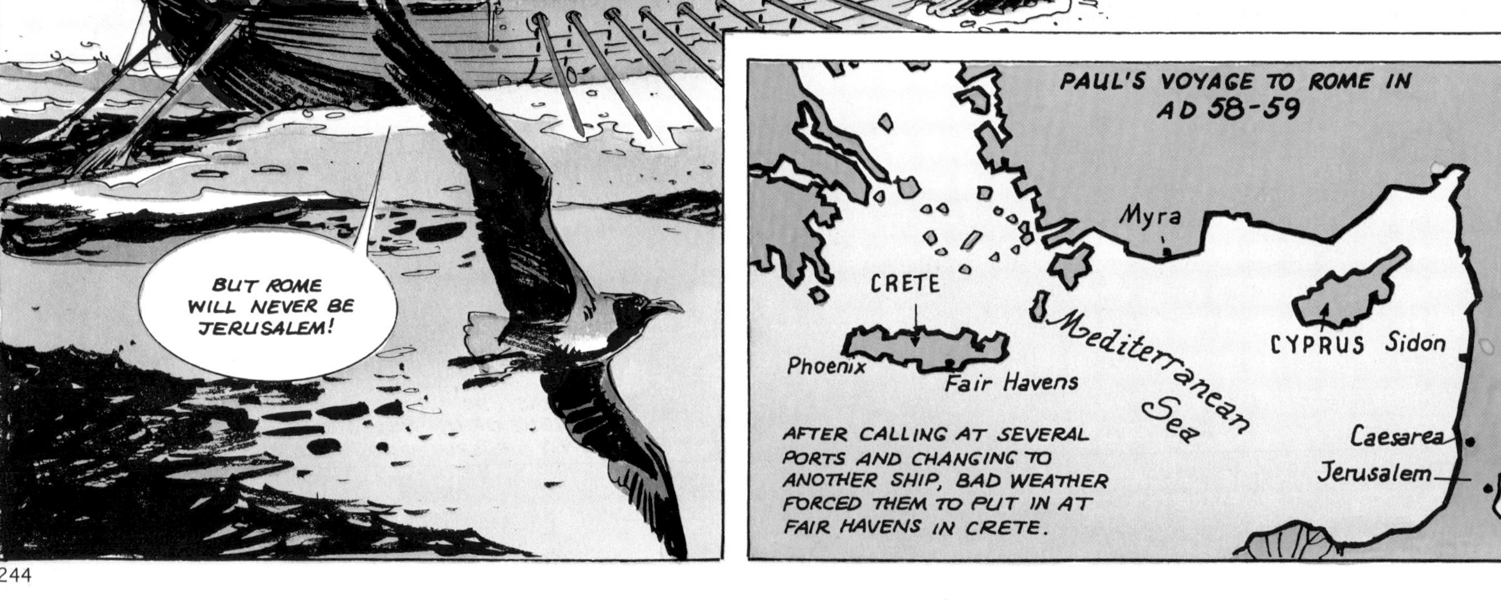
BUT ROME WILL NEVER BE JERUSALEM!
PAUL'S VOYAGE TO ROME IN AD 58-59
Myra
CRETE
Mediterranean Sea
CYPRUS
Sidon
Phoenix
Fair Havens
Caesarea
Jerusalem
AFTER CALLING AT SEVERAL PORTS AND CHANGING TO ANOTHER SHIP, BAD WEATHER FORCED THEM TO PUT IN AT FAIR HAVENS IN CRETE.

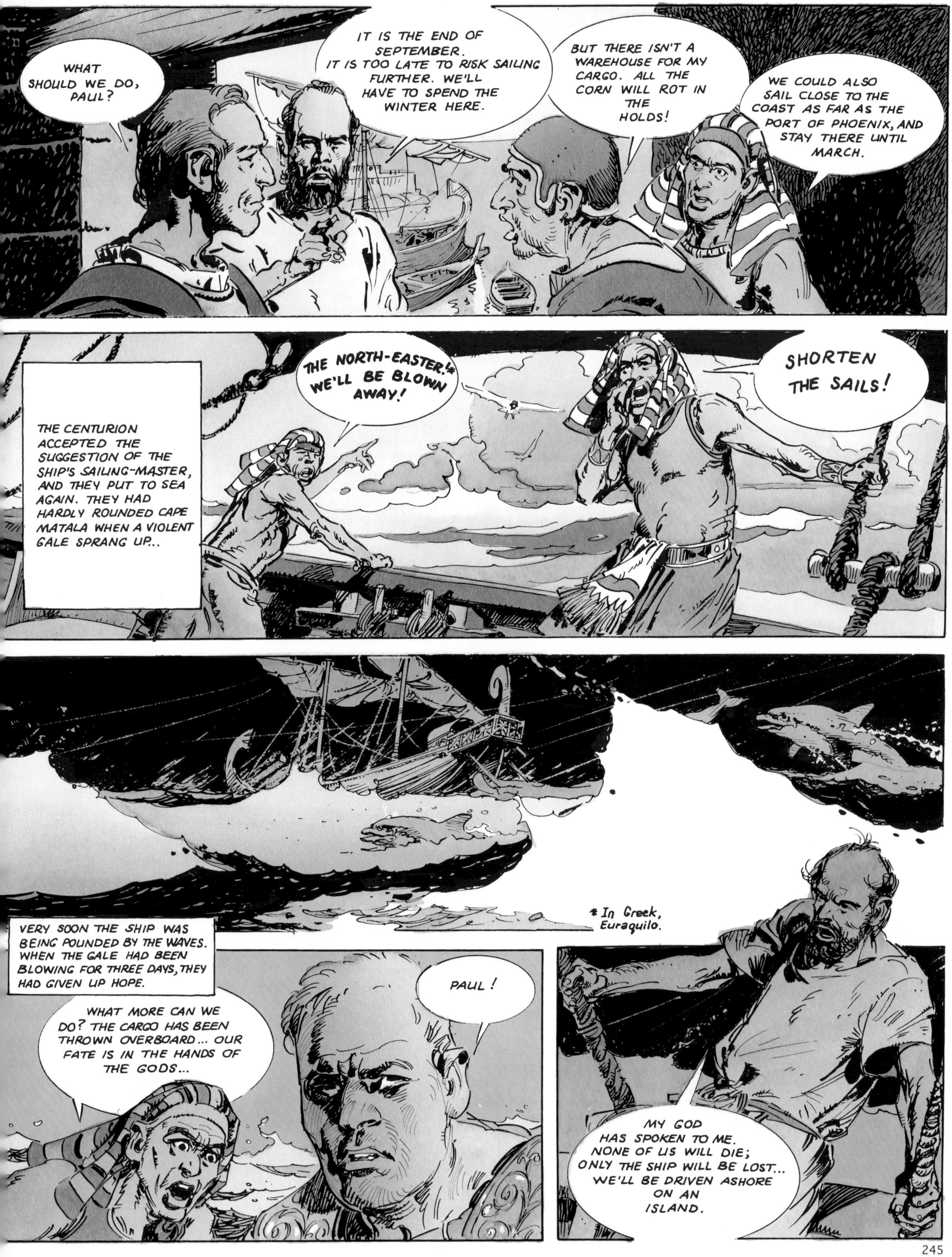

* In Greek, Euraquilo.

VERY SOON THE SHIP WAS BEING POUNDED BY THE WAVES. WHEN THE GALE HAD BEEN BLOWING FOR THREE DAYS, THEY HAD GIVEN UP HOPE.

WHAT MORE CAN WE DO? THE CARGO HAS BEEN THROWN OVERBOARD... OUR FATE IS IN THE HANDS OF THE GODS...

PAUL!

MY GOD HAS SPOKEN TO ME. NONE OF US WILL DIE; ONLY THE SHIP WILL BE LOST... WE'LL BE DRIVEN ASHORE ON AN ISLAND.

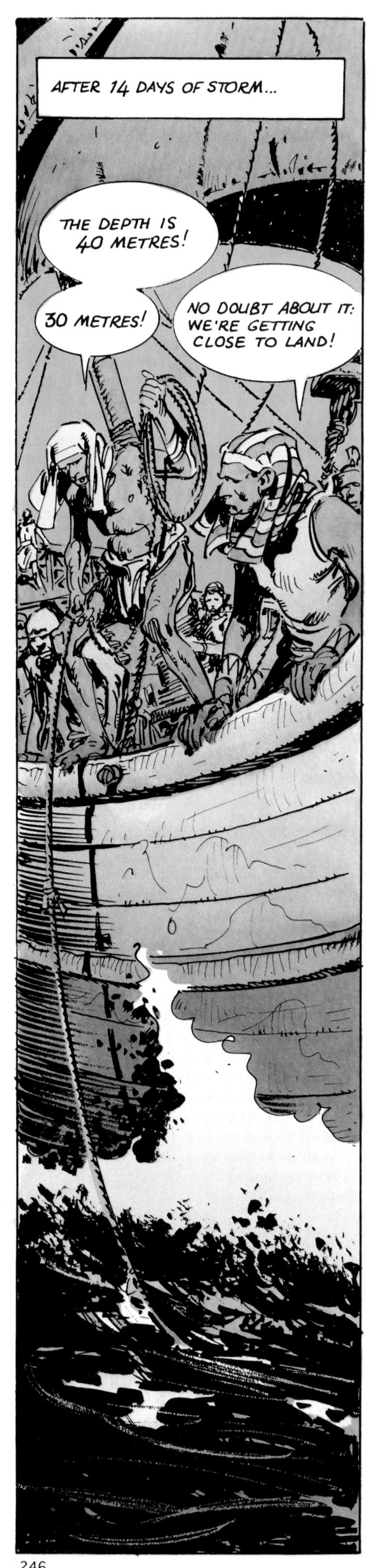
AFTER 14 DAYS OF STORM...
THE DEPTH IS 40 METRES!
30 METRES!
NO DOUBT ABOUT IT: WE'RE GETTING CLOSE TO LAND!

THE NEXT MORNING...
CAPTAIN! A BEACH!
LET'S TRY TO HEAD FOR IT.

BUT SUDDENLY...
JULIUS, WE MUST KILL THE PRISONERS, OTHERWISE...
I FORBID IT! UNTIE THEM, AND LET EACH ONE GE ASHORE AS BEST HE CAN!

AND, AS PAUL HAD PREDICTED, THEY ALL REACHED LAND SAFE AND SOUND.

COME! COME!
WE'RE ON THE ISLAND OF MALTA! WHAT A VOYAGE! *
CENTURION, ALL THE PRISONERS ARE HERE!
* About 1200 kilometres.

PAUL HAD A BUNDLE OF STICKS FOR THE FIRE, WHEN A SNAKE CAME OUT OF IT...
THAT MAN IS CURSED!
THE GODS ARE AFTER HIM!

... AND BIT HIS HAND.

PAUL, LET ME SEE THAT BITE.
DON'T WORRY, LUKE.
WAIT! HE'LL BE DEAD IN A FEW SECONDS!

BUT PAUL CAME TO NO HARM.
THAT MAN IS A GOD!
I'LL END UP BELIEVING IT!

THE GOVERNOR'S HOUSE WAS NEARBY.

GREETINGS, PUBLIUS! A STRANGE GROUP HAS COME ASHORE...

I'VE HEARD ABOUT YOUR SHIPWRECK... MAKE YOURSELVES AT HOME.

...AND ALL THE CASTAWAYS WERE WARMLY WELCOMED AS HIS GUESTS.

I KNOW EVERYTHING THEY SAY ABOUT YOU, PAUL! SERVANT OF THE GOD OF ISRAEL...
...AND OF JESUS, HIS MESSIAH!

I'VE HEARD THAT YOUR FATHER IS VERY ILL. WILL YOU LET ME PRAY FOR HIM?
I WOULDN'T DARE TO ASK - BUT SEEING THAT YOU SUGGEST IT!

WELL, FATHER, HOW DO YOU FEEL?
AS FIT AS A FIDDLE! I'M HUNGRY...

THE NEWS SPREAD. SOON SICK PEOPLE FROM ALL OVER THE ISLAND WERE BROUGHT TO PAUL, AND HE HEALED THEM.

WE WEREN'T LUCKY ENOUGH TO BE IN CAPERNAUM, ARISTARCHUS, BUT THIS IS JUST AS GOOD!

AT THE BEGINNING OF SPRING, PAUL AND HIS COMPANIONS LEFT MALTA FOR ROME.

STAY FAITHFUL TO THE WORD YOU'VE RECEIVED!
GOODBYE, PAUL!

AFTER A VOYAGE WITHOUT ANY PROBLEMS, THE SHIP REACHED PUTEOLI.

THERE'S VESUVIUS!

A LARGE CROWD WELCOMED THE TRAVELLERS.

WHY SUCH A GREETING?

IT IS THE CUSTOM! THIS IS THE FIRST CARGO OF EGYPTIAN CORN THIS YEAR.

HEY! PAUL! OVER HERE!

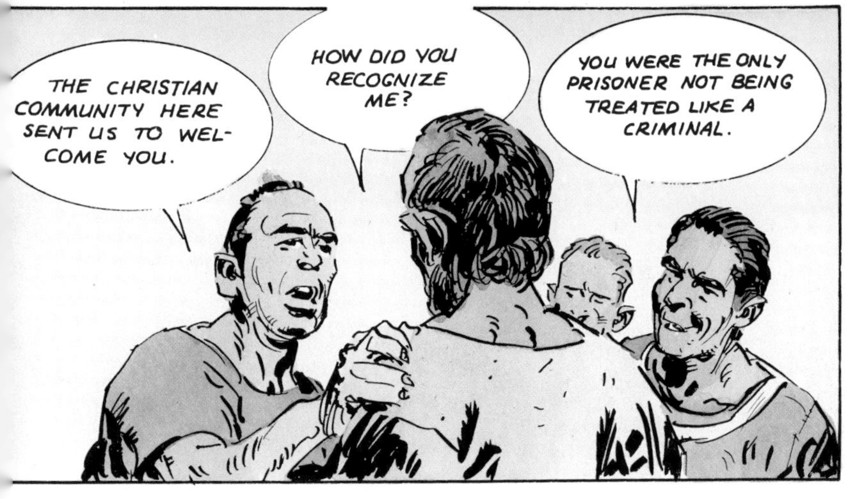

THE CHRISTIAN COMMUNITY HERE SENT US TO WEL-COME YOU.

HOW DID YOU RECOGNIZE ME?

YOU WERE THE ONLY PRISONER NOT BEING TREATED LIKE A CRIMINAL.

CENTURION, I'VE FOUND CHRISTIANS HERE. THEY'VE INVITED ME TO THEIR HOMES...

THAT'S FINE! MAKE THE MOST OF IT. WE SHAN'T BE LEAVING FOR ROME FOR A WEEK.

EIGHT DAYS LATER...
OFF WE GO!
THEY WERE A LITTLE MORE THAN 200 KM FROM ROME.

AFTER WALKING ALONG THE DUSTY ROADS OF CAMPANIA, THE GROUP REACHED THE APPIAN WAY.

SOME ESTATES AROUND HERE HAVE MORE THAN A THOUSAND SLAVES!

THEN, TO CROSS THE PONTINE MARSHES, JULIUS USED THE CANAL BUILT BY AUGUSTUS.
AAAAH! WE'LL BE EATEN ALIVE BY MOSQUITOES!
BETTER THE MOSQUITOES THAN THE LIONS OF THE CIRCUS MAXIMUS!

THE BELIEVERS CAME FROM ROME TO MEET THEM AT THE FORUM OF APPIUS, 65 KM FROM THE CITY.

EVERYBODY GET OFF!

NEXT DAY, AT THREE INNS, 40 KM FROM ROME...
AQUILA! PRISCILLA! WHAT A SURPRISE!

AT LAST, AROUND A BEND IN THE ROAD...

THERE'S ROME!

PRAISE THE LORD! MAY HE BREATHE HIS LIFE INTO THE HEART OF THE EMPIRE!

ROME

Tiber

FLAMINIAN WAY

CAPITOLINE HILL

PALACE OF TIBERIUS

CIRCUS MAXIMUS

APPIAN WAY

TO OSTIA

HE PROCESSION OF PRISONERS FIRST WENT THROUGH THE WORKING-CLASS AREAS.

DON'T EMPTY YOUR BASKET ON THE PRISONERS GOING PAST!

HURRY UP!

LET THEM PASS!

WHEN THEY REACHED THE CIRCUS MAXIMUS, THE CENTURION LEFT THE PRISONERS TO THEIR SAD FATE. THEN HE TOOK PAUL TO THE PALACE OF THE PREFECT OF THE IMPERIAL POLICE.

BURRHUS IS A WISE AND LEVEL-HEADED MAN. YOU'VE NOTHING TO FEAR FROM HIM... BUT I'M GOING TO MISS YOU, PAUL.

I'LL NOT FORGET YOU, JULIUS. YOU'VE BEEN A BROTHER TO ME THROUGHOUT THE VOYAGE.

BURRHUS READ THE LETTER FROM GOVERNOR FESTUS, THEN...

WHILE YOU'RE WAITING OR YOUR CASE TO BE HEARD, YOU CAN BE PARTLY FREE. BUT LET ME KNOW WHAT YOU'RE DOING. YOU CAN GO...

HELPED BY HIS BROTHER CHRISTIANS, PAUL RENTED A SMALL HOUSE.

THE JEWS HAVE A LOT OF INFLUENCE IN ROME. MANY BANKERS, BUSINESS MEN, AND ARTISTS REGULARLY VISIT THE PALACE.

AND NOW WE MUST GO ON WITH OUR WORK. WITH WHOM SHOULD WE BEGIN?

THAT'S HOW, FOR TWO YEARS, PAUL CAME INTO CONTACT WITH MANY PEOPLE, AND STRENGTHENED THE FOUNDATIONS OF THE CHURCH IN ROME

I BEG YOU, BROTHER JEWS, OPEN YOUR EYES AND SEE HOW IN EVERY WAY JESUS OF NAZARETH HAS FULFILLED THE LAW AND THE PROPHETS.

THE TIRELESS APOSTLE NEVER FORGOT THE COMMUNITIES FAR AWAY. HE WROTE...

TO THE COLOSSIANS...
IF, THEN, YOU HAVE BEEN RAISED WITH CHRIST, SEEK THE THINGS IN HEAVEN, WHERE CHRIST SITS AT GOD'S RIGHT HAND.
TO THE EPHESIANS...
I URGE YOU, THEN - I, WHO AM THE LORD'S PRISONER - TO LEAD THE KIND OF LIFE TO WHICH GOD HAS CALLED YOU.

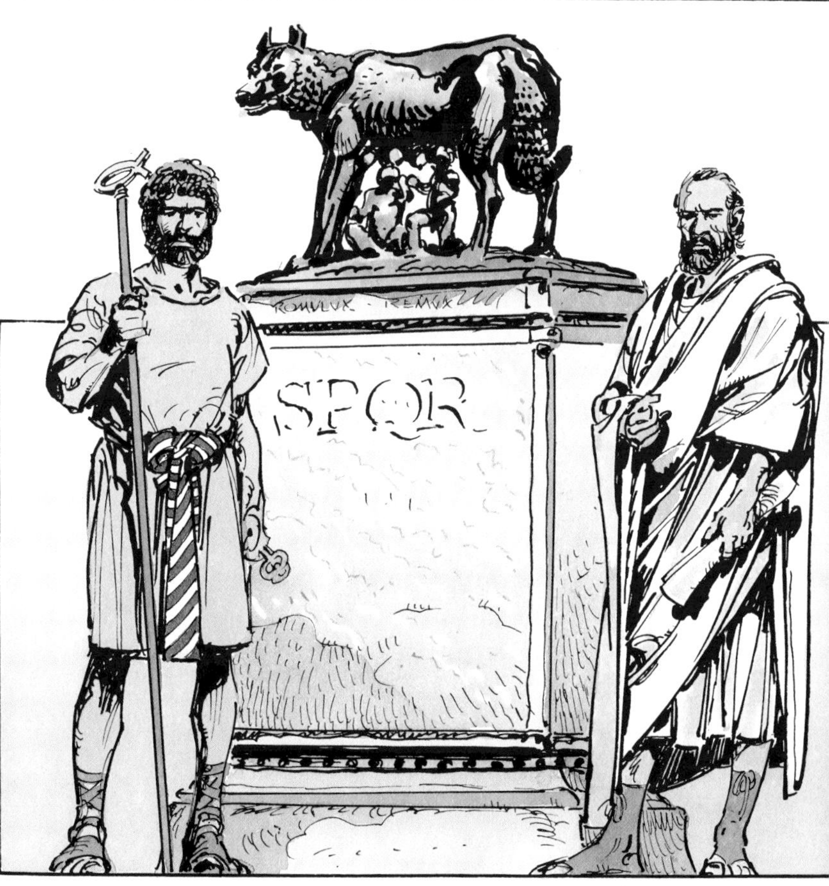

THIS IS WHERE THE ACTS OF THE APOSTLES ENDS. BUT SOME THINGS IN THE LETTERS, AND WHAT WE KNOW FROM HISTORY AND STORIES OF THAT TIME, HELP US TO FOLLOW THE LAST YEARS OF PETER AND PAUL...

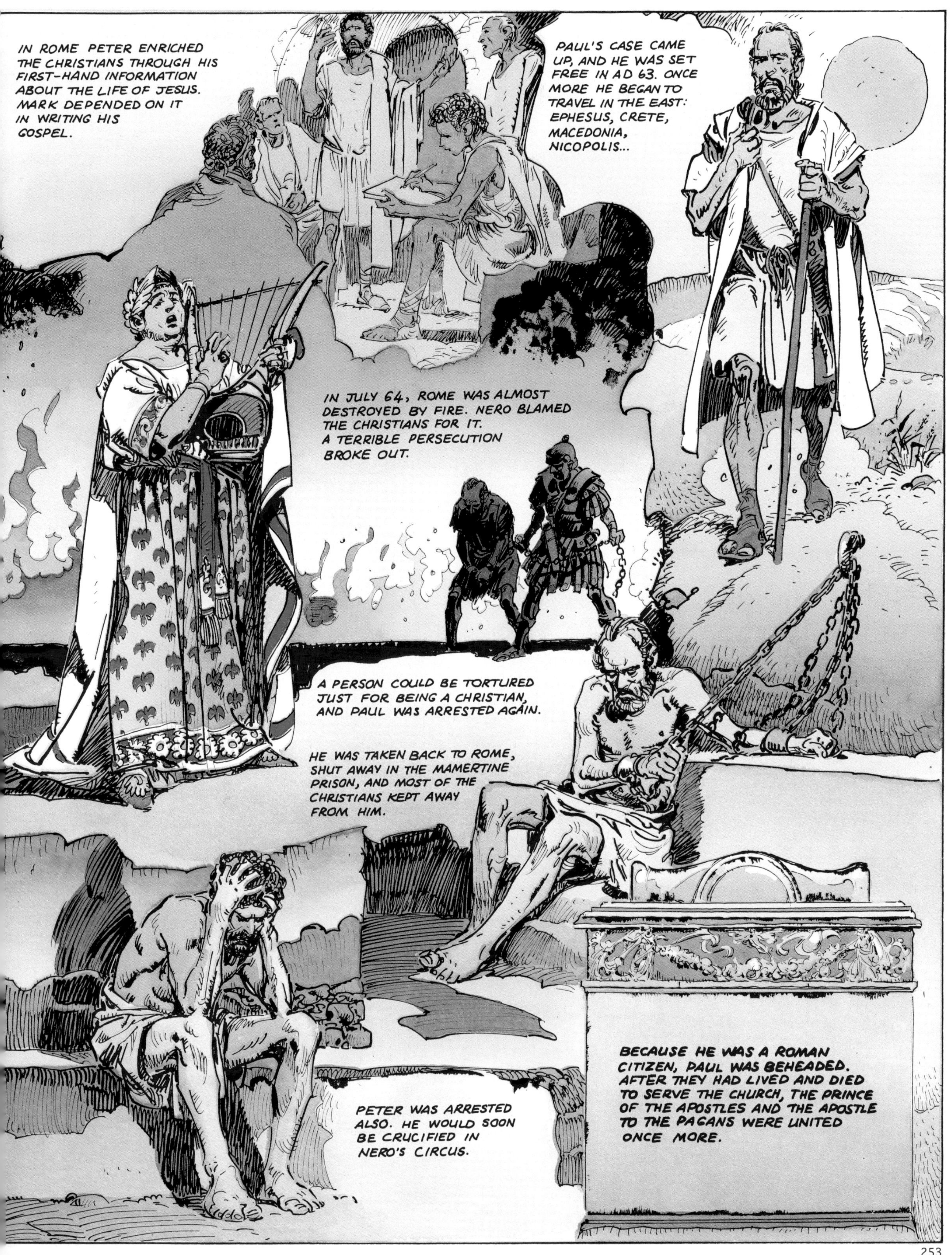
IN ROME PETER ENRICHED THE CHRISTIANS THROUGH HIS FIRST-HAND INFORMATION ABOUT THE LIFE OF JESUS. MARK DEPENDED ON IT IN WRITING HIS GOSPEL.
PAUL'S CASE CAME UP, AND HE WAS SET FREE IN AD 63. ONCE MORE HE BEGAN TO TRAVEL IN THE EAST: EPHESUS, CRETE, MACEDONIA, NICOPOLIS...
IN JULY 64, ROME WAS ALMOST DESTROYED BY FIRE. NERO BLAMED THE CHRISTIANS FOR IT. A TERRIBLE PERSECUTION BROKE OUT.
A PERSON COULD BE TORTURED JUST FOR BEING A CHRISTIAN, AND PAUL WAS ARRESTED AGAIN.
HE WAS TAKEN BACK TO ROME, SHUT AWAY IN THE MAMERTINE PRISON, AND MOST OF THE CHRISTIANS KEPT AWAY FROM HIM.
PETER WAS ARRESTED ALSO. HE WOULD SOON BE CRUCIFIED IN NERO'S CIRCUS.
BECAUSE HE WAS A ROMAN CITIZEN, PAUL WAS BEHEADED. AFTER THEY HAD LIVED AND DIED TO SERVE THE CHURCH, THE PRINCE OF THE APOSTLES AND THE APOSTLE TO THE PAGANS WERE UNITED ONCE MORE.

IN THE SPRING OF AD 70 THE NEW EMPEROR, VESPASIAN, HURLED 60 000 MEN OF HIS LEGIONS AGAINST JERUSALEM, TO CRUSH THE JEWISH REBELLION WHICH HAD LASTED FOR FOUR YEARS.
AT THEIR HEAD WAS HIS OWN SON, TITUS.
THE TERRIBLE NEWS SPREAD THROUGH THE HOLY CITY, FULL OF PILGRIMS COME TO CELEBRATE PASSOVER.
THE ROMANS ARE COMING! BOLT YOUR DOORS!

THE VISIONS OF JOHN
THE BOOK OF REVELATION

SCENARIO: Etienne DAHLER
DRAWING: Raymond POÏVET

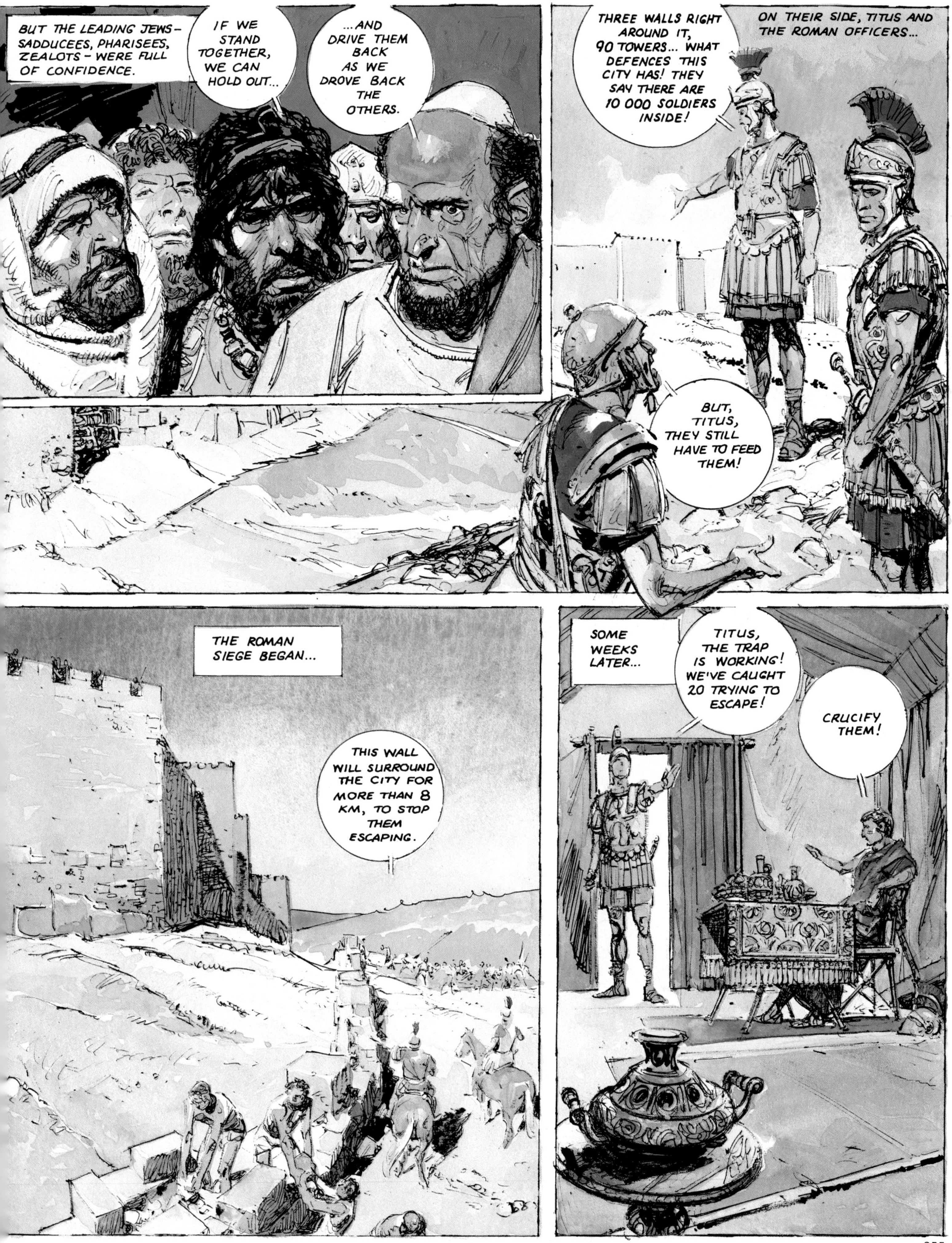

BUT THE LEADING JEWS – SADDUCEES, PHARISEES, ZEALOTS – WERE FULL OF CONFIDENCE.

IF WE STAND TOGETHER, WE CAN HOLD OUT...

...AND DRIVE THEM BACK AS WE DROVE BACK THE OTHERS.

ON THEIR SIDE, TITUS AND THE ROMAN OFFICERS...

THREE WALLS RIGHT AROUND IT, 90 TOWERS... WHAT DEFENCES THIS CITY HAS! THEY SAY THERE ARE 10 000 SOLDIERS INSIDE!

BUT, TITUS, THEY STILL HAVE TO FEED THEM!

WHEN HE HAD LET THE CITY STARVE FOR 100 DAYS, TITUS DECIDED TO ATTACK.
FORT ANTONIA WAS CAPTURED, BUT THE REBELS WHO HAD TAKEN REFUGE IN THE TEMPLE, STILL HELD OUT.
THE TEMPLE... ISN'T IT MAGNIFICENT!
YES, BUT HOW DO WE CAPTURE IT WITHOUT SETTING FIRE TO IT?
THE DOORS OF PRECIOUS CEDAR WOOD WERE SOON BURNING FIERCELY...
...AND THE SOLDIERS WENT INTO THE HOLY PLACE AND KILLED EVERYONE THEY FOUND THERE...
IN THE STREETS OF JERUSALEM...
NO MERCY!
THE PEOPLE WERE SLAUGHTERED, AND THE TEMPLE WAS BURNED TO THE GROUND. AFTER THAT TRAGIC DAY, JERUSALEM NO LONGER HAD A HOLY PLACE.

THE NEWS SOON REACHED EPHESUS IN ASIA MINOR, WHERE THE APOSTLE JOHN HAD BEEN LIVING FOR SOME YEARS.
JOHN, HOW COULD GOD LET SUCH A THING HAPPEN?
THE MASTER FORETOLD IT! HE SAID: 'NOT ONE STONE OF THIS BUILDING WILL BE LEFT IN ITS PLACE.'

HE ALSO SAID: 'THAT WILL BE ONLY THE BEGINNING OF THE TROUBLES. YOU'LL BE PERSECUTED FOR MY SAKE.'

BUT...

I REMEMBER SOMETHING ELSE JESUS SAID: 'WHEN THE GOOD NEWS OF THE KINGDOM HAS REACHED TO THE ENDS OF THE EARTH, THE END WILL COME.'

JOHN, WE'VE BEEN WAITING FOR YOU. MANY OF THE BROTHERS ARE VERY UPSET BY THE NEWS THAT JERUSALEM HAS FALLEN.

I'LL SPEAK TO THEM.

JOHN ENCOURAGED THE CHRISTIANS IN EPHESUS.
PEACE BE WITH YOU! THESE THINGS HAVE TO HAPPEN... WE MUST TELL PEOPLE JESUS CHRIST CAN SAVE THEM. THERE'S STILL TIME.
JOHN, DO YOU THINK THE END OF THE WORLD IS NEAR?
NO ONE KNOWS! BUT WE DO KNOW THAT AFTER THE TROUBLES THE SUN WILL BECOME DARK; THE MOON WON'T SHINE, AND THE STARS WILL FALL OUT OF THE SKY...
...THEN THE SIGN OF THE SON OF MAN WILL APPEAR IN THE SKY, AND ALL THE NATIONS WILL SEE HIS GLORY.
THE LORD HIMSELF SAID THAT HE'LL SEND HIS ANGELS TO SOUND THE TRUMPET AND GATHER HIS CHOSEN PEOPLE FROM ALL OVER THE WORLD.
THERE'S NO TIME TO LOSE! EACH OF US MUST LEAVE EARLY TOMORROW, TO VISIT OUR BROTHERS AND ENCOURAGE THEM.

TROAS
PERGAMUM
THYATIRA
N
SARDIS
SMYRNA
PHILADELPHIA
EPHESUS
HIERAPOLIS
LAODICEA
COLOSSAE
PATMOS
MANY CHRISTIAN COMMUNITIES HAD SPRUNG UP IN ASIA MINOR OWING TO THE WORK OF THE APOSTLES JOHN AND PHILIP.

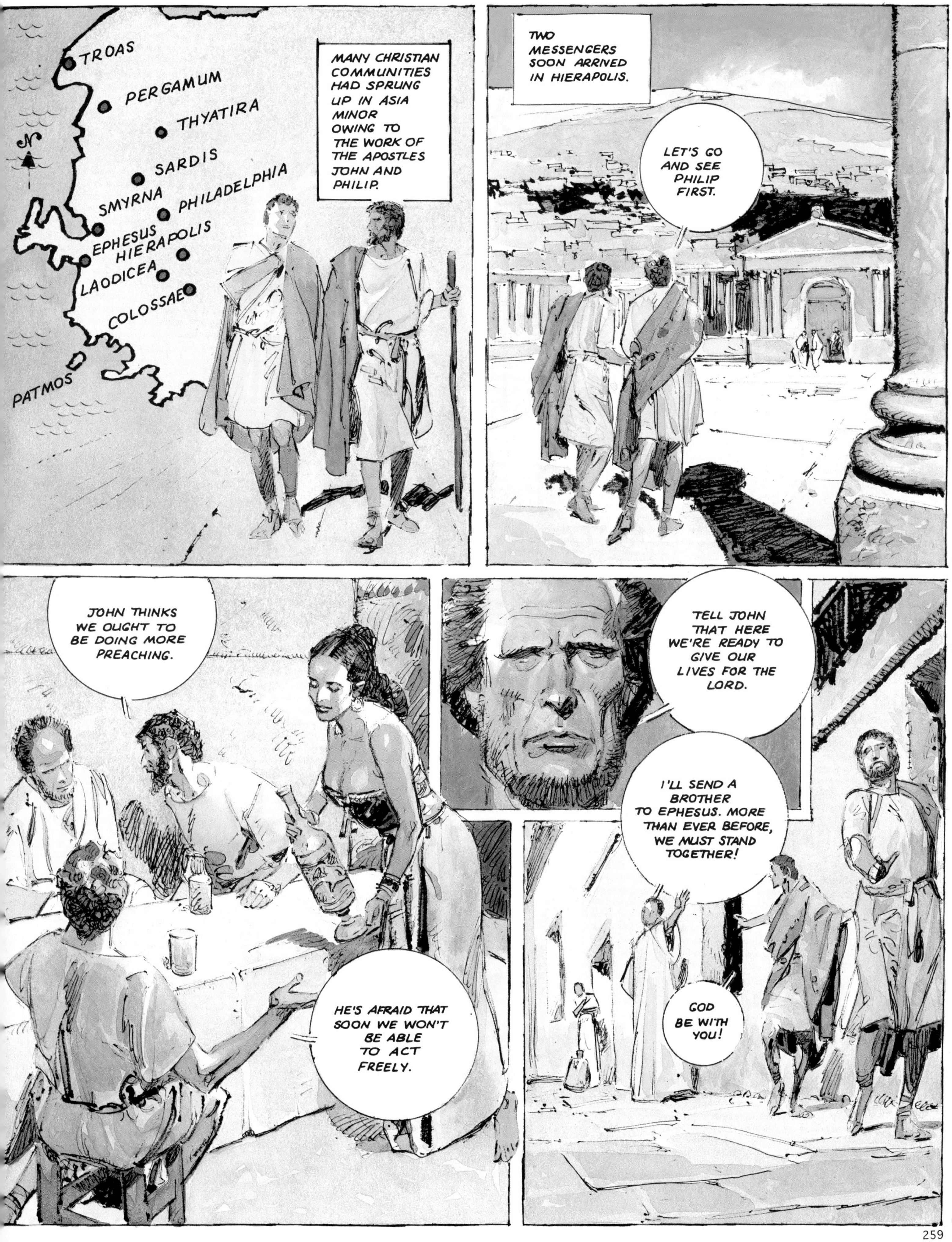

TWO MESSENGERS SOON ARRIVED IN HIERAPOLIS.
LET'S GO AND SEE PHILIP FIRST.

JOHN THINKS WE OUGHT TO BE DOING MORE PREACHING.

HE'S AFRAID THAT SOON WE WON'T BE ABLE TO ACT FREELY.

TELL JOHN THAT HERE WE'RE READY TO GIVE OUR LIVES FOR THE LORD.

I'LL SEND A BROTHER TO EPHESUS. MORE THAN EVER BEFORE, WE MUST STAND TOGETHER!

GOD BE WITH YOU!

TEN YEARS LATER THERE WAS A NEW EMPEROR IN ROME; DOMITIAN, THE BROTHER OF TITUS, BUT THE ROMAN NOBILITY DIDN'T TRUST HIM.
DOMITIAN? HE'S AN UPSTART!
NOT A PATCH ON HIS BROTHER!
IN THE YEAR 88 A CONSPIRACY IN ROME CAME TO NOTHING. BUT IT MADE DOMITIAN FURIOUS.
PUNISH ALL THE CONSPIRATORS WITHOUT MERCY!
AND I'M SURE THERE ARE OTHERS READY TO RISE UP AGAINST ME... PHILOSOPHERS WHO SPREAD DANGEROUS IDEAS...
... JEWS WHO REFUSE TO PAY THE TAX TO JUPITER! AS FOR THE CHRISTIANS...

FROM ROME THE PERSECUTION SPREAD TO THE PROVINCES. IT WAS ESPECIALLY SEVERE IN ASIA MINOR.
HOLD FAST, MY CHILDREN!...REMEMBER THESE WORDS OF THE LORD: 'HE WHO IS ASHAMED OF ME BEFORE OTHER PEOPLE, I WILL BE ASHAMED OF HIM BEFORE MY FATHER.'
JOHN! SOME BROTHERS IN HIERAPOLIS AND SMYRNA HAVE BEEN ARRESTED...
IN SOME PLACES, WHERE THE OFFICIALS HATED THEM, THE CHRISTIANS WERE TORTURED, PUT TO DEATH, OR THROWN INTO PRISON.
THESE ARE THE REAL ENEMIES OF THE EMPIRE! THEY QUIETLY DESTROY OUR ROMAN WAY OF LIFE.
ACCUSATIONS WERE BEING MADE EVERYWHERE.
THEY MEET SECRETLY AT NIGHT...
...YES! TO DRINK BLOOD AND EAT HUMAN FLESH!
IN HIS TURN, JOHN, AT EPHESUS...
I ARREST YOU IN THE NAME OF THE EMPEROR!
WE'LL FOLLOW YOU.

NEXT DAY...
IS IT TRUE THAT YOU REFUSE TO WORSHIP OUR GODS AND TO SACRIFICE TO THE EMPEROR?
QUITE TRUE!
THAT PROVES THAT YOU'RE AGAINST THE EMPIRE!
ONLY OVER OUR WORSHIP! FOR THE REST WE OBEY ALL THE LAWS OF ROME.
THEY SAY THAT YOU WORK FOR THE COMING OF A NEW KING... THE...CHRIST...
DON'T WORRY! HIS KINGDOM ISN'T OF THIS WORLD.
POOR FOOLS! ...NOT MUCH OF A DANGER TO THE EMPIRE!
IN THE NAME OF THE EMPEROR I SENTENCE YOU TO FORCED LABOUR ON THE ISLAND OF PATMOS NOW, GO!

A LITTLE LATER, IN THE HARBOUR OF EPHESUS...
COME ON! GET ON BOARD!
THEY SAILED PAST SAMOS, THEN CAME IN SIGHT OF THE ISLAND OF PATMOS.
THERE'S OUR NEW PRISON!
DON'T FORGET: YOU'RE HERE FOR FORCED LABOUR!
THINK YOURSELVES LUCKY! ... YOU COULD HAVE BEEN THROWN TO THE WILD ANIMALS IN ROME!
SHUT UP!

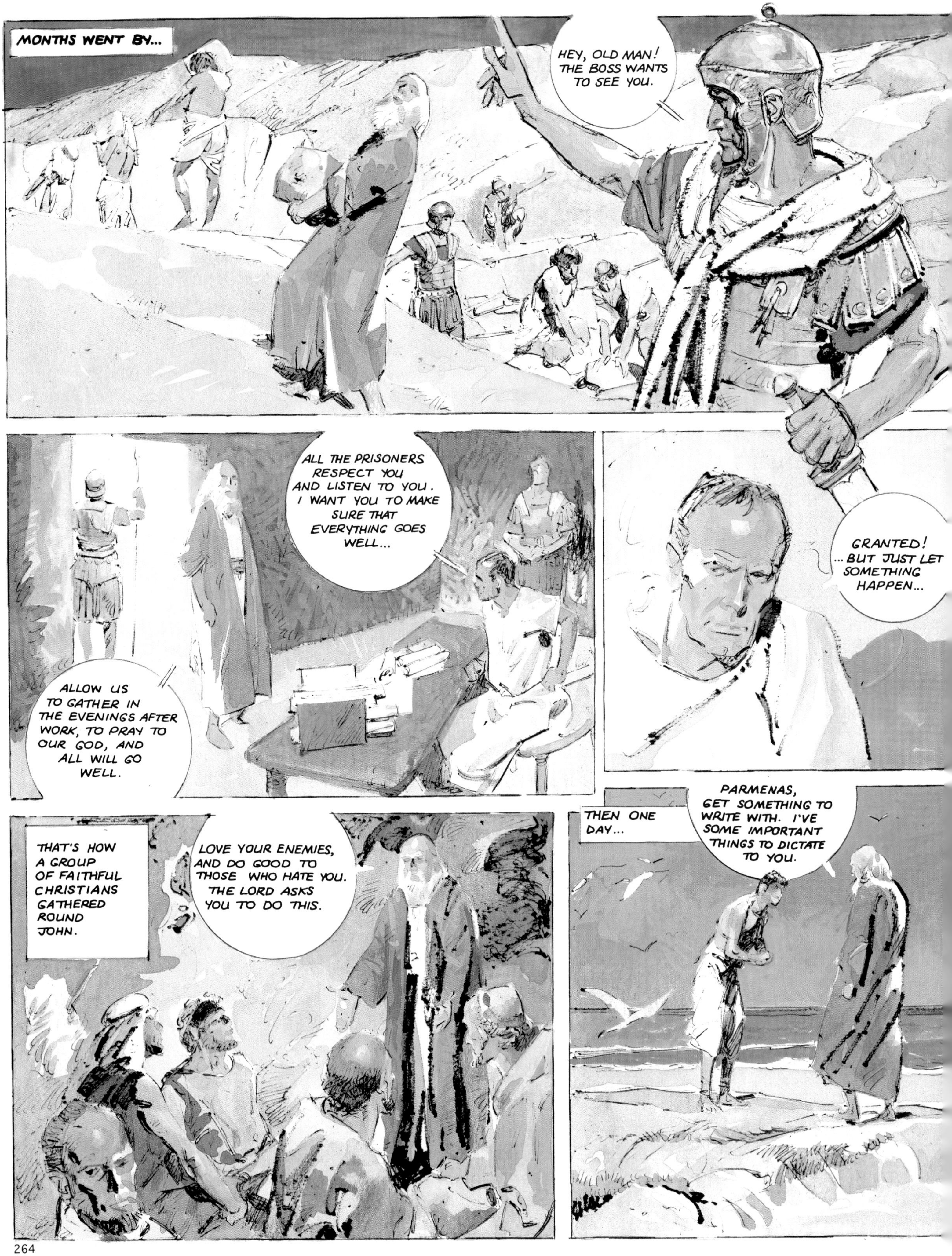

MONTHS WENT BY...

HEY, OLD MAN! THE BOSS WANTS TO SEE YOU.

ALL THE PRISONERS RESPECT YOU AND LISTEN TO YOU. I WANT YOU TO MAKE SURE THAT EVERYTHING GOES WELL...

ALLOW US TO GATHER IN THE EVENINGS AFTER WORK, TO PRAY TO OUR GOD, AND ALL WILL GO WELL.

GRANTED! ...BUT JUST LET SOMETHING HAPPEN...

EARLY THE NEXT DAY...
PARMENAS, THIS IS WHAT HAPPENED TO ME. ON THE LORD'S DAY I WAS GRIPPED BY THE SPIRIT, AND I HEARD A POWERFUL VOICE BEHIND ME, SAYING...
I'M LISTENING, JOHN.

WRITE DOWN WHAT YOU SEE! AND SEND IT TO THE SEVEN CHURCHES: TO EPHESUS, SMYRNA, PERGAMUM, THYATIRA, SARDIS, PHILADELPHIA, AND LAODICEA!
SO I FELL AT HIS FEET, AND HE SAID TO ME: 'DON'T BE AFRAID! I AM THE FIRST AND THE LAST. I WAS DEAD, AND SEE: I AM ALIVE FOR EVER AND EVER.'

I TURNED ROUND TO SEE WHO WAS THERE, AND THIS IS WHAT I SAW...

WELL, THEN! PARMENAS, YOU'RE NOT WRITING?
JOHN, I'M LISTENING!

EPHESUS, POLITICAL AND RELIGIOUS CAPITAL OF THE PROVINCE OF ASIA, PROUD OF HAVING THE TEMPLE OF ARTEMIS, ONE OF THE SEVEN WONDERS OF THE WORLD.
SMYRNA, A FLOURISHING PORT. THE CHRISTIAN COMMUNITY HERE WOULD SUFFER TERRIBLE PERSECUTION. THEIR BISHOP, POLYCARP, WOULD BE MARTYRED IN AD 155.
I KNOW YOUR TROUBLES AND YOUR POVERTY – YET YOU'RE RICH. BE FAITHFUL, EVEN TO DEATH, AND I WILL GIVE YOU THE CROWN OF LIFE.
I KNOW WHAT YOU'VE DONE. YOU'VE SUFFERED FOR MY SAKE AND YOU HAVEN'T GIVEN UP. BUT YOU DON'T LOVE ME AS YOU DID AT FIRST. TURN BACK TO ME, AND LIVE AS YOU DID AT THE BEGINNING.
PERGAMUM, SEAT OF THE ROMAN PROCONSUL, FAMOUS FOR ITS ALTAR TO ZEUS AND ITS TEMPLE WHERE THE CROWDS WENT TO BE HEALED.
I KNOW WHERE YOU LIVE – THERE WHERE SATAN HAS HIS THRONE – YET YOU DIDN'T LOSE YOUR FAITH IN ME. BUT THERE ARE THOSE AMONG YOU WHO EAT FOOD SACRIFICED TO IDOLS AND LIVE IMMORAL LIVES. TURN BACK TO ME!
I KNOW YOUR LOVE, YOUR FAITH, AND YOUR PATIENCE. BUT I BLAME YOU FOR ALLOWING THAT WOMAN TO LEAD MY SERVANTS ASTRAY. HOLD ON FIRMLY TO WHAT YOU HAVE UNTIL I COME.
THYATIRA, A SMALL TOWN. THE FALSE PROPHETESS JEZEBEL HAD A BAD INFLUENCE ON THE PEOPLE LIVING THERE.

SARDIS, A SMALL TRADE-CENTRE, WEALTHY BECAUSE OF ITS GOLD. KING CROESUS KNEW ABOUT THAT...
PEOPLE SAY THAT YOU'RE ALIVE, BUT YOU'RE DEAD! REMEMBER WHAT YOU WERE TAUGHT; OBEY IT, AND TURN BACK TO ME... OTHERWISE I'LL COME LIKE A THIEF AND TAKE YOU BY SURPRISE.
PHILADELPHIA, A TOWN REBUILT BY TIBERIUS AFTER THE EARTHQUAKE IN AD 17.
BECAUSE YOU'VE KEPT MY WORD FAITHFULLY, I'LL KEEP YOU ON THE DAY OF TESTING THAT'S COMING UPON THE WHOLE WORLD. I'M COMING SOON. KEEP SAFE WHAT YOU HAVE.
LAODICEA, A PROSPEROUS COMMERCIAL CROSSROADS, WHERE WEALTH DULLED PEOPLE'S CONSCIENCES.
BECAUSE YOU'RE LUKEWARM, AND NEITHER HOT NOR COLD, I'LL SPIT YOU OUT OF MY MOUTH. BE EAGER TO SERVE ME AGAIN, AND TURN BACK TO ME.
AND WRITE THIS ALSO:
HE WHO HAS EARS TO HEAR, LISTEN TO WHAT THE SPIRIT IS SAYING TO THE CHURCHES.

NOW, PARMENAS, HERE ARE MY VISIONS. THERE WAS A THRONE IN HEAVEN... AROUND IT WERE 4 LIVING CREATURES, AND 24 ELDERS SAT AROUND THEM.
COME UP HERE, AND I'LL SHOW YOU WHAT IS GOING TO HAPPEN.
HOLY, HOLY, HOLY IS THE LORD GOD ALMIGHTY! HE WAS; HE IS; AND HE IS COMING.
LORD, OUR GOD, YOU ARE WORTHY TO RECEIVE GLORY, HONOUR, AND POWER!
WHO IS WORTHY TO BREAK THE 7 SEALS AND OPEN THE SCROLL?
BUT THERE WAS NOBODY IN HEAVEN, ON THE EARTH OR IN THE UNDERWORLD ABLE TO OPEN THE SCROLL AND READ IT. AND I, JOHN, WEPT BITTERLY...

DON'T WEEP! THE LION FROM JUDAH'S TRIBE, DAVID'S DESCENDANT, HAS WON THE VICTORY. HE'LL OPEN THE SCROLL WITH THE 7 SEALS.
THEN I, JOHN, SAW A LAMB APPEAR WHICH SEEMED TO HAVE BEEN SACRIFICED...
THE LAMB WHO WAS KILLED IS WORTHY TO RECEIVE POWER, WEALTH, WISDOM, AND STRENGTH, HONOUR, GLORY, AND PRAISE!
IT CAME FORWARD TO RECEIVE THE SCROLL...
COME!
IT BROKE THE FIRST SEAL, AND A WHITE HORSE APPEARED...

THE LAMB BROKE THE SECOND, THIRD AND FOURTH SEALS, AND I SAW A RED HORSE, A BLACK HORSE, AND A GREENISH-GREY HORSE...
COME!
COME! COME!
THE HORSEMEN WERE GIVEN POWER OVER A QUARTER OF THE EARTH, TO KILL BY THE SWORD, BY FAMINE, OR BY DEATH.
WHEN THE FIFTH SEAL WAS BROKEN OPEN, I SAW UNDER THE ALTAR THE SOULS OF THOSE WHO HAD BEEN MASSACRED BECAUSE THEY HAD PREACHED GOD'S WORD.
MASTER, HOLY AND TRUE, HOW LONG WILL YOU WAIT TO DO JUSTICE?
AND THEN THE SIXTH SEAL WAS BROKEN. THERE WAS A VIOLENT EARTHQUAKE; THE SUN TURNED BLACK, AND THE MOON WAS COMPLETELY RED, LIKE BLOOD...
MOUNTAINS, FALL ON US, AND HIDE US!
THE TERRIBLE DAY OF GOD'S ANGER IS HERE! WHO CAN STAND AGAINST IT?
HORSEMEN, DON'T HARM THE EARTH, UNTIL WE'VE PUT A MARK ON THE FOREHEADS OF THE SERVANTS OF OUR GOD.
AND I HEARD THE NUMBER OF THOSE WHO WERE MARKED - 144 000, 12 000 FROM EACH OF THE 12 TRIBES OF ISRAEL.

WHEN THE LAMB BROKE OPEN THE SEVENTH SEAL, THERE WAS A GREAT SILENCE IN HEAVEN... AN ANGEL TOOK FIRE FROM THE ALTAR, REFILLED HIS CENSER, AND...
...THREW IT OVER THE EARTH. THERE WERE PEALS OF THUNDER AND FLASHES OF LIGHTNING, WHILE TRUMPETS SOUNDED IN HEAVEN.
THEN CAME THE HORSEMEN, THEIR HORSES SPITTING FIRE.
BELIEVE ME, PARMENAS: IN THOSE DAYS IT WILL BE TERRIBLE FOR THOSE WHO LIVE ON EARTH WHEN THE LAST TRUMPETS ARE HEARD!

A GREAT SIGN APPEARED IN THE SKY: A WOMAN WHOSE DRESS WAS THE SUN, WHO HAD THE MOON UNDER HER FEET, AND A CROWN OF TWELVE STARS ON HER HEAD...
A SECOND SIGN APPEARED, A HUGE DRAGON. IT GOT READY TO DEVOUR THE CHILD AS SOON AS IT WAS BORN.
SHE WAS ABOUT TO GIVE BIRTH TO A CHILD...
THE WOMAN GAVE BIRTH TO A BOY.
THE BOY WAS SNATCHED AWAY AND TAKEN TO GOD, WHILE THE WOMAN FLED... THEN THE DRAGON HAD TO FIGHT THE HEAVENLY ARMY...
...IT WAS THROWN DOWN TO THE EARTH. THEN IT ATTACKED THE WOMAN'S OTHER CHILDREN, THOSE WHO KEEP GOD'S COMMANDMENTS...
...AND ARE FAITHFUL TO JESUS.

THEN ANOTHER BEAST CAME UP OUT OF THE SEA, AND THE DRAGON GAVE IT HIS OWN STRENGTH AND GREAT POWER.

SOON THE BEAST RULED OVER ALL TRIBES, PEOPLES, LANGUAGES AND NATIONS.

THEN ANOTHER BEAST CAME UP OUT OF THE EARTH. IT LOOKED LIKE THE LAMB, BUT IT SPOKE LIKE THE DRAGON.
IT DECEIVED THE PEOPLE ON THE EARTH, AND MADE THEM WORSHIP THE FIRST BEAST.

IT PUT A MARK ON EVERYBODY, SMALL AND GREAT, RICH AND POOR...
666
666
...AND NO ONE COULD BUY OR SELL UNLESS HE WAS MARKED WITH THE NUMBER OF THE BEAST, 666.

THEN AN ANGEL CALLED TO ME...
COME! I'LL SHOW YOU THE JUDGEMENT OF THE GREAT PROSTITUTE WHO LIVES ON THE EDGE OF THE OCEANS.

BABYLON
ALL WHO'VE HAD DEALINGS WITH HER WILL FIGHT AGAINST THE LAMB, BUT HE'LL DEFEAT THEM, BECAUSE HE'S THE LORD OF LORDS.

IN THE END THE BEAST ITSELF TURNED AGAINST THE PROSTITUTE.

SHE HAS FALLEN! BABYLON THE GREAT HAS FALLEN!

HOW AWFUL! BABYLON, ONE HOUR WAS ENOUGH TO JUDGE YOU!

THEN I SAW A NEW HEAVEN AND A NEW EARTH, BECAUSE THE FIRST HEAVEN AND THE FIRST EARTH HAD DISAPPEARED...
...AND I SAW THE NEW JERUSALEM, COMING DOWN OUT OF HEAVEN FROM GOD.
NOW GOD'S HOME IS WITH MANKIND! HE'LL WIPE AWAY ALL TEARS FROM THEIR EYES. THERE'LL BE NO MORE DEATH, NO MORE CRYING OR PAIN. FOR THE OLD WORLD HAS GONE...
AND THE TEMPLE? IS THERE A TEMPLE AGAIN?
NO, BECAUSE THE LORD IS ITS TEMPLE.

I AM THE ALPHA AND THE OMEGA, THE FIRST AND THE LAST, THE BEGINNING AND THE END.
LET ANYONE WHO IS THIRSTY COME. TO THOSE WHO WANT IT I WILL FREELY GIVE THE WATER OF LIFE! YES, I'M COMING SOON.
MARANA THA!
COME, LORD JESUS!
Raymond Poivet.